The Shulammite

The Shulammite

PURSUING INTIMACY WITH CHRIST

Michael Walsh

ARCHANGEL PUBLICATIONS

Archangel Publications
10055 FM 1484, Conroe, TX 77303

MercyChristianFellowship.com
936-756-0063

ISBN-13: 978-0-9787018-0-2
ISBN-10: 0-9787018-0-1

Cover design by Angie Kitzman

Unless otherwise identified, all Scripture quotations in this publication are taken from the *NEW AMERICAN STANDARD BIBLE®*. Copyright ©1960, 1962, 1963, 1968, 1971, 1972, 1973, 1975, 1977, 1995 by The Lockman Foundation. Used by permission. (www.Lockman.org)

Printed in the United States of America

To Jesus, the Lover of My Soul

CONTENTS

AUTHOR'S PREFACE

As a pastor, I have endeavored over the last twenty-seven years to inspire the church to seek God with wholehearted devotion, hoping every person would respond by dedicating significant amounts of time to personal prayer and the study of God's Word. At the same time, I have wanted their enthusiastic involvement in helping to fulfill our corporate mission of proclaiming the gospel, establishing community, discipling others, praying corporately and impacting the nations. This apparent dichotomy between personal devotion and service is complicated by each person's own responsibilities to family, work and school.

It is not only church members who struggle with arranging their priorities, but I have felt the tension in my own personal life as well. For regardless of how much I would like to spend time alone with the Lord, I also feel compelled to fulfill the many and varied obligations associated with family and ministry.

However, it does not seem that God would have us choose between prayer and service, when both are so important to him. Jesus' life is the supreme example of one whose active involvement in the lives of others never appeared to interfere with his personal relationship with the Father. On the contrary, his service seemed only to enhance the dynamic exchange between Father and Son.

The choice between active Christian ministry and a devout prayer life is often described in terms illustrated by the encounter Jesus had with Mary and Martha when he came to visit them. Mary, the devoted worshipper of Jesus, chose the *good part*, while Martha allowed herself to be *worried and bothered* by so many things in her attempt to serve the Lord.[1] The inference is often made, and rightly so, that one's personal devotion to the Lord is far superior to his service for the Lord.

---

[1] Luke 10:41

Testimonies of broken lives *burned out* on Christian service seem to underscore the danger of becoming distracted from one's personal devotion to the Lord while being actively involved in his service. Sometimes, the only solution seems to be a reluctant withdrawal from public ministry for a time of rest and restoration. Yet, too many times these wounded souls simply become lost among a faceless sea of churchgoers, hoping that time will heal the disappointment of having given their best in service to a God who seems to provide little comfort in return.

The Shulammite in the Song of Solomon typifies the believer who realizes she has been like Martha, *worried and bothered* by too many things. She cries out to the Lord, asking him to reveal himself more fully and bring her into an intimate relationship with himself. As he responds to her plea, the Shulammite eventually discovers that it is possible to enjoy intimacy with her beloved in the midst of her work. In fact, it is not only possible, but absolutely essential. For if she wants to truly have his heart, the Shulammite must enjoy doing the kinds of things he likes to do. If she wants to maintain his presence and walk in union with him, she must be willing to go to the kinds of places where he likes to go.

Ultimately, the Shulammite realizes that her beloved is a shepherd who loves his people. She learns that if she is going to walk in unison with him, she must be willing to gladly join him as he labors among the souls of men.

My purpose in writing this book is twofold. First, I hope to inspire wholehearted devotion to the Lord so that many saints will be encouraged to seek the path of the Shulammite. I believe this will happen as they receive divine revelation of Christ's incomprehensible love, as revealed in the Song of Solomon.

Second, I want believers to understand some of the ways the Lord might deal with them throughout the maturation process so that they will have the courage to persevere. Hopefully, the reader will see that fruitful service is a necessary ingredient for spiritual development and does not need to be viewed as a distraction from one's pursuit of intimacy with the Beloved.

The Lord Jesus longs to bring every believer into a state of abiding union that does not force them to choose between being a Martha or a Mary. He wants each one to learn to walk intimately with him, taking his presence with them into every aspect of life, including their work and ministry.

May God, through the pages of this book, bless every reader in the most noble of all occupations: the pursuit of divine love.

Michael Walsh

October 25, 2006

INTRODUCTION

Central Theme

Solomon was the third king of Israel, ruling for forty years around the year 1000 BC. Renowned for his extraordinary wisdom, he established his kingdom in peace. Solomon was immensely wealthy, making silver in Jerusalem as common as stone;[1] he built a magnificent palace, luxuriant gardens and pools. The Bible reports that he spoke 3000 proverbs and wrote 1005 songs,[2] the greatest being the subject of this book.

The Song of Solomon is a highly poetic story of the love relationship between a young Shulammite[3] woman and her beloved, Solomon. It is an allegory drama depicting the love relationship between Christ and his many-membered bride. The idea of a marriage union between the second person of the Godhead with the human race was in the heart of God prior to his creation of Adam and Eve; it is a profound subject with vast implications well beyond the scope of this exposition. Suffice it to say, the institution of marriage between humans was given by God in order that human beings might have a conceptual basis for understanding the love story of the ages, the intimate union between Christ and his beloved bride, the church.[4]

The Shulammite is a single representative of this corporate bride of Christ. The song portrays her personal journey into increasing depths of love, so the individual believer might understand the interactions and processes involved at the personal level as one progresses in his quest for full spiritual union with Christ.

The apostle Paul assures the church that she will eventually reach maturity.[5] It is to this end that he labored, that he might present

---

[1] 1 Kings 10:27; 2 Chronicles 9:27
[2] 1 Kings 4:32
[3] Song 6:13
[4] Matthew 22:2; Ephesians 5:32; 2 Corinthians 11:2; Revelation 19:7-9
[5] Ephesians 4:13

every man complete[1] in Christ.[2] Maturity is evidenced by a love for others. As the believer grows in his relationship with the Lord, he finds himself loving others more perfectly. He finds an increasing desire to express the life and love of Christ in his service to others. This writing examines the hesitations, fears and spiritual growth of the Shulammite as her beloved beckons her to enter fruitful fields of service together with him. She discovers that love and service are not antithetical but complementary in her quest for union with her beloved.

Characters

Main characters

The Shulammite (also called bride, darling, beautiful one, my sister, my dove, my perfect one) is representative of the believer who is seeking spiritual union with Christ. The Shulammite is the focus of the entire song. It is from her perspective that events are narrated, and it is her anxieties, longings, joys and fears that the reader is invited to share. The reader experiences the Shulammite's pain in her lover's absence and her joy in his return, for it is her thoughts and feelings that are the primary subject matter of the Song.

King Solomon (most often referred to by the Shulammite as her *beloved*) is representative of Christ (1:12; 3:7, 11; 8:2).

The Daughters of Jerusalem (also called maidens, daughters of Zion)[3] are representative of the church at large, including both male and female members. These observers are led through a series of changes themselves. They love the Bridegroom and rejoice over him (1:3-4); they are admonished not to stare at the Shulammite's weathered condition early in the song (1:5-6); they do not seek the Beloved with the same intensity of desire as does the Shulammite (2:2); they are admonished not to disturb what

---

[1] The Greek word *teleios* means "having reached its end" and is translated *complete, perfect,* or *mature.*
[2] Colossians 1:28
[3] Jerusalem or Zion is frequently described as "mother" to its "sons and daughters" in the writings of the post-exilic prophets (Isaiah 51:20; 60:4; Lamentations 1:4). The daughters of Zion are mentioned in Isaiah 3:16-24.

God is doing in the heart of the Shulammite (2:7; 3:5; 8:4); they, like the Shulammite early in the song, are separated from Solomon by a wall (2:9); they ask the Shulammite to catch the foxes that are spoiling their vineyards (2:15); they call attention to the Shulammite coming up from the wilderness (8:5); they are loving worshippers who learn to gaze upon the beauty of the king (3:10-11); the Shulammite seeks their help in finding her beloved (5:8), and they ask the Shulammite to describe him (5:9); they then desire to seek him with the Shulammite (6:1); they are a very large quantity among those who praise the Shulammite (6:8-10); they desire to gaze upon her (6:13), and they extol her beauty (7:1-5).

Other characters and who they represent

the Shulammite's brothers (1:6)	immature church leaders
companions of the Beloved (1:7; 8:13)	faithful shepherds
shepherds (1:8-11)	church leaders
young men (2:3)	all possible lovers
watchmen (3:3; 5:7)	intercessors
Shulammite's mother (1:6; 3:4; 6:9; 8:2)	the church
sixty mighty men of Israel (3:7)	mature believers
Solomon's mother (3:11; 8:5)	humanity
the guardsmen (5:7)	church leaders
queens (6:8-9)	mature believers
concubines (6:8-9)	attendants in heaven
the Shulammite's noble people (6:12)	mature believers
the little sister (8:8)	unbelievers who will yet be saved
caretakers of the vineyards (8:11)	ministers in the church

Structure and Story Line

In unraveling the basic structure of the Song, it is helpful to recognize the breaks formed by the three nearly identical adjurations (2:7; 3:5; 8:4) supplied by Solomon, the poet-author. Additionally, a major break occurs in the middle of the Song (after 5:1). These divisions form the basis for outlining the central theme as follows:

Act 1: Desire Kindled (1:1-2:7)

Feeling the emptiness of her own soul, the Shulammite pleads with her beloved to draw her after him. Eventually she moves from being a mere spectator at his table to actually enjoying his presence. However, the experience is fleeting, so she asks the shepherds, who have helped her thus far, if they might further strengthen her heart for she is lovesick.

Act II: The Invitation (2:8-3:5)

The Shulammite's beloved invites her to overcome her fears and join him in fields of service. Recoiling from his offer, she loses the sense of his presence, driving her to fervently seek and again find her beloved.

Act III: Desire Realized (3:6-5:1)

Inspired by the bridal procession, the Shulammite embraces the vision for her own spiritual maturity. Eager to please her beloved, she takes great pains to maximize his present and ensuing pleasure in the garden of her heart. Solomon drinks his wine and his milk, filling himself with joy over the life that has been yielded to him.

Act IV: Love Tested (5:2-8:4)

The Shulammite undergoes two tests. First, her beloved visits her at an inconvenient time. Unwilling to disquiet her own comfort, she rebuffs his advances. The Shulammite has a change of heart; but it is too late, for her beloved has departed. Eventually she realizes that he has gone to his favorite place; there she finds him pasturing his flock.

Then the Shulammite encounters her second test: she is tempted to withdraw from the burdens of ministry. However, the daughters of Jerusalem reassure her of her worth, and she recommits herself to the work. The Shulammite realizes that if she is going to experience union with her beloved, enjoying his abiding presence, she must be willing to join with him in doing the things he enjoys: particularly, ministering to those he loves.

Act V: Mature Love (8:5-8:14)

The Shulammite is now totally yielded to her beloved. Her heart has been enlarged with mature love, evidenced by her concern for the spiritual well-being of others. Her beloved is glad that her priorities are now one with his but reassures her that what he desires even more than service is to hear her words of affectionate love.

Setting

The Song of Solomon consists of a number of dreams and other musings experienced by the Shulammite. Three times Solomon admonishes the daughters of Jerusalem that they should not arouse or awaken his love until she pleases (2:7; 3:5; 8:4), and three times the Shulammite is specifically described as dreaming:

1. a night vision: "On my bed night after night I sought him whom my soul loves." (3:1)
2. a night vision: "I was asleep but my heart was awake." (5:2)
3. a day dream or musing: "Before I was aware, my soul set me over the chariots of my noble people." (6:12-13)

Extraordinary events set against a backdrop of suddenly changing scenery contribute to the surrealistic feel of a dreamy state. Thus, the Shulammite is portrayed as experiencing a sort of mystical sleep in which she typifies the heavenly-minded believer, that is, the one who has set his mind on the things above and not on the things that are upon the earth.[1]

Bridal Paradigm

Scripture portrays the church in many different ways. She is the temple of the Holy Spirit, the dwelling place of God; she is a royal priesthood, ordained to offer praise, worship and prayer to God; she is the family of God, many sons and daughters created in the image of the Father and born of his Spirit; she is an army, overcoming the forces of evil and establishing righteousness upon the earth; she is the body of Christ, doing the works of Jesus in his

---

[1] Colossians 3:2

name; she is a holy nation, called out from among the nations to show forth the glory of God. But at the end of the age, the primary identity of the church appears to be that of a bride— the bride of Christ. Significantly, it is the bride (in cooperation with the Spirit of God) who bids Jesus to come,[1] indicating that the church will have, by that time, cultivated a considerable hunger for intimate affection and eternal union with the Son of God.

The concept of deity being joined together with humanity in intimate union is a profound truth that was hidden throughout the ages but has now been revealed to the church. It was foreshadowed by Adam and Eve, whose marital relationship portrayed the eventual union of Jesus and his bride.[2] Since that time, God has increasingly revealed this marvelous truth. He used marital terminology when he spoke through the prophets, telling Israel that the day would come when they would no longer call him *My Master*, but they would call him *My Husband*.[3] That time is at hand.

Jesus clearly understood his role as the coming bridegroom, teaching that the kingdom of heaven is like a king who has a wedding feast for his son.[4] He also specifically likened his second coming to a bridegroom coming for his bride.[5] John the Baptist too, undoubtedly influenced by the writings of the prophets, described himself as a *friend of the bridegroom*.[6] The apostle Paul told the Corinthian church that he had *betrothed* them to Christ and urged them to remain devoted to Christ so that he would be able to present them as a *chaste virgin*.[7] According to the revelation given the apostle John, the church age culminates with a wedding feast.[8] The bridal paradigm is not an insignificant theme in Scripture, but is of paramount importance in helping the church understand her eternal purpose.

---

[1] Revelation 22:17, 20
[2] Ephesians 5:31-32
[3] Hosea 2:16; Isaiah 62:4-5
[4] Matthew 22:1-14
[5] Matthew 25:1-13
[6] John 3:29
[7] 2 Corinthians 11:2-3
[8] Revelation 19:7-9

Minor Themes

Although the Song of Solomon centers around the thoughts and feelings of the Shulammite, all of Scripture is primarily a revelation of Jesus, the second person of the Godhead. The song presents not only the bride's desire for intimacy with her beloved but also the Beloved's desire for intimacy with his bride.

The alluring power of beauty, both of the bride and of her beloved, is also elucidated. Revelations of the beauty or loveliness of Jesus are many: the Desire of the Nations (1:2-3), the All-sufficient One (1:3), the Good Shepherd (1:7; 2:16), the God of all gods (1:16-17), God of Creation (1:16-17), Resting Place (2:3), Lover of My Soul (2:4), Sovereign King (2:8), Husbandman, Vinedresser (2:11-13), Warrior-king (3:6-8), Majestic King (3:9-10), Bridegroom-King (3:11), Affectionate Bridegroom (4:9-11), Possessor of My Heart (4:16), Suffering Savior (5:2), Glorious One (5:10), Prince of Peace (5:12), Powerful (5:14), Compassionate (5:14), Word made Flesh (5:15), My Husband (7:6-9), Consuming Fire (8:6-7) and My Fortress (8:9).

Prominent throughout the song are the Beloved's intentional withdrawals, part of his strategy for drawing the Shulammite into greater depths of intimacy. While apart, the Shulammite's longings for her beloved increase in intensity (2:17-3:4; 4:16; 5:6; 8:14), even to the point that she becomes sick with love (2:5; 5:8). Although painful, these times of separation give the Shulammite opportunity to meditate upon the desirability of her beloved, elevating the degree of pleasure to be experienced in their eventual union.

Nuances of conjugal love, including the delights of sexual intimacy in marriage that would have been understood by a reader of the time, have not been explored. Although there may be value in such a study from the standpoint of validating God's approval of the pleasures of human sexuality, the Song of Solomon is primarily about the ultimate eternal romance between the human and the divine; this will be its enduring theme throughout eternity.

Although human marriage is both beautiful and enjoyable by design, it is merely a representation of Christ and his church.[1] Both the apostle Paul and the Lord Jesus maintained that marriage is not the loftiest ideal and should be subjugated, by those who are able, to the joy of an exclusive relationship with God.[2]

Preparation

In order to gain the most out of this song, one needs to prepare his heart through prayer, asking God to increase the soul's desire to know him. Then, having his heart tender toward God, the reader should continue dialoging with the Lord as he reads, not rushing ahead to gain some nugget of revelation but contemplating the meaning and personal application of the verses. It is helpful to let one's soul steep within the song, absorbing the truth of God's Word until the soul's very nature is transformed.

A desire to both know and walk in true love is key; the message of this song will remain a mystery to the heart that does not love, for "it is absolutely impossible that its expressions of fire be understood by a heart that is frigid."[3]

Punctuation and Capitalization

The Bible translation used is the New American Standard. The quotation marks, which are not in the original Hebrew, have been removed in order to not confuse the structure of this exposition.

The valuable tradition of capitalizing pronouns relating to God has been discarded only because many references are ambiguous, relating both to Solomon and to the Lord. The use of lower case pronouns helps to maintain the intentional ambiguity.

---

[1] Ephesians 5:31-32
[2] Matthew 19:11-12; 1 Corinthians 7:7-8, 24-28
[3] Arintero, *The Song of Songs* (Rockford, IL: Tan Books and Publishers, Inc., 1992) 31

Act I

———

Desire Kindled

Draw me after you and let us run together!

THE GREATEST SONG

<table>
<tr><td>Solomon, the poet-author:</td><td>1:1 The Song of Songs, which is Solomon's.</td></tr>
</table>

Greatest of All Songs

This is the *song of* all *songs*, meaning that it is the most excellent of all songs known to the poet-author, including the 1005 songs[1] written by Solomon himself, but his acclamation, inspired by the Holy Spirit and borne out by experience, has a wider connotation. It is a prophetic statement concerning the excellence of this song in relation to every song ever written or sung, whether on earth or in heaven, whether by angels or by men, whether a song of celebration, exaltation, declaration or adoration. Of all songs, this is the most excellent.

Unequaled Style

Why does this song merit such an appellation of excellence? Firstly, the style and imagery of the song is unequaled. The many plays on words (appreciable only in the original Hebrew language), the provocative yet discreet language, the picturesque imagery, the interweaving of various sub-themes, the rise and fall of emotional tones that increase in intensity as the reader is continually drawn into the vicarious romance of the Shulammite, make this song a timeless work of art.

Unequaled Subject

More importantly, it is the subject matter that sets this song apart from all others. Certainly there is no loftier a subject than that of the love relationship and ultimate union between Deity and his physical creation. What boundless ecstasy awaits those who will

---

[1] 1 Kings 4:32

become the eternal dwelling place of their Creator, the conscious vessel in which resides undefiled and limitless Love!

Consider the quality of this divine love. How can one begin to grasp the profundity of what he has scarcely witnessed, let alone experienced? Who can fathom the fierceness of innocent passion that resides in the heart of an incomprehensible God?

Love is more than a mere characteristic of God; love is the singular quality defining the very essence of Deity. As the apostle John succinctly states, God is love.[1] Do we dare postulate what might be the pinnacle expression of such love? Could we possibly grasp the implications of such conjecture? Surely the possible reward of capturing even a glimpse of divine love far outweighs the risk of appearing foolishly inept. So where shall we begin?

The Father's love for his children

From a human perspective, is there a love more tender in expression, more violent in safekeeping, more altruistic in care or more selfless in devotion than the love of a mother for her child? Can a mother ever forget her nursing child?[2] Can she ignore the cry of one for whom she endured the pain of delivery? Every contemplation of her child's potential brings its own reward. Even so, a mother's love pales in comparison to the inexhaustible love that the heavenly Father feels for each of his children.

It was love that compelled the Father to sacrifice the Son of his eternal delight so that he might receive many sons and daughters upon whom he could lavish his affection. How undeserved is this love! While we were enemies of God, engaged in evil deeds, the Father sent his Son to suffer a humiliating death in our place. Furthermore, with what generosity does the Father reward us for simply acknowledging the truth of our condition and turning to him with a grateful heart? We become one spirit with him, the Holy Spirit taking up residence in us. It is not yet revealed what we shall be, but we know that when we see him we will be like

---

[1] 1 John 4:8-16
[2] Isaiah 49:15

him.[1] Being his elect, we will be like Christ, filled up with all the fullness of the Godhead in our bodily form.[2] Forever we will radiate his goodness, all of creation glorifying God as they witness his beauty, power and love displayed in our physical bodies. How amazing is God's gratuitous love!

Jesus' love for his bride

Yet, in our attempt to understand divine love, the parent-child paradigm is incomplete, for a child is incapable of responding in such a way as to excite the full range of human emotion in the parent. Admittedly, the purity and the vulnerability of a child's love is without compare, and particularly, the love a parent receives from his adult progeny can provoke feelings of satisfaction found nowhere else. Also, from the child's perspective, the sense of significance, security and comfort received from a loving parent is unexcelled in human relationships. However, the parent-child paradigm lacks the passion for intimacy that burns in the heart of the Son of God for his eternal companion.

Therefore, the love that Jesus has for the church is illustrated in this song and elsewhere in the Bible by the love that a man has for his bride. Is there any love more intimate, more satisfying, more calculating, more consuming, more arresting, more invigorating, more thrilling, more intoxicating or more passionate than the affection that exists between two lovers? Yet even this is but a faint semblance of the fierceness of divine love.

With regard to passion, consider the price that Jesus was willing to pay in order to secure his bride. Jesus was from eternity past full of radiant glory, beautiful beyond description, unlimited in power, the sole recipient of the Father's affection and the singular source of the Father's joy, yet Jesus willingly stripped himself of his eternal glory, irreversibly taking on the form of a human. In his attempt to love and restore an insurgent humanity, he was mercilessly tortured and left to die on a cruel cross.

---

[1] 1 John 3:2
[2] John 1:16; 17:22-23; Romans 8:29; Ephesians 4:13; Colossians 1:27; 2:9

Certainly Jesus' devotion to his Father provided sufficient motivation for him to sacrificially lay down his life in order that the Father's heart might rapt with love in the embrace of millions of loving sons and daughters who would manifest his glory forever.

But Jesus' willing participation in this magnificent plan is propelled not only by his love for the Father, but also by his indefinable love for his bride. This is the essence of this song. It is a revelation of the supreme drama of the ages. Whereas the rest of Scripture provides the unfolding of the divine drama in all its intricacies, the Song of Solomon provides a glimpse into the heart that motivates the Savior's activities. He is irresistibly drawn by the beauty he sees in the bride.

This book displays the unashamed pursuit of the bride for her beloved on a road not well-traveled, but revealed by the Holy Spirit in order that we might be, at the end of the age, merely one of a many-membered bride— a bride who has made herself ready and is even now crying out for the return of her beloved.

Eternal intimate love

The significance of an eternal and intimate union between the immortal Son of God with physical beings made in his own image, fashioned with this end in mind, cannot be overstated. God's desire is that he be adorned by his creation, a creation subdued, cleansed, glorified and sustained by the exertion of his own power— forever.

Significance of a Song

Why does this most delightful and intriguing of all stories come not as prose, not even as a poem, but as a song? A song, by its very nature, has the power to arouse the soul; a song is intoxicating. The fact that we have a song before us is an indication that it is intended to be the subject of one's thoughts on a regular basis, a delightful[1] preoccupation of the mind, not mere information, but a spark of divine revelation of God's heart of fiery love for his bride

---

[1] James 5:13

and her passionate and endless longing for him. God intends that this song awaken in his church ardent desire for him, a desire that eternity will only begin to satiate.

Significance of the Author

It's author, Solomon, is a king. Undoubtedly this man had many encumbrances with which to occupy his mind, yet in all his enterprise, he found the time to ponder the excellence of divine love (8:6). Solomon serves as an example to the twenty-first century man or woman, living in a time when knowledge is increasing at a dizzying pace, of the accessibility of the heavenly Bridegroom. Truly, he is accessible if one would but make him the priority and definitive focus of life.

DESIRABILITY OF THE KING

Shulammite: | 1:2 **May he kiss me with the kisses of his mouth!**

Desire for Love

Smoldering passion explodes upon the scene as the Shulammite begins this discourse concerning her beloved. She speaks not as a servant wanting well-deserved praise, nor as a disciple wanting instruction, encouragement and enablement, nor as a child wanting comfort, care and affirmation. She speaks as a lover and a bride wanting nothing less than her beloved.

Kisses from her beloved's *mouth* communicate to the Shulammite his yearning for her. She longs to experience the exhilaration of knowing that she is wholly desirable to him. The Shulammite wants to know his love, feel his love and be enthralled by his love. She wants the feeling of intimacy. Here kisses are a metaphor for intimacy, for romantic love, love that is pleasurable, exciting and fulfilling.

The desire for affectionate love is built into the soul of every human. Every child, every young person and every adult wants to feel loved, valued and special. Love is the most compelling force in the earth because the universal demand to be loved is the most powerful desire of the human heart.

Desire for love is one evidence that man was created in God's own image, created with the potential of being joined together with the one who made him. God is love. He designed humans not only with the capacity to experience the joy of being fully loved but also with the potential of being perfected in love. Still, the Shulammite must *be loved* if she is going to love more perfectly, for only when she feels secure in the love of another will she be willing to fully love. However, at the moment, the Shulammite is not thinking about being perfected in love; her only desire is to know that she *is loved*.

While some may judge the Shulammite to be self-centered or even distastefully sensual, she makes no apology for her unashamed supplication, for she seems to understand intuitively what must be explained to the uninitiated, that love demands expression. In other words, the very nature of love demands that it be given expression, or it can no longer justly be called love.

Though it may appear that the Shulammite is here placing intemperate demands upon her beloved, she thinks otherwise, for she knows that the pleasure she will derive from receiving such expressions of love is not the least at variance with the pleasure he will experience in the giving of such expressions.

The Only Safe Context for Intimacy

Love provides the only safe context for intimacy; for intimacy is built on trust, and love provides the only secure basis for trust. One might trust a doctor, a mechanic or an accountant because of his integrity or competence, but these qualities alone are insufficient as a basis for the level of trust required for intimacy, which involves making oneself vulnerable to the pain of rejection and the shame of exposure.

In the Garden of Eden, Adam and Eve, naked and not ashamed, experienced intimacy. Without having tasted of sin, Adam and Eve were not subject to the woundings and fears associated with false accusations, selfish exploitations, demanding withdrawals or evil intentions.

Now that sin has entered into the world, every relationship has been affected by painful disappointments. Where is the man or the woman who can be totally trusted to act always with the other's best interest at heart? Only God is worthy of such trust. His love never disappoints.

Many Kisses

In a spiritual sense, kisses are the revelations of God's love to the human heart. The Shulammite wants not just one kiss but many. One kiss will try to convince her of her beloved's love for the moment, but her famished heart requires continual reassurances. The Lord's kiss may come as a fresh revelation from his Word,[1] producing impulsive praise, a moment of awe while gazing at a billowy sky or a multicolor sunset, the sheer delight of a child's spontaneous affection, or the warm sense of his presence in a moment of prayer or worship. It may be the convergence of many circumstances in a way that convinces the heart that God is intimately involved in every detail of one's life.

These revelations of God's love reassure the believer of the Lord's undying devotion, causing the flame of desire within the human heart to become an all-consuming fire that melts away one's preoccupation with himself.

Abrupt Beginning

The abruptness with which the Shulammite begins her discourse betrays the fact that she has been meditating upon her beloved for some time. She is yet immature but full of passion. Only the passionate will relate to the Shulammite. She is a soul hungry for God, hungry for union with the Divine.[2]

Like the unnamed sinner who washed Jesus' feet with her tears,[3] the Shulammite has already kissed his feet. In other words, she has experienced repentance from sin, and is now full of longing to possess and enjoy him. She wants to be one spirit with him. Not content to wait for his second coming to be so joined with him, to behold him, the Shulammite longs for his kisses now.

Why does she want kisses from *him* and not from another? The Shulammite answers this question in the passage that follows.

---

[1] God spoke to Moses mouth to mouth (Numbers 12:8).
[2] Galatians 2:20
[3] Luke 7:37-50

For your love is better than wine.
1:3 Your oils have a pleasing fragrance,
Your name is like purified oil;
Therefore the maidens love you.
1:4 Draw me after you and let us run *together*!

Love Better than Wine

Becoming more bold, the Shulammite addresses her beloved directly, declaring that the awareness of his affection is more exhilarating, more tantalizing and more soothing *than wine*. Being far superior to wine, only his love can satisfy the relentless cry within her heart for love. Wine implies a momentary sensual bliss that merely dulls the pain of unfulfilled longings, whereas her beloved's affection completes the soul through the impartation of awaking and restorative life. How superior is his love to wine!

His Oils

The *oils* of the Shulammite's beloved *have a pleasing fragrance*. Whereas men attempt to enhance their desirability by rubbing fragrant oils into their skin, Christ has no need of adding anything to himself. It is the fragrance of his very own nature, the thoughts, feelings and inclinations that arise from within his own being, that makes him wholly desirable.

There are three outstanding characteristics alluded to in this song that make the Shulammite's beloved particularly alluring. They are more like three outline headings under which could be inserted a host of additional characteristics serving to amplify each of the three. Every human being is attracted by these three qualities because they satisfy longings deep within every soul.

Beautiful (1:16; 2:3)

There is something fascinating and compelling about that which is beautiful. Beauty attracts; whereas, that which is ugly or grotesque repels. Every person has a desire to be joined to beauty. Individuals adorn themselves with beautiful things in order to enhance their own personal beauty, believing that the beauty of the object is transferred to the one who is so adorned. For this reason, people decorate themselves with jewelry, a fashionable car, or even well-dressed children or an attractive spouse.

However, beauty is more than physical. Qualities such as wisdom, compassion and humility also beautify an individual. For example, someone might say, "It was beautiful to see the way he took care of his brother" or, "He handled that situation beautifully" or, "It was beautiful to see how he humbled himself in asking forgiveness." The Lord Jesus is unsurpassed and indescribably beautiful in radiant glory, yet it is the inner qualities implied by the oil metaphor that make him so compelling to the Shulammite.

Unlike the beauty of earthly objects, the beauty of the Lord Jesus can actually be imparted to the one who possesses him. This is because he comes to dwell within the believer, his presence permeating the entire being of that person so that he becomes a new creation in which all the old things have passed away and everything becomes new.[1]

The process of transformation begins when a believer receives the Word of God; it is like a seed planted in his heart.[2] As he walks in the truth of the Word, the seed continues to grow, producing a tree of righteousness[3] from which grows the fruit of the Holy Spirit:[4] love, joy, peace, patience, gentleness, kindness and humility, qualities that truly enhance the beauty of the individual.

King David, the father of Solomon, wanted one thing from the Lord, that he might dwell in the house of the Lord all the days of his life, to behold the beauty of the Lord and to meditate in His temple.[5] The Lord is unsurpassed in beauty in every sense of the word and is, therefore, wholly desirable. By beholding his beauty, one becomes transfixed, adorned, and ultimately transformed into Christ's glorious image.

---

[1] 2 Corinthians 5:17
[2] James 1:21
[3] James 3:18
[4] Galatians 5:22
[5] Psalm 27:4

Powerful (2:8-9; 3:6-10)

People generally respect power and despise weakness; most people would prefer to be on a winning team than to be on a losing team. Power is sought out through many avenues: an influential friend, a secure job, an impressive diploma or the increase of knowledge. Wealth is often accumulated for the feeling of power and security it provides the owner.

Everyone wants the ability to successfully make their dreams become reality, to feel safe, protected and secure. Often, although not a rule by any means, women tend to be more concerned about feeling safe, while men strive to feel successful. In reality, success is simply a different way of making a person feel safe, safe from the fears of humiliation and rejection that often follow hard on the heels of failure.

Having all power and all authority, whether in heaven or on the earth, Jesus Christ is the most powerful individual in the universe. He has the power to govern the affairs of men and of nations, to maintain the stars and their courses and to hold every atomic particle in its place. He has the power to create, to impart life and to satisfy the innermost desires of every human being.

Amazingly, because of the great love he has for his bride, Christ offers to share his unfathomable power, riches and authority with those who will trust him with their lives. Jesus said that those who overcome the world will be seated together with him upon his throne forever.[1] This, the highest attainment possible, is the pinnacle of success for any human being. The person joined to Christ becomes strong, successful and safe in him, the eternal Beloved.

Tenderhearted (4:1-15; 5:2-4; 6:4-5)

It is possible to behold someone of stunning beauty and exceptional strength without feeling particularly drawn toward greater levels of intimacy with that individual, for such a person has the capacity to captivate the imagination but not the heart. This

---

[1] Revelation 3:21

is because intimacy requires trust, and trust refuses to rest upon one who is not also perceived to be kind, gentle and tenderhearted.

People gravitate toward those who seem sensitive and responsive to what is important to them. They want to be able to share their dreams, struggles, victories and pains with someone whose response will be comforting and reassuring. Such responses help convince them that they are accepted and enjoyed. Inwardly they desire to be known, to be understood and to be valued by someone they esteem. Tenderhearted affection causes them to feel alive; it awakens hope that they are consequential and that life has purpose.

To be treasured by Christ is the ultimate affirmation. Knowing the affections of Christ has the power to soften the most hardened heart, give hope to the most downcast and heal the most broken. There is no one whose estimation is to be more valued than that of Christ. Knowing that Jesus considers one worth the price of his blood is both humbling and ennobling.

Conclusion

Apart from Christ, the qualities of beauty, power and tenderheartedness are corrupted. The legitimate attraction to beauty ensnares the heart through lust; power preys upon the weak, and feigned affection manipulates the naive through illicit control. Thus, because intimacy presupposes vulnerability, there can be no intimacy in the context of human relationships without substantial risk of injury.

However, with Jesus there is no such risk, for he is no ordinary man. Jesus, the source of the Father's continual delight from eternity past,[1] is love made flesh. To be vulnerable with one who is completely loving and joy-giving, guarantees the rapturous delight of total abandonment to another, without any accompanying fear.

Jesus is unsurpassed in beauty, sovereign in power and uniquely passionate in his love and desire for his bride. There is none like him. Who would not want to know him? Who would not leap at

---

[1] John 1:1-3

the invitation to forsake all other lovers in order that they might gain Christ? Who would not want to joyfully abandon themselves to his tender mercies?

His Name

Jesus' *name is like purified oil;*[1] there is no imperfection in him. He is the Creator of Heaven and Earth, Almighty God, the All-knowing, Ever-present, Eternal, Lawgiver, King and Judge. He is the Lion from the tribe of Judah, the Ancient of Days, Prince of Peace, Provider, Healer, Deliverer, Savior, Lord and Christ. He is the Lamb of God slain from the foundation of the world, the Word of God and the Wisdom of God. He is the Resurrection and the Life, the only Door to the Father, the only Begotten of the Father, Faithful and True. He is King of kings and Lord of lords. He rules with justice, mercy and truth. He never changes; he is the same yesterday, today and forever. He is the Good Shepherd and Heavenly Bridegroom, full of compassion, gracious, slow to anger, tenderhearted, gentle and kind. Words fail to adequately describe the beauty, power and grace that belong to the person of the Lord Jesus Christ. He has a name that no one knows except himself.[2] His glory is beyond knowing. He is worthy to receive all riches, honor, glory, power, might, blessing and dominion both now and forever, so that at the name of Jesus every knee should bow, of those who are in heaven and on the earth and under the earth.[3]

Maidens

It is no wonder that *the maidens love* him! How could all the world not love him? It is impossible to know Christ and not be ravished by his love. The *maidens* in the song symbolize immature believers. Their hearts have not become hardened by years of unbelief and cynicism, but they are tender toward spiritual things. The Shulammite can see that they, like herself, love the Lord and are in

---

[1] *Purified oil* is literally "oil that is emptied (from one vessel to another)."
[2] Revelation 19:12
[3] Philippians 2:10

the process of growing into the measure of the stature of the fullness of Christ.[1]

It will become apparent later that the intensity of the Shulammite's desire for her beloved differs from that of the maidens.[2] At this point, it is sufficient to note that the Shulammite is singled out by the poet-author so the reader can observe the development of her love on a personal level.

Draw Me

The maidens love and praise their king, but the Shulammite's response is more decisive. Longing to be drawn into his presence, she asks for grace. *"Draw me,"*[3] she pleads. The Shulammite knows that her own human affections are insufficient to carry her into the depth of intimacy, love and devotion her heart craves. She asks for grace to be totally abandoned to the purposes of her beloved that she might *run together* with him.

Although the Shulammite desires the freedom that comes with total abandonment of the will, she does not yet realize what complete surrender will entail. Nevertheless, she makes a dual request: *Draw me after you and let us run together.* The Shulammite asks to be drawn into greater intimacy and service; the tension implied in this dual request is a key to intimacy that she discovers only later. This tension between intimate embrace and service underlies the principal theme of the song. But for now the Shulammite does not really want service; she only wants to be near her beloved. In her mind, *running together* simply implies a freedom in the expression of her personal devotion and freedom from fear, anxiety, depression and other sinful encumbrances that might otherwise distract her from enjoying her beloved.

The Shulammite wants to be yoked together with her beloved, but she realizes that the place she wants to go in her walk with God cannot be achieved by human effort alone. Knowing that

---

[1] Ephesians 4:13
[2] The difference is plain in 2:2.
[3] This can also be translated "drag me" (Psalm 28:3; Job 24:22, 41:1).

supernatural grace will be required to bring a mere mortal into union with the living God, she wisely pleads for his help.

Although the Shulammite loves her beloved, she is aware that his desire for her is greater than her desire for him. She is hoping that through the kisses of his mouth (1:2), that is, by experiencing her beloved's love more frequently and more fully, her desire for him will increase, and she will also love him more perfectly. Like the father who brought his son to Jesus to be healed, she might be heard saying, "I do believe; help my unbelief."[1]

Shulammite: | 1:4b **The king has brought me into his chambers.**[2]

Why does the Shulammite's heart long so intensely for her beloved? What is the fascination with her king that compels her to be so boldly assertive? The Shulammite explains: *the king* had previously *brought* her *into his chambers*, the innermost places of his dwelling.[3] These are not places for the casual inquirer, nor the curious onlooker. They are places reserved for those who love and seek him;[4] they are places where he lets himself be known.[5]

At times the Lord grants his elect a special revelation of himself, producing a twofold effect. The incomparable joy of the experience brings a deep sense of contentment to the believer, and at the same time, the believer is ruined for anything else the world may have to offer. This is what happens when a believer is baptized in the Holy Spirit: he experiences the joy of God's wonderful presence so that he is ruined for anything less.

---

[1] Mark 9:24

[2] This can be translated (as it appears in the *New International Version*), "Let the king bring me into his chambers," thus corresponding to "May he kiss me" (1:2). The remainder of Act 1 would then portray the Shulammite coming into the king's various enclosures (1:12 where *table* can be translated *enclosure*; 1:17; 2:4). However, the NASB translation is preferred because the three enclosure scenes seem to describe her present experience, not her unfulfilled pursuit.

[3] Being with the king in his private rooms is a significant theme throughout Act I. The Shulammite is with her beloved in his chambers (1:4): at his table, literally, *enclosure* (1:12), in his houses (1:17) and in his banquet hall (2:4).

[4] Acts 5:32

[5] Philippians 3:10

Jesus told his disciples that they would receive power when the Holy Spirit comes upon them. Therefore, it is fitting that believers expect to receive power when they petition God to be baptized with the Holy Spirit, but it should be noted that the power is merely an effect of the Holy Spirit's coming. For the Holy Spirit is a person, and although he comes in power, he also imparts a revelation of the character and nature of God.

When Moses, hungry to know God more fully, boldly cried out, "Show me your glory," the Lord certainly understood that Moses was asking for more than a manifestation of God's power. Moses had seen the plagues over Egypt, the parting of the Red Sea, the pouring forth of water from a rock and the etching of the ten commandments into stone by the finger of God. What Moses wanted was a revelation of who God is: a revelation of his person. After sheltering Moses in the cleft of the rock, the glorious manifestation of God's presence passed by and God announced himself, "The Lord, the Lord God, compassionate and gracious, slow to anger, and abounding in lovingkindness and truth; who keeps lovingkindness for thousands, who forgives iniquity, transgression and sin."[1] At that moment Moses received a revelation of who God is.

God is, in a word, love.[2] Therefore, when God manifests himself to a soul longing to know him, baptizing him with his Spirit, it is natural that God would make known his love. Such a foretaste of God's love provides the needed motivation for the believer to spend a lifetime, if necessary, in his quest for full and permanent union with the living God.

Knowing that God must escort the believer into his secret dwelling place, the Shulammite acknowledges that it is her king who has opened the way into his chambers for her. The believer knocks, but it is the Lord who must open the door and, by an act of divine grace, escort the believer inside.

---

[1] Exodus 34:6-7
[2] 1 John 4:8, 16

Seeming to leave her story incomplete, the Shulammite does not tell what the chambers are like or what happened in the chambers. This is to illustrate that one's experiences with the Holy Spirit are a private matter. Sometimes the believer has permission to speak of such things, but other times not. Sometimes there are, by divine design, no words to describe what is meant to be kept secret, for secrecy among two parties fosters a sense of intimacy between them.

Chambers are plural because the Lord has many revelations of himself that he would share with the Shulammite. At this point she has learned to appreciate only a minute degree of his overwhelming love, his extravagant beauty, his awesome power, his glorious majesty and his intoxicating joy. She has yet to learn of not only his kindness but also his severity, his justice as well as his mercy, and his sacrificial love as well as his tenderhearted love. There are many chambers in her beloved's dwelling, and eternity will provide insufficient time to exhaust the joy of discovering the innumerable revelations within his chambers. What limitless delights await those who love him!

daughters of Jerusalem to Beloved:	
1:4c	**We will rejoice in you and be glad;**
	We will extol your love more than wine.

Voices of maidens rejoicing in their king sharply interrupt the Shulammite's musings. Although the Shulammite's brief encounter in the king's chambers has no doubt helped to further captivate her heart and increase her hope of the intimacy yet to come, it was not sufficient to alleviate the troubling tendency to become so easily distracted from her quest of making her beloved her every thought.

The maidens agree with the Shulammite in her estimation of her beloved's beauty and power, for they have tasted of his *love* and found it to be sweeter *than wine*. Still, the maidens do not yet know him intimately, evidenced by the fact that they, like the Shulammite, are yet separated from the Beloved by a wall (2:9).

Although enthusiastic displays of devotion can masquerade as true love, the Shulammite interprets the maidens' praise at face value. Unaware that their hearts have not been stirred with the same degree of longing as hers,[1] she is impressed by the freedom of expression the maidens have in their praise of the Beloved. The Shulammite is not surprised that they love him so, for she has just come from his private chambers where she received a profound revelation of his beauty, power and love. Agreeing with the maidens, the Shulammite says, "With just cause *do they love you*." Who would not love him? He is perfect in every way; there is none like him in all the earth.

The maidens (later called daughters of Jerusalem) represent the main body of the church. They are those precious souls who love to give the Lord praise but, as yet, are immature in their knowledge of him. Their faith is real, but has yet to be fully tested. Their praise is heartfelt, but not yet mixed with the bittersweet passion to know Christ more deeply— bitter in its unfulfilled longing, sweet in every contemplation of its divine object of focus.

---

[1] They eventually desire to seek the Beloved with the Shulammite in 6:1.

THE SHULAMMITE'S CONDITION

Shulammite to
the daughters of
Jerusalem: 1:5 **I am black but lovely,**
O daughters of Jerusalem,
Like the tents of Kedar,
Like the curtains of Solomon.
1:6 **Do not stare at me because I am swarthy,**
For the sun has burned me.
My mother's sons were angry with me;
They made me caretaker of the vineyards,
***But* I have not taken care of my own**
vineyard.

Black

The brief moment of bliss in the king's chambers (1:4b) lingers in the mind of the Shulammite. Though both pleasant and impacting, the experience was not completely transforming. The Shulammite remains immature, painfully self-conscious of her obvious shortcomings.

There is a striking coarseness to a life sorely affected by the pressures of the world. The Shulammite says simply, *"I am black."* Her blackness does not describe her natural coloring, but the weathered condition produced by the sun while she has labored in the heat of the day.[1] The sun in this case is a metaphor for the distresses, pressures, anxieties, wounds, rejections, frustrations and agitations that come with attempting to help comfort, encourage, train, counsel and correct others in their relationships with God and others.[2] These afflictions, coupled with the neglect of her personal walk with God, have resulted in the darkening of her own soul.

---

[1] Job's skin too was blackened by the heat of the sun (Job 30:30).
[2] In the book of Ecclesiastes, Solomon refers to the natural realm as that which is "under the sun."

Many saints have spent unimaginably long and difficult hours in faithful service without losing their peace and joy, but they have learned the secret of maintaining their awareness of the Lord's presence with them in all they do. The Shulammite, on the other hand, is like those who become overwhelmed by the concerns of caring for others. Impossibly, they attempt to live the lives of those they want to help. This inability to distinguish their own lives from the lives of those in need results in constant worry. They take upon themselves burdens God never intended them to carry, having not yet learned what Jesus meant when he said that his yoke is easy and his burden is light.[1] Their resulting lack of joy serves only to foster feelings of guilt, frustration, failure and discouragement, thus compounding a cycle of never-ending pressures that weigh heavily against the soul.

But Lovely

Although aware of her blackness, the Shulammite does not abandon hope, but boldly declares the conviction of her intrinsic worth. She offers two images of stark contrast in an attempt to illustrate her condition: black on the outside, *but lovely* on the inside.

1. The black goat hair *tents* of the Bedouins *of Kedar* exposed to the heat of the desert sun possess a coarseness apparent to any casual onlooker, but to the desert nomad such a tent is innately desirable as a place of comfort and rest.

2. Similarly, Solomon's *curtains*,[2] actually pavilions or pleasure-tents, paint a vivid picture of contrasts: darkly somber in appearance yet stunning in luxuriant beauty, a beauty that can be fully appreciated only by its occupant.

---

[1] Matthew 11:30

[2] Keil-Delitzsch, *Commentary on the Old Testament* (Grand Rapids, MI: Eerdmans, 1978) Vol. 6, p. 26. "By this word we will have to think of a pleasure-tent or pavilion for the king . . . spread out like the flying butterfly. This Hebrew word would certainly also mean curtains for separating a chamber; but in the . . . temple the curtains separating the Most Holy from the Holy Place were not so designated."

In likening herself to these black tents of Kedar and of Solomon, the Shulammite is saying, "There is more to me than what you might think; though I am weathered on the outside, I am beautiful on the inside."

Loveliness by design

The Shulammite is aware that, in spite of the coarseness resulting from years of neglect of her spiritual life, there is a loveliness, an innate desirability endowed by her Creator, for she has been made in the image of God, fashioned for the purpose of becoming his dwelling place, destined to manifest his glorious presence in her physical body forever. She does not count herself unworthy of eternal life,[1] but believes there is something intrinsically valuable and ultimately redeemable about her.

Loveliness confirmed through acceptance

Factors convincing the Shulammite of her desirability are not simply theological or intellectual, but also experiential. It was a powerful encounter in the king's innermost chambers (1:4b) that convinced the Shulammite of his love and acceptance. This event at the outset of the Shulammite's quest signifies her immersion or baptism in the Holy Spirit, an experience promised to all of Jesus' followers. Partaking of this heavenly gift, the believer receives overwhelming joy, unimaginable peace, and a firsthand revelation of the Savior's love.

Why are believers often plagued by doubts concerning their salvation? Why do they need constant reassurances of his commitment to them? The answer lies simply in their lack of experience with the Holy Spirit.

When the Holy Spirit descended upon Jesus like a dove, a voice was heard from heaven saying, "This is my beloved Son in whom I am well pleased."[2] Every believer should likewise expect his sonship to be confirmed as a result of his encounter with the Holy Spirit. Although he may not hear a voice from heaven, the believer should expect that in some way, the words of Jesus will be

---

[1] Acts 13:46
[2] Matthew 3:17

fulfilled: "I will ask the Father, and he will give you another Helper, that he may be with you forever; that is the Spirit of truth, . . . you know him because he abides with you, and will be in you. . . . In that day you shall know that I am in My Father, and you in Me, and I in you."[1]

Lovely because of desire

There is yet another reason why the Shulammite deems herself lovely. She believes that because she inwardly longs for her beloved, his love looks past the glaring imperfections all too obvious to those around her. Yes, she has made foolish choices in this journey called life; her darkened soul has shielded her, not only from those who would do harm, but also from her beloved. Walls that she built to protect herself from suffering pain have had the unintended purpose of shielding her from experiencing the joys of unfettered love. The darkness in the Shulammite's life is real, but there is a loveliness defined, not by past achievements, but by the present inclination of her heart. She possesses the beauty of an inner grace, a heart that desires to know God, to be one with her beloved that they might run together. She is convinced that he finds this trait attractive.

Daughters of Jerusalem

"Do not stare at me because I am swarthy," pleads the Shulammite. The daughters of Jerusalem stare because they do not know what else to do. They are not malicious, simply naive, lacking the experience or wisdom to know how to respond. The Shulammite is a mere curiosity to them.

Even still, the Shulammite feels obliged to explain the cause of her blackness to these onlookers. This need to find understanding from those ill-equipped to offer any assistance is an indication of her immaturity. Seasoned saints prefer to remain silent rather than attempt to justify themselves in the eyes of others, having learned that the past is usually best left in the past.

---

[1] John 14:16-17, 20

Caretaker

Being made a *caretaker of the vineyards*, signifies that the Shulammite was in the business of ministering to human souls. How ironic that one who is fully occupied with caring for others should, in the process, neglect the care of her own soul.

Aptly, the Shulammite portrays the contemporary believer who is diligent in the work of the ministry, but then neglects his first love.[1] He starts off well, serving the Lord with gladness, happy for any opportunity to be useful to the One who redeemed him and gave him life, but then fervent service becomes a substitute for obedience in little things. The Holy Spirit is speaking, but the believer is no longer sensitive to the gentle invitations to prayer, forgiveness, self-control and opportunities to humble himself before others. He loses the vitality and freshness of his initial relationship with God and eventually finds himself attempting to point others in a direction that he himself is not moving.

Stepbrothers

The Shulammite's *mother's sons* were likely her stepbrothers, causing one to imagine a cruel environment in which she had no father to whom she could appeal for protection. Although they have a different father, these stepbrothers have the same mother as the Shulammite, meaning that they are part of the professing church.

These sons represent church leaders who do not exhibit the spirit of the heavenly Father in their lives. Being fleshly and worldly minded or immature at best, they do not understand spiritual things; therefore, they tend to substitute activity for heartfelt worship, promotion for prayer, and programs for the power of the Holy Spirit. Deficient in wisdom, understanding and love for the truth, they are unable to lead others into a true knowledge of God. Oblivious to the intensity of the Shulammite's longings, they are unable to help her satisfy them.

---

[1] Revelation 2:4

Although the Shulammite admits to a blackness that resulted from neglecting the needs of her own soul, she views herself as somewhat of a victim. She blames her mother's sons for her condition: they were *angry* with her and *they made* her caretaker of the vineyards.[1] The anger and the coercion of her stepbrothers are indicative of two hardships faced by the Shulammite.

Addressing the angry environment first, sympathy for the Shulammite might seem to be in order. Yet the apostle Peter writes that to patiently endure harsh, unreasonable and unjust treatment finds favor with God.[2] Working for one who is easily provoked can provide opportunity to grow in the graces of humility, gentleness, kindness and patience. Thus, the Shulammite would do well to not view herself as a victim, but accept full responsibility for her own responses to her stepbrothers' anger.

The second hardship faced by the Shulammite, the coercion she felt from her stepbrothers, implies that she had a heavy workload and insufficient time in which to care for her *own vineyard*. She seems to blame her stepbrothers, suggesting that it was because of their coercion that she did not have the time to care for her soul.

However, the facts do not bear out her protestations. The Shulammite was not a slave to the vineyards for she was also a shepherdess. She found time to care for her goats; was there no time to care for her soul? She believes that circumstances beyond her control caused her soul to suffer loss, but there are few moments in life over which one has no control. With rare exception, one's life course is determined by decisions made on the basis of perceived reward or penalty. The Shulammite was not victimized by her stepbrothers, for she, by her own choices, helped to shape the world in which she lived. Something was more important to the Shulammite than taking care of her soul.

At this point it is instructive to note what may have motivated the Shulammite to make choices that were ultimately self-destructive.

---

[1] The *New International Version* is more emphatic: " . . . and made me take care of the vineyards."
[2] 1 Peter 2:18-20

The Hebrew word that describes the stepbrothers' anger (1:6) is telling, for the word *angry* can also be translated *burned*. Thus, the Shulammite was *burned* by her stepbrothers' anger that she interpreted as rejection. Where the Shulammite complains, "*the sun has burned me*" (1:6), the text literally reads, "the sun has *glanced* at me." This searing gaze of the sun is a metaphor for the pressure the Shulammite felt by allowing herself to be dominated by the fear of the opinions of her brothers.

Because believers are supposed to be accepting of one another, even as they have been shown acceptance by Christ,[1] the church should be the last place where someone ought to fear rejection. Nevertheless, believers can feel driven to perform for others in hopes of obtaining their approval. In which case, believers' lives become dominated by the fear of the opinions of men, eventually costing them their peace, their joy and their intimacy with God.

The Shulammite's stepbrothers can also symbolize one's misguided conscience. Because of the weakness of their faith, believers sometimes feel they need to work very hard in order to justify themselves before God and thus gain his approval. However, this attempt completely undermines the sacrifice of Jesus and the blood that he shed for their justification. Believers should not feel motivated to labor in order to gain God's acceptance, but their labor should flow out of a heart of love and gratitude for all that God has already done for them.

Still controlled to a great degree by her fears, the Shulammite has not yet learned how to labor out of love. She does not have the knowledge of God necessary to sustain her in the work; this she will develop later. There is hope for the Shulammite. She admits responsibility for not caring for her own vineyard, decisively breaking free from the fear that had controlled her. She is willing to address the needs of her own soul in order to pursue her beloved with wholehearted abandonment.

---

[1] Romans 15:7

Tell me, O you whom my soul loves,
Where do you pasture *your flock,*
Where do you make *it* lie down at noon?
For why should I be like one who veils herself
Beside the flocks of your companions?

The Good Shepherd

Although the Shulammite has admitted to not tending her own vineyard, resulting in the bedraggled condition of her darkened soul, she insists that she really does love her beloved and that she now wants to take whatever action is necessary to be near him.

Recognizing that she needs healing, the Shulammite comes to her beloved, not as though he were a king, nor an intimate lover, but she comes to him as the Good Shepherd. She sees herself like a little lamb needing to be cared for, nourished and strengthened by the Shepherd and Guardian[1] of her soul.

The Shulammite begs to know where her beloved makes his *flock lie down at noon*. Sheep will not lie down in the heat of the day until their hunger has been satisfied. The Shulammite wants to experience the soul satisfaction and rest that no one can give except her beloved. She has neglected him for too long and now wants to restore the feeling of intimacy she once enjoyed. Like the prodigal son who finally comes to his senses and returns home to be clothed and fed by his father, the Shulammite has come to her senses and is now searching for the road back home to her beloved.

Friendship with God

The Shulammite *loves* her beloved, but because she has neglected their relationship, she now feels far removed from him. When she passes by the flocks of his friends, she feels like an outsider, not free to mingle among them. Ashamed of her darkened condition, she likens herself to a harlot who must cover her face in public,[2] particularly when among her beloved's *companions*, those who

---

[1] 1 Peter 2:25
[2] Genesis 38:15

have already entered into the place of friendship with God. Jesus said that his friends are those who do what he commands.[1] Abraham became a friend of God[2] because he was one whom God could count on to keep his commandments.[3]

Some suppose that God's commandments are impossible to obey, yet Moses told Israel that God's commandments were not too difficult, nor were they out of reach.[4] The apostle John in the New Testament also gives assurance that God's commandments are not burdensome.[5] To maintain that God has issued commandments that he knew were impossible to keep is contrary to the plain teaching of Scripture and accuses God of being unkind and unjust. The accusation relieves man of any sense of responsibility for his disobedience, rationalizing that the commandment was, after all, *unreasonably difficult*. However, God is not unreasonable, nor is he unjust.

Every believer can take comfort in the fact that if he sins, he need merely confess his sin to God in order to obtain forgiveness, for the shed blood of the precious Savior is sufficient to cleanse him from all unrighteousness.[6] However, just because God has made provision for one's failure, does not presuppose that he will fail. To think otherwise is to presume that because there is a fire station located nearby, it is inevitable that one's house will burn.

To live with the constant expectation of moral failure is to set oneself up for defeat, for in any temptation one might rationalize that it is simply one of those occasions in which must come the inevitable failure. A person will live what he believes; he will certainly live no higher than what he believes to be possible. If he believes failure is imminent, he will fail. If he believes he is a new creation, filled with the power of the Holy Spirit, then he will find grace to help in the time of need. For God has promised to not allow him to be tempted beyond that which he is able to endure,

---

[1] John 15:14-15
[2] James 2:23
[3] Genesis 17:9; 18:19
[4] Deuteronomy 30:11
[5] 1 John 5:3
[6] 1 John 1:9

but will in every temptation provide a way of escape.[1] This is the clear teaching of Scripture.

The Christian life was not designed to be a constant struggle with sin, but a life lived in union with Christ. An important key to living an overcoming life is to realize that all of God's commandments are based on the royal law, the law of love.[2] When a person is propelled by love, he finds that God's commandments are not burdensome, for when focusing upon loving God and loving others, he habitually experiences God's righteousness, peace and joy in the Holy Spirit. The psalmists of the Old Testament agree, finding God's commandments delightful, sweeter than honey and more to be desired than gold.[3]

The Shulammite does not want to live as a second class citizen in the kingdom of God. She asks pointedly, *"Why should I be like one who veils herself?"* In other words, "Is there any freedom for me? Is there any hope? Must I always be ashamed? How can my soul be restored? Why should I waste my life in aimless wandering? Is there a way home for me?"

Beloved to Shulammite:		
	1:8	**If you yourself do not know,**
		Most beautiful among women,
		Go forth on the trail of the flock,
		And pasture your young goats
		By the tents of the shepherds.
	1:9	**To me, my darling, you are like**
		My mare among the chariots of Pharaoh.
	1:10	**Your cheeks are lovely with ornaments,**
		Your neck with strings of beads.

Most Beautiful

"If you yourself do not know . . . " The Beloved seems to be gently chiding the Shulammite as if she should already know the answer as to where she might find him, yet he softens this mild reproof by assuring the Shulammite that she is *most beautiful among women.*

---

[1] 1 Corinthians 10:13
[2] Matthew 22:37-40; James 2:8
[3] Psalm 19:7-10; 119:47, 103, 127, 140

His subtle suggestion, that he expected her to have known where to find him, is calculated. He is giving notice that he is never far out of reach to the hungry, searching heart of the Shulammite, for although he may be hidden to some, he has made himself quite accessible to the *most beautiful among women*. It must never be allowed to escape her notice that her beloved has made every provision necessary for the Shulammite's entrance into union with him.

She is desirable. The Shulammite sees herself as weathered and unkempt, but her beloved sees her as *most beautiful*. Throughout the song the Beloved affirms the Shulammite's desirability and worth; there is never even a hint of disapproval. Beginning with this first address, he lavishes praise upon her, wishing to convince her of his love. He knows that if she ever truly believes that she is loved and wanted, she will stop at nothing in her pursuit for union with the one who so completely loves her.

Herein lies an essential key for igniting the hearts of God's people with love for him, a key with which the apostle Paul was well-acquainted. For he prayed that the church would come to know the love of Christ that surpasses knowledge, and that in knowing this love, she might be filled up to all the fullness of God.[1] Thus, Paul understood that for the church to experience the fullness of divine life, she must first receive a supernatural revelation of the incomprehensible love of Christ, a love that is irresistibly uncommon, indescribably excellent and inalterably intense.

Previously, even though conscious of her darkened condition, the Shulammite referred to herself as lovely (1:5), recognizing that there is something redeemable about herself, but when her beloved calls her *most beautiful*, he is not speaking of her potential but of the beauty he presently sees in her.

There is a charming story in the Old Testament of a young woman named Esther who, although chosen to wed King Ahasuerus because of her outstanding beauty, was required to undergo

---

[1] Ephesians 3:19

twelve months of purification and perfuming in order to make herself presentable before entering into the king's presence. Similarly, the Shulammite has yet to experience the purifying process of divinely orchestrated testings that will cause her to become even more presentable to her king. Be that as it may, in the eyes of the king, her present beauty far outshines all that passes for beauty among all other possible lovers; her beloved unhesitatingly hails her as the most beautiful among all women.

In like manner the future bride of Christ is breathtakingly beautiful to him, for he sees his divine nature in her. She has yet to develop the inner graces that will become evident in her fully mature state, but there is no other creature in heaven or on earth so captivating to the King of Heaven than the one who has been created in his own image and within whom dwells the very Spirit of God himself.

The king admires and desires the Shulammite and greatly anticipates granting her the peace that she knows can be found only in his presence (1:7). She will eventually have the one for whom her soul longs, but her immediate step is to find the tents of the shepherds.

Shepherds' Tents

In the previous verse (1:7), the Shulammite expressed her discontentment with merely pasturing her goats beside the shepherds' flocks. Now her beloved tells her that what she could not find in the shepherds' fields of service, she will find where they dwell: *"Go forth on the trail of the flock, and pasture your young goats by the tents of the shepherds."*

If she wants healing and the renewing of her soul, the Shulammite must learn from the shepherds, for they have been commissioned by the Good Shepherd to assist in the noble work of restoring the souls of those who are hungry to know the ways of God more perfectly. The Shulammite is encouraged to no longer remain aloof, lingering on the outskirts of the flocks. She must go to the tents of the shepherds in order to discover how they live. Many believers are willing to go to meetings for their periodic *feeding*, but a smaller number seek to know the way of life that has produced in the shepherd his ability to feed not only his flock but himself as well.

The *trail of the flock* that the Shulammite must travel alludes to two spiritual realities. First, the way that leads to life is not a boulevard but a narrow trail that few press in to find. Because many find it easier to wander on the outskirts of the flock, the Shulammite is encouraged to press in to the narrow way in order to find her beloved.

Second, although it is little-used, the trail is not unexplored. Those searching for God are sometimes tempted to strike out on their own in their attempt to forge a new spiritual path, yet the way to the Good Shepherd is not by some new revelation or new way but is marked out by those who have traveled that way before. Not only does the Shulammite have the examples of the patriarchs— Abel, Enoch, Noah, Abraham, Jacob, Moses, David and the like[1]— but she is encouraged to seek out those of her own generation who have come to know God beyond her present level of experience.

Certainly, the Lord wants to lead each one of his sheep personally, but how can his sheep expect to hear their Shepherd's voice if they cannot also hear it in the ones he sends? In addition, how can they expect to follow in the steps of the Master if they are not willing to follow in the way of those who have already learned to trod in the Master's steps? True shepherds are inspiring examples of faith and obedience who can help shed light on the darkened path to the heart's true home.

These spiritual guides do not always find it necessary to occupy positions of great authority in the church and may be humbly employed. Real spiritual authority is measured by one's standing with God, not their position in the church. True shepherds are able to say with the apostle Paul, "Be imitators of me, just as I also am of Christ."[2] How it must grieve the Lord that more do not avail themselves of the shepherds that he so graciously provides.

---

[1] Genesis 47:3
[2] 1 Corinthians 11:1

Shepherdess

The Shulammite's beloved instructs her, not only to go forth on the trail herself, but also to take her flock with her. An important key to personal spiritual development is to become actively involved in ministering to others. In shepherding others, one learns valuable lessons in self-sacrifice, wisdom, humility and love. These all work to bring one closer in his quest for union with the Beloved.

It is significant that the Shulammite's herd is goats and not sheep. Goats tend to be a bit more stubborn than sheep and here represent those followers who are a little more difficult with which to work. The Shulammite has not yet been able to bring her followers to maturity because she herself is only at the beginning of her great pilgrimage.

At times one may want to complain about the testy and abrasive souls that God sends to be cared for. One might like God to send some who are a little less trouble, more pliable or more godly, but it is helpful to remember that the Lord entrusts his shepherds with various responsibilities based upon two criteria: what they can handle at their present maturity level and what will best help in the process of conforming them to the image and likeness of Christ. Working with immature goats will give the Shulammite opportunities to grow in the graces of love, gentleness, humility, wisdom and patience, thus causing her to become more capable of ministering life to others.

The problem with the Shulammite, however, is that she has been trying to tend her goats alone. To her credit she has not given up, but now her beloved instructs her to find true shepherds who will teach both her and her flock the ways of God.

Darling

Having just directed the young Shulammite to the shepherds (1:8), her beloved does not want her to become discouraged in thinking that he will remain emotionally distant and reveal himself through human emissaries only. Therefore, he takes special pains to reassure her of his deep admiration of her charms: *"To me, my darling, you are like my mare among the chariots of Pharaoh."*

Another reason for his encouragement is that he does not perceive the Shulammite to be as dark as she might appear to others. He considers the likelihood that the shepherds will undervalue the passion and the potential that lies within the heart of this young shepherdess; therefore, he gives her assurances that he sees what others might overlook. *"To me . . . ,"* he asserts.

The king has already praised the Shulammite as the *most beautiful among women* (1:8), but now, in addressing her as *my darling* (1:9), he reveals the effect that she has upon him, that is, the extent to which she stirs his emotions. One familiar with horses can imagine the heart-throbbing allure of brazen power rippling through the flanks of parading stallions. Like the renown horses of Egypt (the finest of which were imported by Solomon), the Shulammite provokes a mysterious motion within her beloved and he decidedly sets his affections upon her.

What is the loveliness that the king sees in the Shulammite? To him she is stunningly beautiful, born for royalty. If the Shulammite were a mare, her beauty would give her no reason to be intimidated, even by the chariots of Pharaoh, for she is in no way inferior to the best the world has to offer. A king's steed is trained to remain steady, even in the din of battle,[1] for he bears the sovereign and majestic ruler of the nation. Here the king sees the Shulammite likewise as too beautiful to be intimidated by even the most powerful of the earth, and, like a king's steed, she too is destined to bear the stately presence of the king.

Her *cheeks*, meaning her facial expressions, particularly her smile, are *lovely* to her beloved. They are not yet fragrant like his cheeks (5:13), for she has merely begun to put on Christ. Although not fully conformed to his image, she is well on her way, and the king is enthusiastic about her progress. Her *neck*, meaning her will, is

---

[1] Job 39:19-25

resolute and has been adorned, having been *made lovely* with *strings of beads*, representing daily strings of right choices.[1]

The intensity of the Shulammite's longing for the king makes her uniquely compelling, and the uncommon humility with which she confesses the wretched condition of her darkened soul (1:5-6), as though blushing at her own deformity, makes her all the more lovely.

| Shepherds to Shulammite: | 1:11 | **We will make for you ornaments of gold With beads of silver.** |

Previously, the Beloved sent the Shulammite to learn from the shepherds where she might find him (1:8). Shepherds represent the true spiritual leaders, particularly apostles, prophets, evangelists, pastors and teachers.[2] They now offer to help the Shulammite become even more beautiful than she is already. Like faithful and selfless eunuchs, they will help prepare the bride for her wedding day.[3] It is their job to nurture and care for her soul, equipping her for service and inspiring her to godliness until she reaches full maturity.

By what standard will her maturity be measured? In other words, how mature will she become? The apostle Paul makes the audacious claim that she will eventually attain to the measure of the stature that belongs to the fullness of Christ.[4] The implications of such a claim stagger the imagination: the fullness of the incomprehensible, infinite glory of the uncreated Christ (far beyond the glory of angels) eternally manifest in human flesh— the Shulammite's flesh!

Shepherds will help the Shulammite understand her glorious and majestic destiny, revealing through word and deed the love of Christ, that she, being rooted and grounded in love, might be able to comprehend with all the saints what is the breadth and length

---

[1] Proverbs 1:8-9
[2] Ephesians 4:11
[3] Esther 2:3, 6, 15
[4] Ephesians 4:13

and height and depth, and to know the love of Christ that surpasses knowledge, that she might be filled up to all the fullness of God.[1] These are glorious promises from God's Word and certainly cannot be accomplished by human effort alone. The shepherds will need to be much in prayer and reliance upon the Holy Spirit to make even the slightest progress here.

Gold speaks of divinity; *ornaments of gold* upon the cheeks of the Shulammite thus represent the nature of Christ manifest in a thousand facial expressions: enthusiastic love, radiant joy, tenderhearted compassion, patient understanding, wise deliberation, resolute conviction, noble humility and soothing peace. How can one be decorated any more beautifully than by the character of Christ? There is none like him in all the earth, nor will there ever be. Let all creation bow down and worship him!

Silver speaks of redemption, that is, the saving work of Christ accomplished by his life, death and resurrection; thus, *strings of silver beads* upon the neck of the Shulammite represent the wise choices that contribute toward the redemptive purposes of God. Her glorious transformation requires continual yieldedness to the person of the Holy Spirit until Christ's nature is fully formed in her. Daily she decides to live for the greatest good, the manifestation of Christ's kingdom in the earth.

---

[1] Ephesians 3:18-19

THE SHULAMMITE'S DESIRE

Although the Shulammite was reluctant to reveal the details of her initial encounter in the king's chambers (1:4), the experience has lingered in its effects, being not an end in itself, but merely a beginning, a doorway into a greater dimension of beholding her beloved. After seeking help from the shepherds, the Shulammite makes significant progress in her walk with the Lord and is now able to provide a glimpse into some of her current experiences. She first describes the longing she feels while remotely in his presence (1:12-14); then she alludes to her various worship experiences (1:16-2:1), and finally, she describes the sheer delight of enjoying her beloved's love (2:3-2:5).

Shulammite: | 1:12 **While the king was at his table,**
My perfume gave forth its fragrance.
| 1:13 **My beloved is to me a pouch of myrrh**
Which lies all night between my breasts.
| 1:14 **My beloved is to me a cluster of henna blossoms**
In the vineyards of Engedi.

The King's Table

The *king* is *at his table*,[1] signifying that it is laden with many choice foods. This table has its fulfillment in the New Covenant and represents the bountiful provision that the Lord Jesus Christ has made available to all believers:[2] unending peace, overflowing joy, ravishing love, unshakable righteousness, far-reaching authority, immeasurable power and a radiant glory that will be experienced throughout eternity.

---

[1] The Hebrew *mesab*, translated table, can also be translated as that which encircles, surrounds, or is round. Thus, the idea of an enclosure may be suggested.
[2] Solomon feasted at a table set from a seemingly limitless supply of sumptuous meats. His daily provision was three-hundred bushels of fine flour, six-hundred bushels of meal, thirty oxen, and a hundred sheep besides deer, gazelles, roebucks, and fattened fowl (1 Kings 4:22-23). The king's table therefore represents a lavish display of God's bountiful provision available to the believer.

Here, at her present level of maturity, the Shulammite is absent from the king's table, meaning that she is not yet fully aware of the promises and the graces that have been laid up for her. The immature are not accustomed to the word of righteousness and can merely drink the milk of the Word of God;[1] solid foods are enjoyed by the mature, those whose spiritual senses have been trained in righteousness.[2] However, unaware as she might be, the Shulammite has received sufficient revelation of the beauty of the king to inspire insatiable longing and undying devotion.

Nard Perfume

Though distanced from her king, the Shulammite's *perfume* (literally, *nard*) *gave forth its fragrance*. Nard, sometimes called spikenard, is Sanskrit for *exhaling a scent* and symbolizes the Shulammite's impassioned praise, adoration and longings for love.

Nard is derived from a plant found in the Himalayas of India and China and imported in sealed alabaster jars. Although very costly, it was lavished upon Jesus by Mary of Bethany while he reclined at table in the final hours before he was crucified, giving a glimpse into the longings that lie not so hidden behind Mary's extravagant devotion. Such abandoned worship is very costly because it is only those who have fixed their affections unreservedly upon Christ that can attain the more sublime dimensions of ardent love.

Nard has a sweet, woody, spicy odor; it also has a slight sourness, suggestive of the angst of unfulfilled longing. In the Shulammite, the tartness of unfulfilled desire combines with the ineffable sweetness of every contemplation of her beloved. One is sometimes tempted to dull the pain of deferred hope by dreaming of houses, lands, success or other comforts— something relatively achievable, but the Shulammite willingly endures the intense disquiet of longing. She has but one desire, and she sets her affections unambiguously upon him. Though the Shulammite is obliged to wait for ultimate union, the fire of her desire does not subside.

---

[1] 1 Peter 2:2
[2] Hebrews 5:14

Myrrh

What is the secret to the Shulammite's loyal persistence? It is thoughts of her beloved continually pressing upon her heart, like a *pouch of myrrh* penetrating and invigorating the inner recesses of her soul.

A sweet and sharply spicy perfume, myrrh is pleasant to the nose, yet bitter to the tongue, an apt illustration of people's diverse reactions to the knowledge of God. Recalling the marvelous works of God is a source of untold delight for those who truly know him, while those who do not know him continually experience the pain of unfulfilled expectations. They are constantly disillusioned because they grievously misunderstand their Maker. His righteousness and justice are oftentimes taken to be harshness or even cruelty; his patience is viewed as indifference, and his unchangeableness is interpreted as insensitivity.

However, the Shulammite delights in her beloved's tender mercies, his sweet compassions, his boundless joy, his enduring strength and his unfailing love. She continually meditates upon his goodness; even the *night* gives no respite from her magnificent obsession.

Between the Shulammite's *breasts* lay a pouch or sachet in which the myrrh is contained, suggesting that the Shulammite's thoughts have been taken captive[1] to do her bidding. The believer who wants to continually dwell upon the Beloved must exercise great determination in continually taking his thoughts captive and focusing them upon the beautiful Lord Jesus.

Henna Blossoms

In Solomon's day, the leaf of the fragrant *henna* plant was commonly made into a red cosmetic and applied to the palms of the hands, the soles of the feet, and sometimes in the hair and beard.[2] The Hebrew word for henna is also translated *atone, redeem*

---

[1] 2 Corinthians 10:5
[2] It was sometimes also applied to the fingernails and toenails.

or *forgive*. Thus, henna represents the forgiving grace of the Lord Jesus Christ manifest in the shedding of his blood on Calvary's cross, by which he purchased forgiveness from sin for every person who will come to him. As the blood ran down his face and flowed from his hands and feet, he was heard saying, "Father, forgive them; for they do not know what they are doing."[1]

When the Shulammite likens her beloved to *a cluster of henna blossoms*, she reveals her particular delight in his forgiving grace. Her beloved offers total forgiveness and never mentions her former sins, not even the time when her soul grew dark from neglect. He speaks only words of comfort and encouragement to this searching soul.

The presence of rose-scented tropical henna blossoms in the hillside vineyards of Engedi is a story of contrasts. The lush Engedi oasis is fed by springs from the rugged desert slopes overlooking the Dead Sea, the delicate pink hue of the henna blossom contrasting strikingly with its torrid wilderness environment. Correspondingly, every thought of the beautiful Jesus, the life-giving spirit,[2] lifts the Shulammite's barren soul into the high places of fruitfulness in the life of the Spirit.

Beloved to Shulammite:	1:15 **How beautiful you are, my darling, How beautiful you are! Your eyes are *like* doves.**

The Shulammite sees herself as weathered, but her beloved sees her as *beautiful*. Apparently, her time with the shepherds has been fruitful. Her beloved is overwhelmed by the Shulammite's devotion. *"How beautiful you are,"* he exclaims. The sheer pleasure he experiences in expressing praise is reason enough for him to immediately repeat his adulation, but he does so with the Shulammite's welfare in mind. His words are intended to be creative; if the Shulammite believes she is esteemed, she will live in such a way as to increase her loveliness. He is aware also that to

---

[1] Luke 23:34
[2] 1 Corinthians 15:45

the degree the Shulammite believes she is desired, she will zealously pursue her beloved, unhindered by any fear of rejection.

The Shulammite's beloved confides why he finds her so beautiful. Her *eyes*, windows to her soul, reveal beautiful dove-like qualities: delicate, unguarded, gentle, innocent[1] and mysterious. A dove mates for life, making it a fitting symbol for the kind of devoted love expressed by the Shulammite. Coincidentally, doves are able to focus both their eyes upon a single object at once, again characterizing the Shulammite's single-eyed devotion that has so captured the attention of her beloved.

Shulammite to Beloved:		
	1:16	**How handsome you are, my beloved,** *And* **so pleasant!** **Indeed, our couch is luxuriant!**
	1:17	**The beams of our houses are cedars,** **Our rafters, cypresses.**
	2:1	**I am the rose of Sharon,** **The lily of the valleys.**

Handsome and Pleasant

Returning the praise she has just received (1:8-10), the Shulammite searches for words that do not come. She readily declares that her beloved is *handsome*, but she lacks the vocabulary to describe his attractiveness in any detail. The Shulammite states emphatically that he is *pleasant*, that is, charming, lovely and sweet, but she cannot yet say what makes him so. This lack of vocabulary is an indication that the Shulammite is merely at the beginning stages of her transformation.[2]

She is typical of a young believer, filled with thanksgiving for the things that God provides: forgiveness, healing, deliverance, love and care— but understanding these things only in a general sense. The Shulammite knows that God is good, but she cannot yet describe his goodness in any great detail. Time spent in God's

---

[1]. Matthew 10:16
[2] Romans 12:2; 2 Corinthians 3:18

Word is crucial for developing a deeper and an abiding knowledge of him at this point.

However, the Shulammite's relative inexperience does not detract from the joy she indulges in her beloved's presence, for she describes their *couch*, the place of intimacy, as *luxuriant*. It is certainly his sweetness and charm that makes it so. What joy, what peace, and what contentment the Shulammite experiences in the luscious exchange of affectionate longings: expressions of love, adoration and praise!

The word translated *luxuriant* can also be translated *lush* or *verdant*, suggesting a springlike pastoral scene, perhaps a fertile grassy clearing encircled by patches of pristine vegetation. The imagery is intended to portray freedom of expression and the joy of abandoned and unhindered worship.

Cedars and Cypresses

The outdoor theme is not merely intimated, but fully exploited as the Shulammite depicts herself meeting with her beloved amongst tall majestic cedars and overshadowing cypresses:[1] "*The beams of our houses are cedars, our rafters, cypresses.*"

The language is reminiscent of the trees under which the Israelites sought their idols, as the prophet Jeremiah declared, "She went up on every high hill and under every green tree, and she was a harlot there."[2] The Lord pleaded with Israel, promising that he would be their lush tree: "It is I who answer and look after you. I am like a luxuriant cypress; from me comes your fruit."[3]

However, unlike Israel, the Shulammite does not seek help from idols, but looks to Jesus to supply all her needs. He is the Tree of

---

[1] This is presumably the *Cupressus sempervirens horizontalis*, a native evergreen, nine to fifteen meters high, with spreading branches, small scale-like leaves and round cones.
[2] Jeremiah 3:6, 9
[3] Hosea 14:8

Life[1] planted in the Garden of Eden, the one who still bears the fruit[2] of salvation for all who would feast upon him.

Upright cedars with cypress rafters also allude to the cross of Christ. Although this cross would not appear in human history for another thousand years, it is the focal point of God's grand design for joining the human heart to deity and is therefore appropriately portrayed overshadowing the trysting place the Shulammite shares with her beloved. It is through the cross that Christ redeemed the souls of men, reconciling them to the Father, that they might become the dwelling place of God. Oh, the wondrous cross, the place where lovingkindness and truth have met together, where righteousness and peace have kissed,[3] and where mercy has triumphed over judgment.[4]

Houses

Though it is not revealed how many *houses* the Shulammite shares with her beloved, there is clearly more than one. Presumably, the houses are distinct from one another, like the rooms of a mansion, each providing an atmosphere suitable to its intended purpose. Diverse houses speak of the many varied experiences the Shulammite shares with her beloved, such as intimate love, victorious faith, glorious worship, joyous thanksgiving, exuberant praise, humble adoration, unshakable peace, attentive contemplation and empathetic tears.

The plural *houses* also suggests that the Shulammite typifies not merely the individual believer, but a corporate bride as well. Jesus said: "In my Father's house are many dwelling places . . . . And if I go and prepare a place for you, I will come again, and receive you to myself; that where I am, there you may be also."[5] Jesus is coming back for a many-membered corporate bride consisting of all those whose affections are uniquely set upon him.

---

[1] Genesis 2:9; Revelation 22: 2, 14, 19
[2] The luxurious couch noted earlier can also be translated *fruitful* couch.
[3] Psalm 85:10
[4] James 2:13
[5] John 14:2-3

Roses and Lilies

Imagining a gently sloping hillside, beautifully carpeted with flowers of brilliant red, delicate pink, flaming orange and deep violet, seemingly cascading into a tranquil pool, clear as crystal and laced about with snowy white blossoms, the Shulammite likens herself to flowers such as these: *the rose of Sharon* and *the lily of the valleys*.[1] Both are beautiful and plentiful in the land of Israel. The Shulammite has been awakened to the fact that she is beautifully crafted in the Master's image with the potential for unfathomable glory, yet, in the flower similitude, the Shulammite also humbly admits that she is merely one of many who are so destined.

Similarly, the believer must avoid denigrating himself so as to think that there is nothing about him worthy of the Savior's love, for every human being is the Lord's handiwork and of inestimable value, evidenced by the price he was willing to pay— the blood of the only begotten Son of God. Yet, neither should the believer's heart be lifted up in pride because of the beauty given him by his Creator, remembering always that the believer possesses nothing that was not given him from above.

The shepherds seem to have done their job well, effectively helping the Shulammite grow, for she has progressed from seeing herself as black but lovely (1:5) to now being a beautiful rose and a lily, albeit a humble blossom, one of many spread out upon the ground before her beloved.

---

[1] The Hebrew word *shoshan* is borrowed from the Egyptian word for water lily (also known as the lotus blossom), the form of which was used to decorate Solomon's temple (1 Kings 7:19, 22, 26; 2 Chronicles 4:5). However, depending on the context, the Hebrew term can refer to other kinds of flowers. Lily of the valleys (Hebrew: *ereq*) is a non-technical term (not excluding water lilies that would naturally be found in the valleys) and is not dissimilar to the lily of the fields (Greek, *agro*: countryside) referenced by Jesus (Matthew 6:28) and, interestingly, linked to Solomon (Luke 12:27).

| Beloved to the | 2:2 | **Like a lily among the thorns,** |
| Shepherds: | | **So is my darling among the maidens.** |

In the preceding verse (2:1), the Shulammite modestly likened herself to a lily, seeing herself as merely one among the many blossoms of a vast pastoral scene. The Shulammite's humility, an indispensable key to her growth in God, does not go unnoticed by her beloved. Since she did not exalt herself, her beloved now honors her, not by addressing her directly, but by openly proclaiming her beauty to the shepherds who had previously offered (1:11) to adorn her. In this he commends the shepherds, who have had a significant hand in helping beautify the Shulammite.

A *lily* may seem insignificant when observed among ten thousand like itself, but it is exquisitely beautiful when found among *thorns*. Her beloved declares that in his estimation there is a radical difference between the Shulammite and the other *maidens*. The maidens, or daughters of Jerusalem, are those in the church who desire the blessings of God in their lives but are still looking for happiness and fulfillment from things other than the Lord. They love the Beloved in a measure (1:4), but they have not yet begun their quest to know him absolutely. Like the Shulammite, their love is immature, but unlike the Shulammite, they have not yet fully extricated themselves from their love for the things of this world.

Jesus said that the Word of God sown among thorns is choked out by the cares of the world and becomes unfruitful. The maidens are likened to thorns because their anxious hearts are divided, continually distracted by the cares of this life, so that the Word of God has little effect in them.

A lily naturally contrasts with thorns, for while the thorn promises only unpleasantries, the lily delights the senses of sight, smell and touch. Spiritually speaking, the lily suggests the beauty of the Shulammite's humility, the preciousness of her longings and the tenderness of her devotion to her beloved. How stunningly beautiful she is among the capricious hearts of the young maidens!

2:3 Like an apple tree among the trees of the forest,
So is my beloved among the young men.
In his shade I took great delight and sat down,
And his fruit was sweet to my taste.
2:4 He has brought me to *his* banquet hall,
And his banner over me is love.
2:5 Sustain me with raisin cakes,
Refresh me with apples,
Because I am lovesick.

Apple Tree

Outstanding among the trees

In the preceding verse (2:2) Solomon extolled the Shulammite as the most beautiful among women and like a lily among the maidens. The Shulammite now returns the compliment: her beloved is outstanding *among the young men*. There is none like him. She imagines herself passing through the *forest*; every tree is barren and incapable of providing any relief from her hunger. Suddenly she eyes an *apple tree:* how rare, how sweet, how pleasant, and most importantly, how satisfying!

The young men, the other *trees of the forest*, represent all other possible lovers. Unlike Israel, who lusted after the paramours of Egypt,[1] the Shulammite reserves her affections for her beloved. It is under the overarching branches of his love, a canopy of divine affection, that her soul finds exhilaration and rest. However, her beloved has not yet captured her exclusive gaze, for in comparing him with others, it is evident that, however dimly, others are still in her view. The Shulammite has yet to come to the place where she sees nothing other than her beloved's incomparable beauty (5:10-16).[2]

---

[1] Ezekiel 23:20

[2] The Shulammite lacks understanding when she compares her beloved because there is no one worthy to be compared to him. Whereas, he encourages the Shulammite (something he does not need from her) by telling her she possesses a degree of devotion that sets her apart from the maidens (2:2). Later, he comforts her to know that she has attained to the stature of the most noble members of the bridal company (6:8-9); she is in fact one of a many-membered bride. Her comparison is unworthy of him and tends to diminish his glory since he is incomparable. Whereas, his comparison of her tends to elevate her glory.

Rest in it's shade

Convinced that her beloved is most excellent, the Shulammite lacks the vocabulary to explain what makes him so. Her attraction to her beloved is still somewhat experience-based, that is, motivated by the peace and the joy she feels in his presence. This is not to say that either her experiences or her motivations are wrong or misguided, merely incomplete. (Although, before this song is over, the Shulammite will grow tremendously in understanding and wisdom concerning her relationship with her beloved.)

At this point the Shulammite greatly enjoys the tranquilizing peace and the warm tenderhearted love she experiences in her beloved's presence: *In his shade I took great delight and sat down.* Here the Shulammite echoes King David's ovation: "In your presence is fullness of joy and in your right hand there are pleasures forever!"[1] Sitting in the shade of her beloved, the Shulammite finds rest. She has never known such peace; there is no striving, no anxiety and no fear under the overarching love of her beloved. Here she is shaded from the burning sun, the self-imposed tyranny of the opinions of men that had previously been a major cause of her weathered condition (1:6). She finds respite from the thorny irritations stemming from everyday life among the maidens (2:2).

It is no coincidence that the Shulammite finds this place of rest[2] immediately following her humble admission to being merely the rose of Sharon and the lily of the valleys (2:1). For it is only after one abandons his desire for recognition from men that he is able to experience the divine peace promised by Jesus when he said, "Come to me, all who are weary and heavy-laden, and I will give you rest. Take my yoke upon you, and learn from me, for I am gentle and humble in heart; and you shall find rest for your souls."[3]

Some are always striving, hoping for recognition and acceptance, unable to find contentment in the love that comes only from the

---

[1] Psalm 16:11
[2] Hebrews 4:1-3
[3] Matthew 11:28-29

beloved Savior, Jesus; but, as for the Shulammite, she has finally found the peace she was looking for when she asked her beloved to reveal where he pastures his flock and where he makes them lie down at noon (1:7). She has learned that there is rest under the canopy of the revelation of his love.

Sweetness of it's fruit

His fruit was sweet to my taste. If it was an ordinary apple tree that the Shulammite found in the forest, there would be nothing spectacular about it's fruit, but because this tree symbolizes Jesus, who is the Tree of Life, its fruit is extraordinary. The apples represent the knowledge of God revealed through his Word, for the Word of God is nourishing and life-giving, enlightening the heart and healing the soul. Jesus' words of love and desire for his bride and his promises concerning her eventual union with him are more to be desired than apples of gold in settings of silver.[1]

Banquet Hall

After having expended great energy in seeking her beloved (1:8), longing for him continually (1:12-13), the Shulammite now luxuriously dines under his protective and comforting shade (2:3). It would seem that the Shulammite might take some satisfaction in having finally succeeded in obtaining a new level of intimacy with her beloved, but instead, she abruptly credits her beloved as the one who is responsible for drawing her to himself:[2] *"He has brought[3] me to his banquet hall."*[4]

Her great king conquered the Shulammite's will by revealing the strength of his love, a love so commanding that it is illustrated by the military imagery of a *banner*. In Solomon's time, a banner typically portrayed the specific mission, skill or patron deity of an army. However, in this case there is no marching army, but only

---

[1] Proverbs 25:11

[2] Psalm 65:4

[3] The word translated *brought* often has a violent connotation as in the hauling away of prisoners (Ezekiel 12:13; 17:4, 12; 20:35) or booty (2 Chronicles 36:18).

[4] Although she takes no credit, it was the Shulammite's primordial cry for intimacy (1:4) that provoked this determined response from her beloved.

the beloved king himself, carrying a banner representing a kingdom of which he is the patron deity.

His is not an earthly kingdom, but his kingdom is universal and otherworldly. It is administrated by the royal law of love,[1] more than a guiding principle, but an all-pervasive reality legitimizing authority, governing justice, creating purpose and defining beauty.

The banner under which the Shulammite boasts, identifies the very essence of her king as well as his mission. Though the Shulammite, driven by an insatiable thirst for love, views herself as the pursuer, it is the king who emptied himself, leaving his throne in glory and entering the earth as a man in order that he might capture the Shulammite's heart by *love*.

In his banquet hall,[2] literally *house of wine*, the Shulammite feasts upon the sweet fruit of God's love, tasting the overwhelming joy of fellowship with her beloved. The experience is pleasurable but momentary. The banquet hall is still not the bridal chamber, and her lovesick soul cries for more.

Lovesickness

The Shulammite is obsessed with the desire to know her beloved's love and has lost all interest in other things. She lacks the strength and motivation for even the necessary affairs of life. *"Sustain me,"* she begs, hoping the shepherds[3] will nourish her soul with *raisin cakes* and *apples*, metaphors for precious revelations of her beloved.

Biblically, raisin cakes are associated with sacrificial meals,[4] thereby indicating the divine nature of her beloved and the sanctity of their union. Since raisins and wine are both derived

---

[1] James 2:8
[2] This is the last of the enclosure scenes, a major theme of Act 1 (Song 1:4; 1:12-14; 1:16-17; 2:4).
[3] This final scene is addressed to the shepherds and not to the Shulammite's beloved, for the verbs are masculine plural imperatives. Additionally, there is never a response from the Shulammite's beloved and, more notably, only at risk of insult would the Shulammite tell her lover that she is lovesick while in his presence.
[4] Solomon's father, King David, distributed raisin cakes to those who helped bring the ark of God's presence back to Jerusalem (1 Chronicles 16:3; 2 Samuel 6:19).

from grapes, raisin cakes are also a subtle reference back to the banquet hall, literally, *house of wine* (2:4). Although raisin cakes, lacking the intoxicating effect of wine, are a poor substitute for the bliss she enjoyed feasting on her Savior's love just moments earlier in his banqueting hall (2:4), the Shulammite is desperate.

As her longings intensify, the pain becomes almost unbearable. The looming temptation is that she might turn to worthless activities to distract and thus dull the pain of her wistful yearnings. Pleading with the shepherds to nourish her, the Shulammite hopes they can supply comforting reassurances of her beloved's desire for her with inspiring revelations of his beauty, strength and love that will invigorate her quest for greater intimacy. She languishes for sweet morsels that promise to refresh her soul: an inspiring book, a stirring message, a prophetic word, stories of a divine encounter or revelations of heavenly realities.

Predictably, the Shulammite suffers the inevitable disappointment, for although the shepherds can inspire, they can never satisfy her longing for intimacy. Just as raisins lack the intoxicating effect of wine, so also the revelations required from the shepherds are inferior to the Shulammite's firsthand encounters with the Lord himself. It is normal and even healthy to receive comfort and encouragement from others in one's spiritual pursuit; however, the Shulammite's soul is craving a level of intimacy that only her beloved can supply. Her increasing desire is evidence that her beloved is indeed drawing her as she had requested (1:4). Judiciously he delays satisfying her craving in order that her longings might increase still more, thus adding to the pleasure of their ultimate union.

It is here that the Shulammite can easily fall into a snare. She must not become despondent in her quest for greater intimacy, for if that be the case, she will undermine her own objective. If she becomes despairing, she cannot at the same time persevere in faith to enter into the union for which she so longs. The Shulammite must cling to the fact that Jesus desires his bride even more than she does him, and she must resist the temptation to think that he is unfairly withholding himself from her.

Growing in faith requires that the believer appropriate the knowledge of the love of God that has already been demonstrated by the Savior when he voluntarily emptied himself of his eternal weight of glory, became man, and submitted to a cruel death on the cross. Ascending into heaven, he sent the Holy Spirit to come and do what is so marvelous as to be incomprehensible. The same wonderful Holy Spirit who indwelled Jesus has now come to live inside the believer, imparting the true knowledge of God enjoyed by Jesus and revealing to the believer the riches of the glorious future he will experience in union with Christ throughout eternity.[1]

> Shulammite: | 2:6 *Let* **his left hand be under my head
> And his right hand embrace me.**

With intense desire the Shulammite sighs, resigned to the realization that what she wants from her beloved must come directly from him by the power of the Holy Spirit. There is no other cure for her lovesickness except his personal embrace; the Shulammite longs for the exhilaration of being totally yielded to his control.

Like an animal taken from the wild and now so docile as to allow her head to fall freely backward, baring her neck to the will of her master, the Shulammite wistfully dreams of experiencing the freedom of complete vulnerability in the hands of the one she loves and is learning to trust. *"Let his left hand be under my head,"* sighs the Shulammite as she enjoys a furtive thrill at the thought of trusting her beloved implicitly.

Her beloved's hidden left hand represents the many divine supports or enabling graces of the Lord Jesus calculated to help the Shulammite remain focused upon him. Recklessly, she abandons her will unreservedly to him.

Having yielded her future to her beloved, the Shulammite further dares to submit to the *embrace* of his *right hand*, emblematic of God's power. Thus, she imagines free-falling into the arms of God, unafraid of how she might be treated in the relationship, for she

---

[1] Ephesians 1:18-19

knows that he is gentle and kind toward those he loves. She is confident that the same hand that executes vengeance upon his enemies can impart genuine love and tender affections to his bride. The same hand that destroys his enemies is able also to draw his bride nearer to him in tender embrace.

CLOSING

Beloved to the daughters of Jerusalem:

2:7 **I adjure you, O daughters of Jerusalem,**
By the gazelles or by the hinds of the field,
That you do not arouse or awaken *my* love,
Until she pleases.

The events of this song are too fantastic, and the scenes change too rapidly, to be the literal account of real life situations. The song is better understood as a series of dreams and daytime mental excursions. Twice, the Shulammite is specifically mentioned as dreaming (3:1; 5:2), and once she seems to be daydreaming (6:12). The verse now under study is one of three nearly identical verses that also contribute to the ethereal dreamlike feel of the song.

Here Solomon solemnly charges the daughters of Jerusalem to not disturb the Shulammite until she is ready to be awakened. It is when the Shulammite is in her dreamy state that she experiences and expresses her longings and actual encounters with her beloved. Being asleep then, in this song, is an expression of being in the spirit, removed from that which is merely natural or physical, thinking on those things which are above.[1] To be asleep is to be detached from the cares of this life, the things that so easily distract and entangle the believer. It is to be dead to the world, but alive unto God.[2]

Receiving his series of visions, the prophet Zechariah was apparently so overwhelmed that when the angel of the Lord returned to discuss with him what he was seeing, he had to be roused as a man who is awakened from his sleep.[3] For the Shulammite to awaken when *she pleases* means that she will have extracted from her present experience all her soul could absorb and all that God had intended for the moment. For the Shulammite

---

[1] Colossians 3:1
[2] Romans 6:11; Galatians 6:14
[3] Zechariah 4:1

to voluntarily awaken is an indication that she is ready to walk out her experience in a life filled with God.

Solomon adjures the *daughters of Jerusalem* (the church at large) to not disturb the Shulammite, for they, because of their immaturity, have a propensity for interfering with the work God is doing in the hearts of his elect. They often encourage involvement in activities or relationships that are mere distractions to the lovesick soul. At other times, chancing upon a soul struggling with a recently awakened but clouded conscience, they glibly offer uninformed assurances of God's approval. Although well-meaning, their words of counsel often demonstrate a lack of understanding concerning spiritual realities and can hinder rather than aid the soul in its divine pursuit. Mature souls, those who have passed through times of lovesickness and the commensurate dealings of God, are not so quick to try and alleviate the inevitable discomfort that must come as the Lord brings his elect into total conformity with his will.

By charging the daughters of Jerusalem *by the gazelles or the hinds of the field*, Solomon yields a glimpse into what he values and what he believes the Shulammite will become. Gazelles are strong, swift, and graceful. (The Hebrew word translated *gazelles* literally means *beauty* or *glory*.) They are everything that the Shulammite is not in the eyes of the daughters of Jerusalem at the moment. At this point she seems weak, dull and awkward, but the king knows she is in the process of becoming the most glorious of all creatures.

Gazelles are also suggestive of the gentleness required when relating to the Shulammite during this season in her life. Like the hinds of the field, she can be easily startled by harsh opinions and untried spiritual ideals, and thus distracted from her amorous pursuit. Smitten with love, her beloved jealously watches over and guards the Shulammite's progress.

Solomon's three nearly identical warnings to the maidens (2:7; 3:5; 8:4) each close a major segment of the song. These natural dividers, fortuitously provided by the poet, help the reader unravel the underlying structure of the song and allow him the opportunity to make the mental and emotional shift for each succeeding drama that threatens to unfold.

Act II

The Invitation

Arise, my darling, my beautiful one, and come along.

MISSED OPPORTUNITY

Shulammite to the
daughters of
Jerusalem:

2:8 **Listen! My beloved!**
Behold, he is coming,
Climbing on the mountains,
Leaping on the hills!

2:9 **My beloved is like a gazelle or a young**
stag.
Behold, he is standing behind our wall,
He is looking through the windows,
He is peering through the lattice.

2:10 **My beloved responded and said to me,**

"Arise, my darling, my beautiful one,
And come along.

2:11 **For behold, the winter is past,**
The rain is over *and* **gone.**

2:12 **The flowers have** *already* **appeared in the**
land;
The time has arrived for pruning *the vines,*
And the voice of the turtledove has been
heard in our land.

2:13 **The fig tree has ripened its figs,**
And the vines in blossom have given forth
their **fragrance.**
Arise, my darling, my beautiful one,
And come along!

2:14 **O my dove, in the clefts of the rock,**
In the secret place of the steep pathway,
Let me see your form,
Let me hear your voice;
For your voice is sweet,
And your form is lovely."

He Hastens

The Shulammite's lovesick cry (2:5) touches the heart of her beloved and he responds like a swift-footed *gazelle or a young stag,* springing *on the mountains, leaping* and skipping upon *the hills.*

Passionate love sends him speedily to the soul that seethes with fragrant longings for her beloved (1:12).

However, the Shulammite's beloved is still a king, meaning, as she will soon discover, there is more to him than simply helping her know she is loved. She sees him bounding effortlessly over mountains and hills, formations that represent the governments of nations[1] over all of which this King of kings and Lord of lords reigns triumphantly, giving the Shulammite her first indication that her beloved has interests other than her own. This is not to say that he has been preoccupied or detained, but merely that his wider interests suggest a dimension of adventure yet to be revealed to the Shulammite.

"Listen!" cries the Shulammite. What was it she heard? It matters not. Whether it was his voice or the pounding of his feet,[2] the meaning is that, while others debate his wisdom, question his care and challenge his authority, the Shulammite listens eagerly for his advance and excitedly calls out to the daughters of Jerusalem, alerting them of his coming.

The Shulammite likens her beloved to a *gazelle*. There seems to be a deliberate play on the word gazelle, literally meaning *beauty* or *glory*, in order to suggest his inner graces. He is a young wild *stag*:[3] alert, swift, confident and capable. He stands ready for action, determined, focused, a glorious yet gentle intruder. Marching outside the house, *looking through the windows*, he surveys her condition; he gazes upon her beauty. In response to the Shulammite's cry, her beloved has come on a mission to escort her into greater levels of intimacy.

She Hides

Why is it that the Shulammite's beloved finds her together with the daughters of Jerusalem hiding *behind* a *wall*, requiring that he peer through undisclosed openings in the *lattice* to feast his eyes upon

---

[1] Isaiah 2:2
[2] Genesis 3:8; 1 Kings 14:6
[3] The gazelle is not to suggest fragility, as in the case of the Shulammite who is also identified with the hind of the field (2:7), for he is a wild stag.

her? Why does the Shulammite not come out to meet her beloved? Why does she, like Adam and Eve in the garden at the approach of the Lord,[1] remain sheltered from his presence?

The answer is that the Shulammite is yet immature, hiding behind walls of self-defense mechanisms she has built up over the years, carefully cultivated habits of self-protection: withdrawal, domination, image-making, self-deprecation, anger, rigidity and self-justification. The walls, with their manmade latticework covering the windows, are not difficult for others to see through and do not provide any real protection as she might imagine.

Unbeknown to the Shulammite, the very defenses designed to protect her from others also shield her from her beloved. If she wants to experience intimacy with her beloved, the Shulammite will have to forsake the mechanisms designed to protect her from the inevitable pain that comes with making herself vulnerable to others. She must be willing to come out of hiding and love others even as Christ has loved her. This requires a willingness to risk the possible pains of rejection, misunderstanding and neglect that too often accompany interpersonal relationships, for the very mechanisms that protect her heart from feeling pain, so desensitize the heart that it becomes incapable of feeling love and, therefore, incapable of giving love.

Mankind's condition on the earth and the design of the human heart are such that love is perfected through interactions with other people.[2] For if one was to focus on loving God only, it would be easy for him to believe that he loves God more than he really does. Heart issues that hinder one's ability to love can often remain hidden in his relationship with God, whereas they are quickly exposed when dealing with other people.

The Shulammite wants intimacy, but she is incapable of experiencing greater intimacy until she is willing to overcome her fears. Because the very fears evident in her relationships with others also hinder her relationship with her beloved, he now comes

---

[1] Genesis 3:8
[2] Matthew 5:46-48; Ephesians 4:16; 1 Thessalonians 3:12-13; 1 John 4:12

to bring the Shulammite into greater freedom, gently coaxing her out of her comfort zone.

He Calls

"Arise, my darling, my beautiful one, and come along" (2:10). The one who admonished the daughters of Jerusalem to not awaken the Shulammite (2:7) now attempts to awaken her himself. Her beloved has heard the desperate cry of the Shulammite's heart and emerges to help her overcome the obstacles that hinder the development of her capacity to experience love.

The *winter* season of her hiddenness is past, and the Shulammite has entered the springtime of her soul, a time of joyful[1] and productive fruit-bearing. The temporary separation from the presence of God that rained down feelings of abandonment, neglect and isolation upon her soul has ended, and it is now time for her to experience a greater expression of the fruit of the Holy Spirit's presence in her life. The Shulammite does not realize the degree to which she has grown and is unaware of the new, rewarding experiences that await her in ministry: incessant joy, enduring peace and a stubborn kindness that flows unreservedly toward others.[2]

Her beloved calls the Shulammite to arise and join him in fruitful service. Her time with faithful shepherds (1:8-11) has helped to groom the Shulammite for a new type of ministry, not simply the caring for people's needs, but the reproduction of divine life in others.

Opportunities abound, for *flowers have already appeared in the land.* Fields of blossoms (a metaphor for the lives of other believers) beg for pollination, meaning that souls are prepared and waiting to receive the ministry that will lead to further fruit-bearing in their lives. Already *the voice of the turtledove,*[3] other joyful laborers, *has been heard in* the *land.*

---

[1] The Hebrew *zamir*, translated *pruning*, can also mean *songs*.
[2] Romans 14:17
[3] The Shulammite is also likened to a dove (Song 1:15; 2:14; 4:1; 6:9).

It is time for *pruning* (2:12), better understood here to mean *tying up of the vines.*[1] Budding grapevines are carefully lifted and tied up off the ground so that the fruit can be protected from insects and rot. Similarly, the souls of men need to be lifted up, strengthened and encouraged so that they might bring forth the fruit of the Holy Spirit. The Shulammite's own soul has been restored sufficiently to now be able to minister to others in many ways: a smile, encouragement, instruction, and kind expressions of affection and fellowship.

However, the Shulammite remembers her previous experience of laboring in the vineyards (1:6). Busily engaged in her work, she was all the while hiding, not really giving her heart to those she was serving. It was a job, a duty, a rung on the ladder of spiritual success. In the process she lost the presence of God in her own life.

Reluctant to again risk personal loss, she hesitates.

He Calls Again

Clefts of the rock

The Shulammite's beloved coaxes her a second time, repeating the invitation he made moments earlier: *"Arise, my darling, my beautiful one, and come along"* (2:13). He reassures the Shulammite of her loveliness; she is again his *dove* (as in 1:15). But this time the characteristic he admires specifically is her hiddenness, for she dwells high up in the *clefts of the rock.*[2] The rock speaks of Christ,[3] whom the Shulammite has found to be her strong tower, a hiding place[4] in her times of trouble. She has learned to dwell in the shelter of the Most High,[5] experiencing the peace and rest that comes from being in his presence. The secret place of the Lord's

---

[1] The Hebrew *zamir* usually refers to the cutting back of the grapevines in winter or the grape harvest in late summer. Because the setting here is middle or late spring (The heavy rains finish by May, and figs ripen as early as May.), *zamir* (translated *pruning*) is better understood as *tending* or *tying up.*

[2] This is reminiscent of when the Lord sheltered Moses in the cleft of the rock as his glory passed by (Exodus 33:22).

[3] 1 Corinthians 10:4

[4] Psalm 27:5; 31:20; 32:7; 119:114

[5] Psalm 91:1

presence[1] is discovered up a steep pathway, a road not well traveled, an arduous journey not for the fainthearted, for it takes courage and determination to leave the comforts of familiar surroundings and venture out into the high places. Not everyone is willing to give up time with friends, recreation, work or entertainment to invest in their pursuit of the Beloved.

If the rock represents Christ, then the clefts of the rock suggest the wounds of Christ by which believers are healed, for in his suffering, death and resurrection, Jesus obtained physical[2] and spiritual healing for all those who would believe in him. For the Shulammite to take refuge in the wounds of Christ means that she has learned to appropriate the healing benefits that Christ has obtained for her. Particularly, her soul has been cleansed and healed of the inner wounds that caused her to go astray in her heart, and she is now wholly devoted to the Shepherd and Guardian of her soul.[3]

Doves make their nests in cliff-side clefts and caves. When frightened, they are reluctant to emerge. The Shulammite's beloved is asking her to give up the cloistered lifestyle she has enjoyed behind her walled enclosure (2:9) and begin to give herself to others. He asks her to be willing to give up even some of her precious time alone with him, for he knows that without ministry to others, her times of seclusion can become self-serving, an opportunity for insulating and even justifying secret fears.

Form and voice

Her beloved senses the Shulammite's need for a clarification of her identity and purpose if she is going to be persuaded to come out of hiding. She needs to know that she is desirable, that she is valuable and has something of value to offer others. He encourages the Shulammite in this regard, asking to see her *form*, which speaks of an outward beauty exhibited in her smile, bearing, attentiveness and tranquillity. Actually, this outer beauty is a mere reflection of

---

[1] Psalm 27:5; 31:20
[2] Isaiah 53:4-6; Matthew 8:17
[3] 1 Peter 2:24-25

the nature of Christ that is being formed within,[1] a beauty that must not remain hidden, but deliberately shared with others.

Asking to hear the Shulammite's *voice*, her beloved affirms the purity of her spirit;[2] there is an inner sweetness that finds expression in the words she speaks. If she would give herself to thoughtful conversation, she could raise the level of others' awareness of spiritual realities, for she has the potential of inspiring them with words of encouragement, comfort and occasional instruction. Whether limited by a predisposition to shyness, or simply a lack of confidence when it comes to authentic communication, the Shulammite has more to offer than she has been willing to acknowledge.

Just as the Shulammite can take no credit for her form[3] or voice, which were given her by the Creator, neither can the believer take credit for the work that the Holy Spirit has wrought in him. It is Christ in his church that makes her glorious; everything that exists has come into being by him and for him.[4] The bride of Christ is beautiful because she is the work of God in the earth, and although she must cooperate with the Holy Spirit in the beautification process, she cannot add to or take away from the value that the Savior has placed upon her.

In praising the Shulammite's form and voice, her beloved intends for her to understand he wants *her*, not just her ministry. The invitation to display her beauty[5] in his vineyard is for her sake. She wants intimacy, and her beloved knows that for her desire to be realized, she must overcome the fears that keep her hidden from others.

The Shulammite heard her beloved's voice[6] as he came to her (2:8); now he wants to hear her voice as she goes to others. The sound of

---

[1] Galatians 4:19; 2 Corinthians 4:10-11
[2] Proverbs 16:23; Matthew 12:34; 15:18
[3] The Hebrew word *mareh* is literally *appearance* and is sometimes translated *face* (as in the *King James Version*) as in Genesis 29:17 and Esther 2:7.
[4] Colossians 1:16
[5] Esther 1:11
[6] The Hebrew word *qol* (usually translated voice or sound) is used in three places in this first section of Act II: first, to describe the sound of the Shulammite's

turtledoves, other mature laborers, are already being heard in the land, but her beloved wants to hear the voice of the Shulammite. He desperately wants her to believe that she has something valuable to offer others. Whether in singing, preaching, teaching, prophesying, public prayer or encouragement, the Word of God gives life, and it is time for the life-giving voice of the Shulammite to be heard.

Unexpectedly, there is yet another sound that now intrudes upon the scene; it is the voices of the daughters of Jerusalem.

daughters of Jerusalem:	2:15 **Catch the foxes for us,** **The little foxes that are ruining the vineyards,** **While our vineyards are in blossom.**

Overwhelmed by the *little foxes* that threaten to ruin their vineyards, a metaphor for their souls, the daughters of Jerusalem call out to anyone who might be willing to help.[1] Little foxes, commonly about fifteen inches long, chew at the base of the vines and also burrow under the roots, causing the vines to become barren or possibly even die. The foxes represent a wide variety of problems that threaten to upset the inner well-being of the soul.

Typical of new believers, the daughters of Jerusalem are zealous in their love for God. They have survived the long winter season of their souls' separation from God and are now enjoying a springtime season in which they are experiencing rapid personal growth. Because of their immaturity, they can be easily overwhelmed by small irritations that eventually turn into very large difficulties when not properly addressed. Lacking experience in handling their own problems, they often look for someone else to solve their many problems for them. Most often, they simply need love, encouragement, wisdom and some healthy friendships with other members of the body of Christ.

---

beloved coming (2:8), second, to describe the voice of the turtledoves (2:12), and third, to describe the voice of the Shulammite that her beloved now wants to hear (2:14).

[1] The verb *catch* is in the imperative, masculine, plural form.

The Shulammite could help, but her beloved has already attempted twice to coax her into the vineyards (2:10-13). She could not be persuaded by love; can she now be compelled by need? She remembers what it was like previously when she was working in the vineyards (1:6). It was hot, unthankful, and left her no time for herself or for her relationship with God. Afraid of making the same mistake she made before, the Shulammite is inclined to ignore the cry of the daughters of Jerusalem. She is enjoying her relationship with God too much to let others disturb it now.

| Shulammite to the daughters of Jerusalem: | 2:16 **My beloved is mine, and I am his;**
He pastures his flock among the lilies. |

Denying the Maidens

The Shulammite has enjoyed great personal freedom since she quit working for her brothers in the vineyards and is no longer saddled with tiring ministry responsibilities.[1] She has resisted the gentle pleadings of her beloved to come along and join him in the vineyards; now she resists the pressure being applied by the daughters of Jerusalem to come and catch the bothersome foxes.

The manner of the Shulammite's response to the maidens' plea for help is woefully inadequate, even shocking. She is unmoved and abrupt. The daughters of Jerusalem need personal attention, but she cannot be bothered. The Shulammite is still driven too much by the desire to satisfy her own personal needs. She has come a long way since those dark and dreary days of her previous futile labors, and she does not want to lose the ground that she has gained in her relationship with her beloved. Any activity that might threaten her present state of well-being is suspect and will be avoided at all cost.

---

[1] However, earlier she cared for a flock of goats (1:8). There are four possibilities: (1) she may no longer be caring for the goats or (2), the goats may have been a reference to her own unyielding will and not other souls at all or (3), her beloved wants her to shift the focus of her ministry to those who are more teachable or (4), she may still be caring for a few goats or sheep but her beloved is calling her to a wider, and thus more costly, field of service. The fourth option seems the best fit.

Ignoring the maidens' immediate needs, and seemingly oblivious to any sense of responsibility to help meet them, the Shulammite undertakes to describe her relationship with her beloved.

Defining her Relationship

Experiencing peace and joy in God's presence is all that matters to the Shulammite at this time. *"My beloved is mine,"* she says, as she reflects upon her time in the presence of God (2:14), rich times in the Word, in prayer and in worship.

She takes comfort in her beloved's commitment to her, remembering that when she was languishing in unfulfilled desire (2:5), her beloved responded like a swift-footed gazelle and came running to find her.

However, her beloved's dedication will not in itself satisfy the longing of the Shulammite's heart, for no matter how many times she experiences his love, they are but fleeting moments without a reciprocal commitment of love on her part. Mutual commitment is required for there to be an effective exchange of life between them, so the Shulammite adds, *"And I am his,"* thus defining her relationship with her beloved. The Shulammite has secured her new identity as one who belongs to God. Some people attempt to define themselves by their occupation, ministry, nationality, subculture, domestic role, music, clothing or accomplishments, but the Shulammite sees herself primarily as one who loves God, possessing his presence in her life.

"I am his" is the Shulammite's first statement of commitment to her beloved, but her understanding is somewhat shallow. She is yielded for the purpose of experiencing his presence, but she is not yielded for the purpose of selfless service. The Shulammite rejoices in the fact that she has been chosen and now belongs to her beloved, but when confronted with his invitation to productive service, she balks. Up to this point, she seeks her beloved for what she will receive; she does not yet see that union with her beloved is going to cost her everything.

The Shulammite's unwillingness to *come along* with her beloved and help minister to the daughters of Jerusalem reveals that she has not yet fully grasped the words of Jesus when he said, "Whoever wishes to save his life shall lose it; but whoever loses his life for my sake shall find it."[1] Although in her mind she belongs to her beloved, she has not really learned what it means to *lose* or *give up* her own life in order that she might be wholly his.

Directing the Maidens

Although unwilling to get involved personally with the daughters of Jerusalem, the Shulammite is willing to instruct them on where they can find her beloved, for she has discovered the answer to her earlier question (1:7) about where he pastures his flock. Because sheep will not drink from turbulent streams, her beloved brings them to still waters where the *lilies*[2] grow.

Lilies typify those who have learned to abide in God's peace. They are gentle souls who have found their rest in him, souls in whom there is no posturing for position, recognition, or control. Their trust is in God, who provides abundantly beyond what they can ask or think and works all things according to his good pleasure. Jesus said, "Consider the lilies, how they grow; they neither toil nor spin; but I tell you, even Solomon in all his glory did not clothe himself like one of these."[3] If God takes care of the lilies, so God will take care of his children who ought not worry needlessly.

In this song thorns are contrasted with the lily (2:1-2). Thorns signify the anxious cares of this life,[4] while the lily signifies one who is at peace and able to rest in God, trusting him and giving thanks to him in everything.[5] The Shulammite acknowledges and even values the lilies, the many others who, like herself, have learned to rest in the Beloved.

---

[1] Matthew 16:25

[2] Since the author makes no attempt to qualify the term, water lilies are assumed (as in 4:5; 6:2-3). Refer also to the note on 2:1.

[3] Luke 12:27

[4] Luke 8:14

[5] Believers are instructed to give thanks in all things (1 Thessalonians 5:18) and for all things (Ephesians 5:20).

Although she has consecrated her heart to her beloved, the Shulammite fancies herself further along in her spiritual journey than she is actually, for she is not yet willing to give herself to the less mature. Earlier, when the Shulammite asked her beloved where she might find rest from the tormenting sun, he directed her to the tents of the shepherds, from whom she learned wisdom concerning the care of her soul, but she is not willing to help other similarly afflicted souls who are looking for relief from the foxes that now threaten their well-being. A true shepherd is one who is willing to lay down his life for his sheep; the Shulammite is not yet a true shepherdess, for she still cares more about herself than she cares about the needs of others.[1]

"He pastures[2] his flock by the still waters where the *lilies* grow." The Shulammite directs the daughters of Jerusalem to the Beloved, intimating that, as many others have already discovered, peace and rest are to be found only in him. She speaks the truth well enough, telling the maidens where her beloved can be found, but she does not provide the help they need to actually get there.

"If the daughters of Jerusalem are bothered by little foxes," she seems to reason, "then they should simply trust God. After all, this is what the lilies have learned to do, so why can't the daughters of Jerusalem do the same? If they would simply love God more, they would find him quite able to take care of all their needs." One finds it tempting to offer such glib responses to those in need, as though the solution was that easy to come by. If the truth be known, the Shulammite herself is still struggling to discover the secret of abiding in his presence.

The Shulammite's aloofness toward the daughters of Jerusalem reveals a hint of disdain for those who are not fully committed and lack the understanding or even the desire to pursue the Beloved with greater abandonment. She is unwilling to become more personally involved because she has yet to appreciate the

---

[1] Philippians 2:3

[2] The verb *pastures* can be intransitive, suggesting that when the Beloved pastures his sheep, he too is fed. This thought is explored in verses 5:1 and 6:2-3.

inestimable value that her beloved places upon his relationship with each one of these precious souls.

<table>
<tr><td>Shulammite to
Beloved:</td><td>2:17</td><td>**Until the cool of the day when the shadows**
       flee away,
Turn, my beloved, and be like a gazelle
Or a young stag on the mountains of Bether.</td></tr>
</table>

The brief encounter the Shulammite has just experienced with her beloved, punctuated with cries of distress from the daughters of Jerusalem, was not enough to move her out of her comfort zone. Unwilling to heed her beloved's invitation to *come along*, the Shulammite now finds herself without his presence.

Bether means to *cut in two, separate,* or *divide.* The word has several applications in this verse. First, it speaks of the apparent separation the Shulammite is now experiencing from her beloved. Although she can tell others where her beloved pastures his flock, the Shulammite herself has not learned how to abide in that place of rest. She experiences his peace from time to time, but has not yet learned fully the secret of the lilies, for lilies grow in still waters. Her fears and insecurities prevented her from yielding to her beloved's invitation and now he is gone. She calls out to her beloved, imploring him to return once again (2:9).

Second, the *mountains of Bether* are a veiled reference to the Shulammite's separation or consecration to her beloved. She quietly protests that she has disentangled herself from the cares of this world that threaten to distract her from singlehearted love and devotion to the one her soul desires, but the truth is that she still needs to be separated from the inner fears that hinder her from following her beloved into his vineyards. By seeming to withdraw his presence, her beloved creates an apparent distance designed to gently coax the Shulammite out of such fears.

Third, with the mention of Bether, the Shulammite introduces covenantal language, for Bether is the word used to describe Abraham's severing of the sacrificial animals when he made a covenant, or literally, *cut* a covenant with God upon a mountain in the land of Moriah.[1] When the Shulammite asks her beloved to *turn* back *like a gazelle or a young stag on the mountains of Bether*, she presents a picture of the Lord Jesus responding to the believer who calls out to him on the basis of covenantal relationship. Jesus has promised to never leave nor forsake those who are his. He always draws near to those who by faith humbly hold him to his covenantal promises.

The Shulammite's plea infers a confidence in her beloved's faithfulness to her, but she is learning that she cannot presume upon his grace and that he will not be controlled. He comes when he wills, and he goes as he wills. That is, the sense of his presence seems to come and go as he wills. The Shulammite will learn to trust him more completely, knowing that even when the sense of his immediate presence is lifted, he is not out of reach. She will eventually learn to walk in the truth spoken through Isaiah: "Can a woman forget her nursing child, and have no compassion on the son of her womb? Even these may forget, but I will not forget you."[2]

Boldly, the Shulammite importunes her beloved that he might not delay his coming. She begs that he turn back[3] before[4] the evening breeze *when the shadows* lengthen and eventually dissolve into the black of night. Still in the first moments of feeling her beloved's seeming retreat, the Shulammite pleads that he return while it is still called today, as though she is plagued by a foreboding of his complete withdrawal, which would be to her the darkest of all nights imaginable.

---

[1] Genesis 22:2

[2] Isaiah 49:15

[3] The unusual description of shadows fleeing and a gazelle turning back combine to present a picture of a gazelle stopping and turning back to look as he flees. However, the Shulammite wants more than a studied glance; she hopes for a complete change of mind.

[4] The Hebrew *ad*, here translated as *until*, can also be translated *before*.

FRANTIC RECOVERY

Shulammite to the
daughters of
Jerusalem:

3:1 On my bed night after night I sought him
Whom my soul loves;
I sought him but did not find him.

3:2 'I must arise now and go about the city;
In the streets and in the squares
I must seek him whom my soul loves.'
I sought him but did not find him.

3:3 The watchmen who make the rounds in
the city found me,
And I said, 'Have you seen him whom my
soul loves?'

3:4 Scarcely had I left them
When I found him whom my soul loves;
I held on to him and would not let him go,
Until I had brought him to my mother's
house,
And into the room of her who conceived
me.

What the Shulammite used to call *our* bed (1:16), she now calls *my bed* (3:1). Having entered into a time of separation, represented by a series of long and restless nights, she feels alone.

Insecure Love

Night after night the Shulammite dreams that she has lost her beloved; she seeks for him but cannot find him. As often happens with most people, the Shulammite's fears and insecurities are acted out in her dreams. She boasts of her beloved's love (2:16), but when faced with his absence, her insecurities begin to surface. Her doubts and fears arise from the very nature of the relationship. The Shulammite is love-starved and emotionally needy; at this stage she perceives the relationship primarily in terms of how it will benefit her. She does not yet believe that what she offers her beloved is of great value to him, for indeed, her contribution has had more to do with her desire to *be* loved than her desire to love. Her love is intense but lacking in substance.

The immaturity of the Shulammite's love is typical of how people commonly relate to one another. In human relationships one is not truly free to love while dependent upon the other for his sense of well-being. As long as one is dependent upon what he receives from others, to that degree, he is not free to love because he is more concerned about what he will receive than what he will give. Of course, the love and affection received from others is a wonderful blessing from the Lord, but it is an incomparably greater blessing when it is given freely than when it has been demanded out of a feeling of neediness.

Whenever one feels intimidated or threatened in a relationship, he would do well to ask himself, "What is it I want from the other person that I am afraid he will not give me?" For when one loves others perfectly, he has no fear of others because, as the apostle John has noted, "Perfect love casts out all fear."[1] Love considers what is best for others, putting their needs above its own.[2]

This kind of love should be the goal of every believer in his relationship with others, for indeed, it is the command of the Lord Jesus and the very essence of what it means to be a Christian, a follower of Christ. Jesus instructed his disciples that they were to be perfect in love, even as their heavenly Father is perfect in love.[3] In fact, Jesus went so far as to say that his followers will love even their enemies.[4] To walk in union with Christ is to be perfected in love, for "God is love, and the one who abides in love abides in God, and God abides in him."[5]

For someone to love others unreservedly requires that he be rooted and grounded in the love of God, for only God can fulfill the longings for love that lie deep within the heart of every human. To grow in love is to become less dependent upon what one receives

---

[1] 1 John 4:18
[2] Philippians 2:3
[3] Matthew 5:48
[4] Matthew 5:44; Luke 6:27; Luke 6:35;
[5] 1 John 4:16

from others and more dependent upon what he receives from the Lord, for only God is inexhaustible in his supply and his desire to impart love.

This is the reason for one's existence, to know the life and love of God, and to experience that life flowing out toward others. God is love, and his desire is to so unite lives with his that they might manifest his love, not only in this age but throughout all the ages to come.

Loving God wholeheartedly presupposes that one believes God is good and worthy to be trusted. As one comes to know God's faithfulness, kindness, gentleness, tenderheartedness, mercy and wisdom, he learns that God is trustworthy. When one trusts God, he experiences peace and security in his relationship with him, even in the times when God seems to be distant. The Lord will actually lead his elect through times of apparent darkness in order that they might learn to lean more heavily upon him, as the prophet Isaiah says, "Who is among you that fears the LORD, that obeys the voice of His servant, that walks in darkness and has no light? Let him trust in the name of the Lord and rely on his God."[1] The one who trusts God is able to give thanks in everything[2] and be anxious for nothing,[3] even during times of distress.

The Shulammite will eventually enter into mature love, but for now she must have constant reassurances that her beloved is with her. She needs always to hear about his love and desire for her, and she must be continually comforted by the conscious awareness of his presence. Her present feeling of abandonment has become intolerable. Fearing that her beloved may have withdrawn permanently and frustrated because she cannot find him, the Shulammite anxiously scours the *streets* of the *city*.

---

[1] Isaiah 50:10
[2] 1 Thessalonians 5:18
[3] Philippians 4:6

The Watchmen

Full of love and compassion, her beloved meets the Shulammite at her point of need. Since the Shulammite does not know how to *find him*, he sends watchmen to find *her*.

Faithful shepherds[1] make their *rounds* throughout *the city*, watching over the condition of men's souls and the quality of their interactions. They previously helped beautify the Shulammite (1:8), and like faithful eunuchs they will continue laboring to prepare the bride of Christ for the consummation of the relationship at his return. In the end the shepherds shall receive their reward (8:12), an unfading crown of glory.[2] The Father is generous in rewarding these humble shepherds because there is nothing more precious to the Father than his children, nor more precious to the Son than his bride. Absolutely nothing!

There is no greater joy[3] than to labor together with the Holy Spirit in helping to bring about God's eternal purpose, the restoration of his creation. Albeit, in this case the restoration exceeds the quality of the original, for the bride of Christ, being one body together with the Son, will radiate the unfathomable glory of the Son forever. All praise be to God who has chosen to redeem creatures of flesh and make them sons and daughters through the sacrificial outpouring of the life of his Son!

Previously, the Shulammite had asked the shepherds to sustain her with raisin cakes and apples (2:5), hoping to mollify her lovesickness. Now she asks if they can tell her how she can find her beloved. The Shulammite has grown, evidenced by the fact that she is no longer looking to the shepherds to meet the need of her heart, but instead, she looks for them to teach her how to find her beloved for herself. She remembers that the secondhand revelations of raisin cakes and apples, although inspiring and refreshing, did not cure her lovesickness.

---

[1] Isaiah 62:6; Ezekiel 3:17; Hebrews 13:17
[2] 1 Peter 5:4
[3] Philippians 2:2; 1 John 1:4

There is yet another reason why the Shulammite seizes the initiative in seeking out her beloved. Earlier, when he came for her, she declined his invitation to *come along* (2:10, 13). Now, feeling responsible for driving him away, she is frantic to undo the consequence of her reticence; eagerly, she seeks to restore the relationship with her beloved.

Relationship Restored

Able to find her beloved

Presumably, the shepherds have been praying for the Shulammite, their private intercession aiding her in the quest to find her beloved. It is not difficult also to imagine the shepherds encouraging the Shulammite to believe that her beloved is readily accessible and that she must learn to exercise faith in apprehending him, for no sooner does she ask for their help than she finds her beloved! Thus, the Shulammite makes an extremely important discovery: she can find her beloved on her own! She learns that Jesus is never out of reach to all who call upon him from a hungry, sincere heart.

The Shulammite is growing in faith and beginning to wean herself from dependency on the comfort and encouragement of others. This is not to minimize the importance of teachings, revelations, prophecies, consolations, admonitions, words of wisdom and encouragement, for God has so designed the body that all the members are to participate in building up one another in love. (Unquestionably, the *watchmen* were a tremendously important gift sent from the Lord to help the Shulammite along the way.) The point is that as the Shulammite grows closer to the Lord, she moves away from a dependency upon men to a greater dependency upon Christ. The purpose of all true ministry is to aid in this process.

Unwilling to let go

Although the Shulammite is growing, she remains insecure in her relationship with her beloved. When she finally finds him, she holds on to him and does not let him go. She is like Mary who, upon seeing the risen Savior, had to be told, "Stop clinging to me for I have not yet ascended to the Father."[1] Mary clung to Jesus because she thought she had lost him, and she did not want to lose him again.

Mature love, confident of the value it contributes to any given relationship, is secure and does not fear abandonment. This is a confidence the Shulammite will develop over time. However, at this stage, because she neither loves perfectly, nor is she appreciably aware of the joy she provides her beloved, the Shulammite has less than total confidence in his commitment to her. Therefore, she remains in infantile grasping, clinging love; she is more concerned with containing the relationship than in contributing to it.

Believers often struggle similarly in their relationship with God. The loss of the sense of his immediate presence is unsettling because they are not fully convinced of his commitment to them. They understand intellectually that he demonstrated his love by paying an infinitely great price to redeem their souls from sin, but they do not appreciate, at the emotional level, the depth of joy he experiences in every thought over them. The Lord reveals a glimpse of his love for his people through Isaiah, saying, "As the bridegroom rejoices over the bride, so your God will rejoice over you."[2] And again, Zephaniah the prophet says, "He will exult over you with joy, . . . he will rejoice over you with shouts of joy."[3] Can the human mind begin to comprehend the resounding effect throughout the heavens when the Godhead shouts with joy? What unfathomable love the Father has for his children!

The Shulammite is only at the beginning stages of her development. Soon she will be showered with the praises of her beloved, and she will begin to understand that she is desirable to him and has something of value to contribute to the relationship.

---

[1] John 20:17
[2] Isaiah 62:5
[3] Zephaniah 3:17

Reassured of his love

When the Shulammite finds her beloved, she brings him into her *mother's house*. The Shulammite's mother is the city of God, Zion,[1] also called Jerusalem above,[2] and is represented here by the church on earth. Earlier, the Shulammite saw the church as a place of work (1:6); now she sees it as a place of spiritual conception, a place of hearing the gospel and of receiving life through the Word implanted. The Lord is the husband and father who begets believers; the church is the wife and mother who, in cooperation with the Holy Spirit, conceives[3] and rears[4] them.

Notably, the Shulammite brings her beloved all the way into the privacy of her mother's bedroom. This allusion to the time when she was *conceived* reveals the Shulammite's fundamental concern. While her beloved seems to have abandoned her, the Shulammite seriously questions whether she is really born of God. "For if I am really his," she reasons, "then why do I no longer experience his presence like I did before? Is it possible that I have fallen out of favor with God and no longer have his Spirit within me?"

When a person gives his life to Christ and is baptized, the Holy Spirit reveals to his heart that he is loved by God, that his sin is forgiven and that he is now a child of God.[5] However, this knowing is very subjective, and there are times when believers are plagued with doubt and fear concerning their standing with God. Fortunately, the apostle John reveals three external evidences the believer can look to for reassurance that he is born of God.[6] One is that he loves God and keeps his commandments;[7] the second is that he loves and identifies with the people of God,[8] and the third is that he confesses Christ openly before men.[9]

---

[1] Psalm 87:5
[2] Galatians 4:26
[3] Galatians 4:19
[4] 1 Thessalonians 2:7-12
[5] Romans 5:1; 8:15-16; 1 John 3:24
[6] 1 John 5:13
[7] Matthew 16:24-25; 1 John 2:3-5; 3:7-8, 10
[8] Matthew 7:17-18; 1 John 2:19; 3:14, 19
[9] Matthew 10:32-33; 1 John 2:23; 4:15

Unfortunately, the Shulammite does not pause to consider whether her life bears the marks of eternal life, for if she had, she would become more firmly established in her faith. Instead, she simply contents herself in having the sense of her beloved's presence again restored to her.

Holding on to her beloved, the Shulammite does not let go until she brings him into the safety of a private chamber within her mother's house. Still too frightened to join her beloved in his vineyard, the Shulammite retreats to the inner sanctum of her own heart, a place where she previously felt safe behind defensive walls of her own making (2:9). She was willing to venture out for a little while, but only out of desperation at the loss of her beloved's presence.

Summary

In summary, the Shulammite was unwilling to go with her beloved to work in the vineyards, resulting in the loss of the sense of his presence. Upon again finding him, she holds on to her beloved until she brings him into a private chamber within her mother's house.

The Shulammite typifies the believer who is invited by the Lord to extend his love in ministry to others but, because of inner fears, recoils. After suffering the loss of the Lord's presence, he begins to fervently seek the Lord, after which, he is rewarded with a renewal of God's presence that rejuvenates the believer's times of prayer and worship.

CLOSING

| Beloved to the daughters of Jerusalem: | 3:5 | **I adjure you, O daughters of Jerusalem, By the gazelles or by the hinds of the field, That you will not arouse or awaken *my* love, Until she pleases.** |

Solomon repeats[1] his solemn admonition to the *daughters of Jerusalem* that they not disturb the Shulammite from her mystical sleep until she is ready to *awaken*. Again it forms a natural closing. This second act finishes with the Shulammite firmly clutching her beloved. She is satisfied that his presence has been restored.

Significantly, the Shulammite receives no rebuke for having rejected her beloved's invitation to come labor with him. He is gentle and patient, giving her time to make a voluntary choice to go deeper with him without feeling pressured by the fear of his disapproval.

In the next act, her beloved will begin to heap lavish praise upon the Shulammite, inspiring her to make a greater commitment of obedience to him (4:6). He will challenge the Shulammite, but he will not push too hard. He has purposed to sift from her life anything and everything that hinders her from experiencing the thrill of abandoned love, but like a wise miller, he is careful to not thresh too hard or too long lest he damage the grain.[2]

---

[1] This adjuration is explained at its first occurrence (2:7).
[2] Isaiah 28:28

Act III

———

Desire Realized

Eat, friends; drink and imbibe deeply, O lovers.

THE BRIDAL COMPANY[1]

<table>
<tr><td>Shulammite:</td><td>3:6</td><td>What is this coming up from the wilderness
Like columns of smoke,
Perfumed with myrrh and frankincense,
With all scented powders of the merchant?</td></tr>
<tr><td></td><td>3:7</td><td>Behold, it is the traveling couch of Solomon;
Sixty mighty men around it,
Of the mighty men of Israel.</td></tr>
<tr><td></td><td>3:8</td><td>All of them are wielders of the sword,
Expert in war;
Each man has his sword at his side,
Guarding against the terrors of the night.</td></tr>
<tr><td></td><td>3:9</td><td>King Solomon has made for himself a sedan chair
From the timber of Lebanon.</td></tr>
<tr><td></td><td>3:10</td><td>He made its posts of silver,
Its back of gold
And its seat of purple fabric,
With its interior lovingly fitted out
By the daughters of Jerusalem.</td></tr>
</table>

Exclaiming in amazement, "*What is this* . . . ?" the Shulammite wonders breathlessly at the approaching processional. Instantly, she answers her own rhetorical question:[2] "*It is the traveling couch of Solomon.*"[3] Unquestionably, this is no ordinary couch, for it bears the presence of the king; but never before has the Shulammite seen her beloved king quite like this, surrounded by exotic perfumes from Arabia, India and other distant lands, perfumes of such

---

[1] There are three representations of the bridal company in this section: the traveling couch (3:7), the sixty mighty men (3:7), and the crown (3:11).

[2] Since the speaker is close enough to recognize the scents, she is also close enough to identify the object being observed, leading the reader to conclude that this is a rhetorical question.

[3] The Hebrew word translated *this* is in the feminine form and must refer to either the Shulammite or the couch. The couch is preferred since it is the object identified in response to the question. Additionally, the Shulammite is not perfumed with myrrh and frankincense until she responds in wholehearted obedience (4:6, 14).

abundance and extravagant luxury that their sweet aromas ascend *like columns of smoke* above the horizon.

Spiritually speaking, the *couch* or palanquin represents that body of mature believers who carry the presence of Christ wherever they go, saints whose hearts have become a resting place for the Beloved. They loathe all inner striving and are counted among the friends of God. These precious souls have attained a level of intimacy with the Beloved that the Shulammite dreams was hers. They are the bridal company.

Perfume from the Wilderness

Spices that so lavishly perfume Solomon's traveling couch[1] are descriptive of the nature of the bridal company.

Myrrh was the primary ingredient in the anointing oil prescribed for consecrating (that is, separating for service to God) the priests and the many articles in the tabernacle of Moses. The couch drenched in myrrh is, therefore, descriptive of those who have yielded their wills in voluntary obedience and thus have separated themselves totally to God.

Frankincense was burned as incense before the Lord and represents prayer that ascends before the Father.[2] The aroma of frankincense, rising from the traveling couch like columns of smoke, describes the bridal company as a people of prayer, those who walk in continual communion with the Father.[3] For them, prayer is more than a periodic activity; it is a way of life, an expression of the heart's affections that remain constantly centered upon the Beloved.

Although myrrh and frankincense (obedience and prayer) are singled out as the most important of all the spices, the bridal company is not lacking in any quality that graced the life of the Lord Jesus, for she is endowed with *all the scented powders of the merchant*. In other words, the bridal company emits not only the

---

[1] In Solomon's time, it was not uncommon for a woman to perfume the bed she intended to share with her lover (Proverbs 7:17).
[2] Psalm 141:2
[3] Ephesians 6:18; 1 Thessalonians 5:17

pleasing aroma of voluntary submission and unbridled communion, but also the fragrances of love, joy, peace, patience, kindness, goodness, faithfulness, gentleness, self-control, humility, wisdom and every other noble quality. There is no duplicity or compromise in their lives, only perfect and unfeigned devotion to the Father.

Interestingly, myrrh and frankincense, both essential to the Mosaic system of worship, were imported by adventurous spice traders from Arabia and North Africa.[1] Thus, Israel was dependent upon foreign trade for the continuance of its prescribed order of worship and, consequently, its very survival as a nation. Unquestionably, God had purposed from its inception that his house should be called a house of prayer for *all* the nations.[2] Similarly, the myrrh and frankincense accompanying the bridal company hint at its global constitution; that is to say, the bridal company is made up of souls from among the nations of the world.

This international flavor of the bridal company is reinforced by the fact that they possess all the scented powders of the merchant. The inherent interaction with international traders suggests that the bridal company is developed, not in a cloister, but through active involvement with those of the world. God so loved the world that he sent his only begotten Son into the world that the world might be saved through him.[3] In like manner, the Son sends his followers into the world[4] that the world might be saved through their testimony concerning the Son.

The bridal company is seen coming up from the wilderness, the place of testing. Just as the nation of Israel was tested in the wilderness before being led into the promised land, as to whether they would obey God or not,[5] and just as Jesus was tested in the wilderness prior to his time of public ministry, every believer must pass through times of personal testing in order to be refined and

---

[1] Jeremiah 6:20
[2] Isaiah 56:7; Mark 11:17
[3] John 3:16-17
[4] John 17:18
[5] Deuteronomy 8:2; Psalm 66:10

proven for greater levels of responsibility and privilege in the kingdom of God.

Solomon's presence upon his traveling couch (3:9-11) reveals that the bridal company does not come up from the wilderness alone, for they have enthroned the Lord Jesus upon their hearts. His promise to never leave them nor forsake them has become for them a living reality through the exercise of persevering faith. How tragic and how wasteful it is when believers go through wilderness testings and forget the Lord's promise to always be with them, for it is by faithfully enduring the wilderness that the believer accumulates myrrh (proven obedience), frankincense (a developed prayer life) and the most precious of all the other scented powders of the merchant.

Eventually, the Shulammite joins this great bridal company and is herself seen coming up from the wilderness leaning on her beloved (8:5), but for now, she remains awestruck by the richness and splendor of the king's procession.

Sixty Mighty Men

Around Solomon's luxuriant couch is an elite corps of the royal army, *sixty* battle-hardened veterans who, in league with their magnific warrior-king, have triumphed through the fiery trials typified by the wilderness. As part of the entourage bearing the presence of their king, they too are members of the bridal company. They typify mature saints,[1] those who have become expert in wielding the Word of God and have overcome the fiery testing of their faith. These are fearless champions who accompany the king wherever he goes.[2]

These valiant warriors have long ago passed through the training phase of their spiritual adolescence. They have engaged and overcome the evil one[3] in the battle over their own souls and now emerge as a formidable challenge to any would-be attacker. Their

---

[1] Six is the number representing man; ten represents completeness. Sixty (6x10) represents completed man.
[2] Revelation 14:4
[3] 1 John 2:13-14

mere presence causes the enemy to cower, for they walk in perfected love that conquers every fear,[1] tenderhearted mercy that triumphs over judgment,[2] unfeigned humility that keeps their souls from presumptuous sins[3] and unconquerable wisdom that delivers cities.[4] These meek and humble warriors rest their *swords* at their *sides*, always alert to an unexpected attack from an unseen foe, but enjoying the peace that comes through trustful obedience to their king.

Just as the reign of King David, a man of war, was succeeded by the reign of King Solomon, a man of peace, so the Christian life moves from a place of striving with the enemy toward a place of peace and rest in union with God. Both phases are necessary. Israel could not dwell peacefully within the promised land until her enemies had been subdued. Solomon could not have reigned in peace if his father David had not destroyed the enemies before him. Nevertheless, because David was a man of war, God would not use him to build the tabernacle. Correspondingly, the fullness of God's presence does not abide in those still struggling to overcome the enemy in their own souls, but is manifest through those who have triumphed in battle and have found their rest in God.[5]

Solomon has a name meaning *peaceful*. He typifies the Lord Jesus who, while walking upon the earth amidst a wicked and tumultuous generation, remained perfectly calm within. Jesus said to those who would follow him, "Take my yoke upon you, and learn from me, for I am gentle and humble in heart; and you shall find rest for your souls. For my yoke is easy, and my load is light."[6]

How many worry about what others think, only to discover that they can never please everyone? How many are chronically fatigued, expending their emotional energies by continually replaying their own actions and the actions of others in a vain

---

[1] 1 John 4:18
[2] James 2:13
[3] Psalm 19:13
[4] Ecclesiastes 7:19; 9:15;
[5] Hebrews 4:11
[6] Matthew 11:29-30

attempt to justify themselves in their own minds? How many are chronically self-absorbed, constantly seeking the latest convenience by which they can avoid personal discomfort or improve their public image? These are not the Lord's yokes, but are representative of the many burdens that can be quickly lightened when a soul humbly yields control of his life to Christ.

Many souls, lacking the wisdom and ability to secure their own happiness, labor under the burden of trying to govern their own lives apart from God. The resulting inner turmoil can always be traced to some underlying and unnecessary fear. It may be the fear of failure, rejection, abandonment or pain, or it may be the fear of being afraid. In saying, "Take *my* yoke," Jesus offers the key to experiencing his peace.

In the previous visit from her beloved (2:9), the Shulammite was afraid to follow him outside the security of her own walls, and she discovered how easy it is to lose the sweet sense of his presence when otherwise persuaded by troublesome and persistent fears. She viewed her beloved's love for others as daring, adventurous, unnecessarily risky and definitely not safe. He beckoned her to join him, but no, for the Shulammite, the sense of adventure was not worth the loss of her peace. However, now she is made to see that, unlike herself, those in the bridal company enjoy perfect peace precisely because they were willing to face their fears and overcome them.

Sedan Chair

King Solomon comes up from the wilderness, the place of testing, in a *sedan chair*,[1] clearly communicating his victorious and peaceful reign. Likewise, the Lord Jesus Christ, having overcome the malevolent power of the world,[2] is now seated on his eternal throne from where he rules with absolute authority and perfect peace. In addition to conquering sin and death, Christ has also

---

[1] It is unclear whether the chair is another name for the couch, a part of the couch, or a separate transport. It is assumed here to be a part of the couch Solomon made specifically for himself.
[2] John 16:33

subdued through love the barbarous hearts of those who are now the bridal company.[1] Who can be compared with Christ— such mercy, such grace and such indomitable love!

The materials Solomon uses to construct his sedan chair typify three essential qualities of the reigning Christ.

Made *from the timber of Lebanon*, the cedar framework becomes a metaphor for Christ's humanity.[2] The second person of the Godhead, infinitely full of glory, power and wisdom, the uncreated and only begotten Son of God, deliberately descended to the earth and became a man. Suffering the indignities of the human condition in a world wracked with sin, Jesus remained perfectly obedient to the Father, even to the point of a torturous death by crucifixion. As a result, "God highly exalted him, and bestowed on him the name which is above every name, so that at the name of Jesus every knee will bow, of those who are in heaven and on earth and under the earth, and that every tongue will confess that Jesus Christ is Lord, to the glory of God the Father."[3] Jesus is the unique God-man. Though fully God, always existent in the bosom of the Father from eternity past, he is also fully man. How Jesus has ennobled the human race[4] by choosing to take on the form of flesh and blood and become a man!

The golden *back* of the sedan chair represents the divinity of Christ and the quality of his reign. His kingdom is an everlasting kingdom,[5] one in which he wields absolute authority with unerring justice, matchless wisdom and unending love.

Silver, sometimes called *ransom money* in the Bible,[6] represents the work of Christ in redemption. Thus, the *silver posts* supporting the sedan chair indicate that the lovingkindness, justice and righteousness upon which Christ's throne is established[7] is

---

[1] Philippians 3:21
[2] Psalm 1:3; Jeremiah 17:8; Daniel 4; Mark 8:24
[3] Philippians 2:9-11
[4] Albeit, only those who are joined to him are so ennobled.
[5] Isaiah 9:7
[6] Numbers 3:49, 51
[7] 2 Chronicles 9:8; Psalm 9:7; Isaiah 9:7; 16:5

validated or upheld by his willingness to give his life as a ransom for many. In the apostle John's Revelation, the angels, the cherubim and the twenty-four elders around the throne of God in heaven declare this singular work of the precious and wonderful Savior. While the holy and eternal Father is hailed worthy to receive glory and honor and power because of his work in creation,[1] Jesus, the Lamb of God, is hailed worthy to receive power and riches and wisdom and might and honor and glory and blessing because he was slain and purchased for God with his blood men from every tribe and tongue and people and nation.[2]

The *daughters of Jerusalem* add to the extravagance of the procession by lovingly dressing the *interior* of the sedan chair with *purple*, a color representing the grandeur of royalty. These maidens represent the main body of the church, those who love the Lord and glory in the power of his majesty. Through extravagant and loving praise, they invoke the Lord's presence in their midst,[3] but they have not yet learned how to abide in his presence. Though they revel in worshipping him among the throng as King of kings and Lord of lords, the daughters of Jerusalem lack the revelation enabling the heavenly bridegroom to be enthroned within their hearts.

In this discourse the Shulammite is focused primarily upon the bridal company. She recognizes her beloved's redemptive work and his enthronement (3:9-10), but her report is dispassionate, a mere statement of fact.[4] What intrigues the Shulammite is the company of believers who have entered into a dimension of intimacy with the Beloved for which she has cravingly dreamed. Observing their obedience, their overcoming faith and their repose, she begins to see the implications of her salvation and eventual union with her beloved. The Shulammite is inspired to the bridal

---

[1] Revelation 4:8-11. Of course, both the Father and the Son were involved in creation (Genesis 1:26; Colossians 1:15-17), just as both of them were involved also in redemption (John 3:16).

[2] Revelation 5:8-12

[3] Psalm 22:3

[4] Earlier, she rejoiced in *his love* (1:16; 2:3-5), but she does not yet know him well enough, nor does she have the vocabulary, to exult in *him*. That is coming.

call. Furthermore, she realizes she is not alone in her quest; there is a bridal *company*, others who have overcome. She is encouraged to believe that her dream *is* obtainable!

Shulammite to
the daughters of
Jerusalem:

3:11 **Go forth, O daughters of Zion,**
      And gaze on King Solomon with the crown
      With which his mother has crowned him
      On the day of his wedding,
      And on the day of his gladness of heart.

The King's Crown

Excitedly, the Shulammite calls out to the daughters of Jerusalem by a new name: *daughters of Zion*. The most distinguished part of ancient Jerusalem was Zion; it typifies the joyous and triumphant reign of Christ. Addressing the maidens as the *daughters of Zion*, the Shulammite attempts to inspire them to greatness, hoping they will begin to think of themselves as royalty, those chosen to be seated together with Christ upon his heavenly throne as joint heirs of his eternal kingdom.

Enjoining the maidens to *gaze* upon the king, one might wonder why the Shulammite is addressing worshippers, those who love to sing his praises (1:3; 3:10). Why does she here encourage them to look upon the one they are already quite eager to worship? The Shulammite wants the maidens to see the king *with the crown*, that is, with the bridal company that has become for him a crown of beauty and glory,[1] testifying to his role as the heavenly bridegroom.

The Lord Jesus has many crowns[2] or appellations by which he might be praised, and each of the many facets of his glory has a unique transforming effect upon the worshipper.[3] The Shulammite wants the maidens to contemplate the loveliness of Jesus as their heavenly bridegroom: his heart of boundless affection and his joyful anticipation of unbridled intimacy with those who love him.

---

[1] Isaiah 62:3; 1 Corinthians 11:7; Philippians 4:1
[2] Revelation 19:12
[3] 2 Corinthians 3:18

It is this revelation of the bridegroom that satisfies the longing within every heart for love. There is no other relationship on earth able to appease the rabid hunger which God has placed within the soul of man for communion with deity. Many try to satiate this hunger apart from God,[1] ending sooner or later in their hurt. Only in knowing God is love finally and fully realized.

Oftentimes women (or for that matter, men) adorn themselves with gold and precious gems, vainly hoping to beautify themselves. In reality, true and eternal beauty emanates from within and cannot be produced externally by mere accouterments of gold or costly stones.[2] Unlike jewelry, however, a crown is not intended to add beauty, but merely to accentuate the glory intrinsic to the wearer. A king's crown, for example, is meant to draw attention to his authority. An athlete's crown is meant to draw attention to his unexcelled prowess. Jesus is all glorious within and without; nothing can be added to and nothing can be taken away from him. The bridal company does not bejewel the king as though they could add even an ounce of beauty to the one who is breathtakingly resplendent. Instead, they become as a crown to him; their faithful devotion to the bridegroom draws attention to his incomparable worth as savior, lover and friend— qualities he already possesses.

The bride never thinks of claiming her beauty as her own, realizing that it is merely the outworking of the Beloved's presence in her. When she loves, it is the bridegroom loving through her. When she pursues him, it is by the grace that he supplies. When she is deemed beautiful, it is his beauty radiating through her. It is the bridegroom's glory imparted to the bride with which he is crowned.

It was noted earlier that Solomon's name means *peaceful*, but it also means *completion* or *fulfillment*. Thus, Solomon typifies Jesus, who is the fullness of Deity dwelling in bodily form and in whom every believer has been made complete.[3] Jesus is returning for a

---

[1] Jeremiah 2:13
[2] Proverbs 11:22; 1 Timothy 2:9
[3] Colossians 2:9-10

corporate bride, a body of believers who have become mature, to the measure of the stature which belongs to the fullness of Christ.[1] By faith the last days church will enter into the fullness of love, power, joy, wisdom and grace that Jesus has both modeled and obtained for her.

The King's Wedding

Jesus' mother, Mary, while still a virgin, miraculously conceived the Christ child when she was overshadowed by the Holy Spirit. Because Jesus' mother was a human (and his father was God), King Solomon's mother represents Jesus' humanity.[2] In presenting the crown (the mature church of the last days) to her son, Solomon's mother demonstrates that it is humankind (specifically, the people of God) who supply the bride for Christ's wedding day.

This obvious, though subtle, reference to Christ's humanity makes several important statements. Firstly, it was a man who walked on the earth two thousand years ago, overcoming all his enemies and inspiring a host of mighty men to overcome as he also did. Secondly, as a man and as the offspring of David, Jesus is well-qualified to rule the earth upon his promised return when he reestablishes David's throne in Jerusalem.[3] And thirdly, though he be divine, Jesus' humanity speaks of his suitability as a bridegroom for the Shulammite. Though she feels distant from God, Jesus bridges the gap; in becoming a man, he gained for humans the opportunity to access the riches of the knowledge of the glory of God.[4]

Gladness of heart may well understate the indescribable jubilation the Lord Jesus will experience when he is finally united to his beautiful bride. Since the creation of man, the Son of God has eagerly anticipated and longed for the moment when he is forever

---

[1] Ephesians 4:13

[2] In the Bible Jesus is specifically referred to as the *seed* of a *woman* (Genesis 3:15).

[3] Dominion over the earth, originally given to Adam and Eve (representatives of all mankind), was lost through sin but regained through the obedience of Christ (a second representative for all of mankind).

[4] This truth, an essential pillar in the bridal paradigm, deserves greater amplification than is possible in this book.

joined in intimate love with his many-membered bride. Observing the wedding procession, the Shulammite undoubtedly glimpsed this joyous preoccupation upon the face of her beloved.

However, it was the bridal company that made the greater impression upon the Shulammite. Seeing the Beloved crowned by a company of selfless devotees has profoundly impacted the Shulammite, resulting in a radical shift in her thinking: life is about more than what she can *get from* him; it is about what she can *be for* him. As exquisitely crafted platinum highlights the beauty of a diamond, so the bride's life of consecrated obedience, affectionate prayer, overcoming faith, profound peace, uncommon joy and sacrificial love magnifies the beauty and worth of the king.

Embracing the vision for spiritual maturity in her own life, the Shulammite remains painfully aware of her own deficiencies. There are still too many times when she is unloving, irritable, impatient, comparing, complaining or self-justifying. Although no longer black like the tents of Kedar (1:5), she is not yet numbered among the bridal company. Her life is still much too dominated by secret fears yielding to moments of indiscretion.

The triumphant faith and unsullied devotion of the bridal company far outshines the Shulammite's self-centered approach to spirituality. She has been zealously seeking comforting reassurances of her beloved's love while indifferent to his desires (which happen to include the needs of others). Gentle coaxing by her beloved— first by invitation (2:10-14), then by feigned withdrawal (3:1-2)— had not persuaded the Shulammite to come out of hiding to help draw precious souls to him. Now, inspired by the bridal company, the Shulammite overcomes her reticence and urges the daughters of Zion to *go forth* and *gaze on King Solomon with the crown*. This marks a major turning point for the Shulammite and prompts an immediate response from her beloved.

THE SHULAMMITE'S BEAUTY

Beloved to
Shulammite:

4:1 How beautiful you are, my darling,
How beautiful you are!
Your eyes are *like* doves behind your veil;
Your hair is like a flock of goats
That have descended from Mount Gilead.

4:2 Your teeth are like a flock of *newly* shorn ewes
Which have come up from *their* washing,
All of which bear twins,
And not one among them has lost her young.

4:3 Your lips are like a scarlet thread,
And your mouth is lovely.
Your temples are like a slice of a pomegranate
Behind your veil.

4:4 Your neck is like the tower of David
Built with rows of stones,
On which are hung a thousand shields,
All the round shields of the mighty men.

4:5 Your two breasts are like two fawns,
Twins of a gazelle,
Which feed among the lilies.

How beautiful you are, my darling! As though spellbound, the Shulammite's beloved delays elaborating. Intent on savoring the delight of her fascinating charm, he merely repeats, *"How beautiful you are!"* Previous adulation (1:15) merely hinted at the Beloved's admiration for the Shulammite that now breaks forth in a torrent of praise.

Her beloved realizes that the Shulammite is not fully mature, but, understanding the power of affirmation, he extols what are the mere beginnings of the Shulammite's maturation process. He encourages the Shulammite by describing seven physical characteristics that are particularly attractive to him, each one portraying a spiritual quality absolutely essential to her spiritual growth.[1] Although her shortcomings are not hidden from his sight, she is not defined by her shortcomings. Her beloved focuses on the Shulammite's qualities, confident that the good work he has begun in her, he will be able to complete.[2]

Devoted

Doves, a symbol in the ancient world of romantic love, represent the Shulammite's *eyes* and, by implication, her affections. They are veiled from the world, as though to say, they are reserved solely for her beloved.[3] They look to him for love, for understanding, for her sense of value and significance. Without him, her life is empty, meaningless and destitute.

In striking contrast to the brazen face of the boisterous harlot described elsewhere by Solomon,[4] the Shulammite's discreet demeanor suggests a heart that seeks after wisdom[5] and not the approval of men.[6] The Shulammite does not crave to be known by men, nor to be understood, nor does she take satisfaction in the honors and praises bestowed by others. Not wishing to mitigate the praises she will receive from her beloved, the Shulammite shuns every opportunity for public acknowledgment, content to live for an audience of one.

---

[1] There is a striking correlation between the qualities of the Shulammite listed in this discourse and the characteristics of those Jesus comforts in his Sermon on the Mount (Matthew 5:3-10). Jesus said that the poor in spirit are blessed; the Shulammite is devoted, recognizing she is needy without her beloved. Jesus said the gentle or meek are blessed; the Shulammite is humble. Jesus said those who hunger and thirst for righteousness are blessed; the Shulammite's teeth indicate that she is reflective. Jesus said that the merciful are blessed; the Shulammite is merciful. Jesus said that the pure in heart are blessed; the Shulammite is pure of heart. Jesus said that the peacemaker is blessed; the Shulammite is steadfast, the shields around her neck indicating that she is at peace, a requirement of those who would bring peace to others. Jesus said that the persecuted are blessed, teaching also that they should love their enemies (Matthew 5:44); the Shulammite is tenderhearted.

[2] Philippians 1:6; 1 Thessalonians 3:13; 5:23-24; Jude 1:24

[3] Psalm 123:2; 1 Corinthians 2:2; 2 Corinthians 11:2

[4] Proverbs 7:11-13

[5] Proverbs 8:12; 11:22

[6] 2 Corinthians 10:12

Humble

Lustrous black *hair*[1] crowns the Shulammite,[2] illustrating the meek and quiet spirit that graces her soul.[3] Meekness is sometimes interpreted by the uninitiated as weakness, but is more justly defined as the self-restraint of one's inner strength. The Shulammite's hair is alive and flowing, like a *flock of goats* happily descending from Mount Gilead, a place celebrated for its good pastureland and vigorous flocks. The picture is not one of a weak and compliant will, stripped of all vitality and desire for life, but of a robust and determined will in voluntary submission.

Sheep would seem to be a more likely representation of meekness than goats (which tend to be less yielding than sheep), but these goats are not ascending but descending, clearly signifying the Shulammite's unassuming approach toward life: her willingness to listen, to learn, to receive correction and to be the least.

Knowing that all authority is established and maintained by God, the Shulammite is careful to obey, even commands which seem unreasonable or unjust, without the habit of complaining that is so commonly found among souls less distinguished.[4] Although gracious toward all, she is particularly careful to give honor to those whom God has positioned as authority figures in her own life.

Goats are stately in their walk[5] and illustrate the way in which humility ennobles the human spirit. Although a person who is genuinely humble is aware of the grace upon his life, he does not consciously attempt to form such an opinion of himself in the minds of others. Obviously, boasting of one's humility is self-defeating, but even self-effacing attempts at projecting an image of fearless transparency contain within them the subtle desire for self-advancement.

---

[1] See Song 6:5; 7:5 for a further explanation of the Shulammite's hair and Song 4:14 (cinnamon) for more on her humility.
[2] 1 Corinthians 11:15
[3] 1 Peter 3:3-5
[4] 1 Peter 2:13-25
[5] Proverbs 30:29-31

Humility is the cornerstone of the Christian life, the single most important criteria for knowing God. If love is the goal,[1] humility is the means for achieving it. Without humility a soul cannot even begin its advance toward spiritual maturity, for God actively resists the proud, while generously extending grace upon grace to the humble.[2] The importance of humility is impossible to overstate.

Reflective

Sheep have a penchant for ruminating (bringing up and chewing again what has already been chewed slightly and swallowed). In likening the Shulammite's teeth to sheep, her beloved alludes to her capacity for the ruminations of the heart, otherwise known as meditation, that is, the rehearsing of a matter in one's mind by silent reflection or speaking aloud to oneself.

It is fitting that her reflective heart be portrayed by sheep, which are docile and peaceful, implying that the Shulammite has learned to quiet her soul before God, for probably the greatest hindrance to the soul's advancement in God are the many distractions afforded by the world. Like a blanket of wool covering the eyes of the heart, the cares of this world hinder one's ability to interact with God,[3] but the Shulammite's teeth are like *newly shorn ewes*, shorn of the burden of earthly cares and affections that rob the soul of precious moments in the Savior's presence.

In her pursuit of righteousness, the Shulammite carefully guards the thoughts that enter her mind by controlling what her eyes see and her ears hear. She works at constraining her mind to dwell upon only those things that are true, honorable, right, pure, lovely, of good repute, excellent and worthy of praise.[4]

Like *ewes which have come up from their washing*, the Shulammite's heart and mind are cleansed by the water of God's Word.[5] By meditating upon the Scriptures, one's heart, mind and body are

---

[1] 1 Timothy 1:5
[2] James 4:6; 1 Peter 5:5
[3] God prohibited the Levitical priests from wearing wool while ministering in the inner court lest they sweat in his presence (Ezekiel 44:17-18).
[4] Philippians 4:8
[5] Ephesians 5:26

brought into alignment with the Spirit of God, resulting in transformation into the very image and likeness of Christ. Thought patterns are changed, the heart is renewed, fresh vision is appropriated, hope is restored, faith is enlarged, love is imparted, discipline is inspired, peace is appropriated and joy is released. God's Word is nourishing and life-giving, indispensable to one's growth in faith.[1]

In addition, as the Shulammite reflects upon life's events and her own responses in the light of God's Word, she discovers wonderful life-changing truths about the motivations of her heart and God's wonderful love for her.

Searching for meaning in the many circumstances of life, the Shulammite even looks to creation as a source of revelation concerning the character and nature of God. His voice is heard in the thunder; lightning becomes flashes of revelation; flowers speak of his delicate and tender mercies, his beauty, his unlimited creativity and his regard for diversity. The rocks, a timeless witness to the truth, speak of his veracity, strength and steadfastness. All the heavens merely begin to tell of the glory of God.[2]

All of the ewes *bear twins*, meaning that the Shulammite's meditations are fruitful, resulting in greater revelation of the nature of God and of his Christ. Twins speak of corresponding truths. To know God fully is to know him in all his ways. His presence can be so terrible as to cause Moses to say, "I am full of fear and trembling,"[3] and yet Moses also knew him to be compassionate and gracious, slow to anger, and abounding in lovingkindness and truth.[4] He is both the Author and the Finisher of one's faith. He is a mighty Warrior,[5] and he is the Prince of Peace. He is awesome in power, yet gentle and meek. He both purifies and comforts. He wounds and he heals.[6] He is the Ancient

---

[1] Joshua 1:8; 1 Timothy 4:6; Romans 10:17
[2] Psalm 19:1
[3] Hebrews 12:21
[4] Exodus 34:6
[5] Exodus 15:3; Isaiah 42:13
[6] Job 5:18; Hosea 6:1

of Days and yet new every morning. He is the Righteous Judge of all the earth and the sacrificial Lamb slain from the foundation of the world. He is a glorious King and a suffering Servant. He is the Redeemer and Deliverer, but he also executes vengeance upon all his enemies. He is everywhere present and yet hides himself so that he must be sought out. He is the Alpha and the Omega, the Beginning and the End. He is slow to anger yet quick to forgive. There is none like him; he is unique, the only Begotten of the Father, full of grace and truth. Who can resist his loveliness? To whom can he be compared? In his temple everything cries, "Glory!"[1]

More than a source of information and insight, the Word of God is a fountainhead of divine illumination. Through protracted meditation, truths continue to unfold,[2] taking the Shulammite deeper and deeper into the never-ending expanse of the knowledge of God and of his ways. Increasing light causes her heart to burn with explosive passion,[3] oftentimes erupting in a torrent of loving praise, thanksgiving or vehement preaching.[4]

Merciful

Scarlet, the color of the Savior's blood, speaks of the mercy of God manifest in his work of redemption. For while we were sinners, enemies of God and engaged in evil deeds, Christ died for us.[5] So undeserving is the love of God! This is the essence of mercy, the withholding of punishment that is justly due. The Shulammite practices mercy, not only in her actions, but also in her thoughts toward others. Like the Savior, she is slow to anger and quick to forgive. She intentionally forgets offenses, knowing that vengeance is best left to divine Justice.

Mercy is not a lackadaisical indifference toward others' sin, but a realization that love is stronger than the law. There are times for correcting, even rebuking, but the Shulammite looks for

---

[1] Psalm 29:9
[2] Psalm 119:130
[3] Psalm 39:3; Luke 24:32
[4] Jeremiah 20:9; Acts 4:20
[5] Romans 5:6-8; Ephesians 2:1-5

opportunities to extend mercy, knowing that to the degree she is merciful in her judgments toward others, God will be merciful in his judgments toward her. Mercy triumphs over judgment. The Shulammite is generous in giving others the benefit of the doubt, believing the best about them until proven otherwise.

Scarlet *lips* signify the gracious and redemptive quality of the Shulammite's words. Her heart does not tend toward criticism, but toward the building up of others. She follows the New Testament admonition of letting no unwholesome (literally, *rotten*) word proceed from her mouth,[1] but only such a word as is good for edification according to the need of the moment, that it may give grace to those who hear.[2] She does not give in to idle gossip or the pointing of the finger, nor does she use *the truth* as a justification for slander (that is, assertions or innuendoes that may be damaging to the reputation of another). She attempts to speak only that which imparts life to the hearer, causing hearts to be moved nearer to God. In conversation involving matters of everyday life, she endeavors to speak with such grace that the hearer is nevertheless drawn to the Master, who caused his generation to wonder at the gracious words that fell from His lips.[3]

Pure of Heart

Pomegranates are packed with seeds, each covered with an extremely juicy edible flesh, deep pink in color, luscious and very sweet. When Solomon describes the sides of the Shulammite's face as *a slice of pomegranate*, he likely has in mind her oft-blushing rosy complexion.[4] Because of her habitual obedience and resulting purity of heart, the Shulammite is easily flushed by the thought of shameful activities. The prophet Jeremiah rebuked the prophets and priests of his day whose consciences, through many false dealings, had become seared[5] to the point where they no longer

---

[1] The Hebrew *midbar* is related to *dabar* (literally, *word*) and appears only this once in the Bible.
[2] Ephesians 4:29
[3] Luke 4:22
[4] 1 Samuel 16:12; 17:42
[5] 1 Timothy 4:2

blushed over sin.[1] In contrast, the Shulammite works at cultivating a sensitivity to the Holy Spirit and experiences many inner heart-blushings that others never see.

The Shulammite's *veil* represents her inaccessibility to the world, meaning that she has rejected its value system and cannot be lured by its fleshly wisdom, deceitful scheming and lustful pleasures. She has a fierce love for the truth and conducts herself in holiness and godly sincerity, not allowing her mind to be entertained by thoughts or images alien to God.

Those who have clean hands, pure hearts and have not lifted their souls to falsehood nor sworn deceitfully are promised the opportunity to ascend into the hill of the Lord and stand in his holy place.[2] This promise remains for all who love truth and maintain a blameless conscience before God and men:[3] quickly acknowledging their faults, asking forgiveness of those they have sinned against and attempting to restore any resultant damage.

Steadfast

The Shulammite's *neck* represents her will; it is strong *like the tower of David*.

When warriors go into battle, they bear their shields; when they return, they enter the tower and hang their shields on the outside. Therefore, the *shields* of a *thousand* mighty men of valor hanging on the tower wall are an indication that the Shulammite is not at war, but at peace. She has subdued the inner strivings with her flesh, having triumphed in the battle over her own will. The Shulammite is not double-minded, but steadfast, unwavering in her commitment to pursue her beloved with wholehearted abandonment.

Moments earlier, the Shulammite was awed by the fearless mighty men of the bridal company (3:7-8), but in this passage, she is assured by her beloved that the spirit of the mighty men resides

---

[1] Jeremiah 6:15; 8:12
[2] Psalm 24:3-4
[3] Acts 24:16

within her. How encouraging it is to be commended by the Lord in even the smallest of ways! In the Shulammite's mind, she does not see herself as a mighty overcomer, knowing that there are many battles yet to be won, but the Shulammite has had numerous opportunities to place her trust in God by yielding her will to him in voluntary obedience. Her resolute spirit has been strengthened by these righteous choices (represented by the *rows of many stones* that make up the tower), resulting in an elegantly peaceful and stately charm.

Tenderhearted

The Shulammite's virgin *breasts* signal her recent transition into womanhood. Like *twin fawns of a gazelle*, gentle and responsive, the Shulammite's breasts illustrate her tenderhearted and affectionate love.

Easily moved by the joys and sorrows of others, the Shulammite laughs with those who laugh and cries with those who cry. She no longer hides herself from those in pain, as she did earlier when faced with a cry for help from the daughters of Jerusalem (2:15), but her heart is becoming instinctively responsive. As a nursing mother tenderly cares for her child, the Shulammite is quick to identify with the need of others, whether it be a child or the aged, the rich or the poor, whether for consolation, encouragement, a warm embrace or a knowing smile. When needed, it is with the utmost of care that she gently corrects those in opposition that they might come to repentance and a knowledge of the truth.

Because of their tender age, *fawns* are particularly vulnerable, illustrating that the way of gentleness and kindness is the way of perpetual vulnerability. Through practiced innocence the Shulammite is learning to approach human relationships with an unguarded heart. She chooses to believe the best about others, refusing to act on judgments that may be nothing more than mere suspicions. Like the rain that falls on the just and the unjust alike, the Shulammite is kindly affectionate toward all,[1] risking the

---

[1] Matthew 5:43-48

inevitable pain of rejection and betrayal that too often accompanies human relationships.

What allows the Shulammite to be so trusting toward others? Actually, it is not people whom she trusts, but God. She is willing to distrust even her own ability to defend herself, and chooses instead to place her confidence in a loving Father who will not allow his children to be tempted or tried beyond what they are able to endure.[1]

The Shulammite's tender and affectionate heart is developed and maintained through continuous contemplation upon the love of God. She feeds upon Christ as do the *lilies*, those mature souls who have learned to abide in the peace and love of God (2:16). Her staple diet consists of daily meditations in the Scriptures, an intellectual and spiritual ballast for her soul. Romantic meditations on the nature and character of God deepen her desire, and refreshing respites in the presence of God replenish her soul with momentary excursions into his love, his peace and his joy.

---

[1] 1 Corinthians 10:13

NEW HEIGHTS

4:6 **Until the cool of the day**
When the shadows flee away,
I will go my way to the mountain of myrrh
And to the hill of frankincense.

Early in the song, the Shulammite reveled happily in her beloved's presence, though she found that presence to be fleeting (3:1). Nevertheless, she seemed content to exploit each opportunity to remain hidden away with her beloved as though the moment would last forever (2:14; 3:4).

However, upon seeing the bridal company (3:7-11), the Shulammite realizes that her earthly destiny and ultimate fulfillment lie not in being cloistered in the presence of God, but in manifesting his glorious likeness to the world. Excitedly, she embraces the vision for her own spiritual maturity.

Although inspired by the bridal procession, the Shulammite realizes she is far from ready to be received into such a glorious troop. Sensing her undisclosed disquiet, her beloved sets out to encourage the Shulammite about how far she has progressed in her spiritual development; he raves about her beauty (4:1-5). Still, the Shulammite is painfully aware of her inadequacies. She could protest the acclamations of her beloved, arguing that she is not as perfect as he seems to think, but to what end? He continues to speak only of the divine nature that has been worked in her as though he were blind to her many shortcomings.

The effect is predictable; her beloved's gushing praise inspires the Shulammite to become all that he believes her to be and more. A palpable hope surges within her breast as the Shulammite, unwilling to disappoint her beloved, determines to ascend into the high places in God— the way of obedience and unbroken communion.

Remembering the bridal company drenched in myrrh (obedience) and frankincense (prayer) (3:6), the Shulammite pledges with the utmost urgency, "*Until the cool of the day when the shadows flee away,* that is, while it is still called today, before[1] the evening breeze when the shadows melt into the darkness, *I will go my way to the mountain of myrrh and to the hill of frankincense.*"

The Hebrew root of the word *myrrh* means *bitter* and conveys the idea of the personal cost of obedience. For the Shulammite there awaits a cross, a way of affliction that will help remove all that hinders singlehearted devotion and prepare her soul for the union with her beloved she so desperately desires. At this point, somewhat naive to the ultimate ramifications of her consecration, the Shulammite agrees to lay her will upon the altar of sacrifice. With joyful abandonment she gives herself in wholehearted obedience to her beloved, whatever the cost. All she knows and cares is that he loves her, he desires her, and he will be with her.

Jesus was tested while he was on the earth and was found to be obedient through the things he suffered, even unto death.[2] For this obedience he receives all praise, blessing, glory, honor, riches, wisdom, power, dominion and might both now and forever. He has become more than an example, but also an indwelling strength sustaining all who would aspire to walk in total obedience to the Father even as he did.[3]

A *mountain* of myrrh might seem a great challenge, but the Shulammite does not say that she will *climb* this mountain, as though to imply some outstanding achievement on her part. She says merely that she will go her *way* toward the mountain. Jesus is the way. To be yoked together with Christ in the way of obedience is to enter into God's grace. The *mountain* of myrrh is not to suggest its difficulty, but rather the abundant supply of myrrh (obedience) that is available in the grace of God. The Shulammite is

---

[1] See note at Song 2:17.
[2] Hebrews 5:8
[3] Philippians 4:13

confident that through humble obedience, an expression of human weakness, Christ's strength will be perfected in her.[1]

Frankincense, meaning *white* or *pure*, is a white or clear tree resin[2] that was burned as incense before the Lord; it speaks of prayer[3] rising from a pure heart.

The Shulammite's vision of the bridal company (3:6-11) and the effusive praises from her beloved (4:1-5) have served to strengthen her resolve to devote quantities of time to prayer. In order for her time to be qualitative, she will learn to experience many different activities in prayer: jubilant praise and thanksgiving, heartfelt contrition, intercessory petition, reflective meditation, trusted dialogue, reverential worship and simple waiting in quiet before God. She is committed to the process of change, hoping to be transformed into the very image of Christ and joined to him in intimate fellowship to the maximum degree possible in this life.

Ascending the mountain of myrrh and the hill of frankincense, the Shulammite may have had opportunity to reflect upon Abraham ascending Mount Moriah to sacrifice his son Isaac as commanded by the Lord. Abraham said to the young men who were with him, "I and the lad will go yonder; and we will worship and return to you."[4] Abraham was willing to sacrifice that which was most precious to him, his only son, in whom were all the promises that God had made to him. Isaac represented Abraham's dreams, ambitions, desires, affections, everything that he might have loved in this life. By giving Isaac back to God, Abraham was demonstrating that his entire life, all that was dear to him, belonged to God.

True worship is a humble acknowledgment of God's right to supremacy and, as a corollary, the sincere acknowledgment of man's dependency upon God. Therefore, the intensity of one's worship will be directly proportionate to the degree to which he

---

[1] 2 Corinthians 12:9
[2] Frankincense is obtained from trees of the balsam family that grow on both sides of the Red Sea.
[3] Psalm 141:2; Revelation 5:8
[4] Genesis 22:2-5

recognizes that dependency in his life. Abraham stretches out his faith in radical obedience, reaching for the very pinnacle of worship: the acknowledgment that God is the sum total of all things considered. To have him is to have everything, and to have anything without him is to have nothing at all.

As the Shulammite ascends the mountain of myrrh and the hill of frankincense, she embraces a life of worship, a life in which she daily presents her body as a living sacrifice to God in order that God might be all and in all.[1]

Myrrh is a mountain and frankincense a hill. A mountain is greater than a hill just as obedience is greater than prayer. For what good is it to spend hours in prayer but never obey the word of the Lord? Jesus said: "Not everyone who says to Me, 'Lord, Lord,' will enter the kingdom of heaven, but he who does the will of My Father who is in heaven."[2] However, neither does one have the strength to fully obey the Lord unless he is filled with a passionate love for him, a love cultivated through prayer. The Christian life is not meant to be a constant struggle of obedience, but a continual pursuit of knowing God. Although this pursuit necessitates obedience, it is not a struggle, but a joy, to obey the object of one's affections.

Having been assured of his love, the Shulammite is spurred on to pursue with total abandonment a life of continual fellowship with her beloved, her God and king, her lover and her friend. His words of love have set her free from every fear, every doubt and every worry. He is powerful and he loves her. His effusive praises have convinced the Shulammite that he eagerly anticipates sharing a common life, longing to be intimately joined with her forever.

---

[1] Romans 12:1
[2] Matthew 7:21

4:7 **You are altogether beautiful, my darling,**
And there is no blemish in you.

4:8 **Come with me from Lebanon, my bride,**
May you come with me from Lebanon.
Journey down from the summit of Amana,
From the summit of Senir and Hermon,
From the dens of lions,
From the mountains of leopards.

4:9 **You have made my heart beat faster, my sister,**
my bride;
You have made my heart beat faster with a
single glance of your eyes,
With a single strand of your necklace.

4:10 **How beautiful is your love, my sister, my**
bride!
How much better is your love than wine,
And the fragrance of your oils
Than all kinds of spices!

4:11 **Your lips, my bride, drip honey;**
Honey and milk are under your tongue,
And the fragrance of your garments is like the
fragrance of Lebanon.

Purity

Never before has her beloved's praise risen to such heights as here, where he declares the Shulammite *altogether beautiful*! Like Enoch, who walked with God and was taken up because he was found pleasing to God,[1] like Noah, a righteous and blameless man who walked with God,[2] and like Job, a blameless and upright man,[3] there is *no blemish* in her. The Shulammite's surrender to a life of obedience and prayer (4:6) has worked in her a remarkable degree of purity.

Her beloved invites the Shulammite to come down from the mountains of *Lebanon*, meaning in Hebrew *white*[4] and signifying

---

[1] Genesis 5:22, 24; Hebrews 11:5
[2] Genesis 6:9
[3] Job 1:1, 8; 2:3
[4] There is an interesting play on words: the Shulammite had determined to go to the hill of *frankincense* (Hebrew: *lebonah*) (4:6), and now her beloved invites her to come down with him from *Lebanon*. *Frankincense* and *Lebanon* come from the same

her separation from the world (a system of thought and action antithetical to the kingdom of God). All that empowers the world system— greed, sensuality and pride— are not from the Father. Those who love the world do not have a true love for God and come under the control of the evil one.[1] The Shulammite's life of loving obedience has worked to replicate the righteousness of the Son of God in her, evidenced by his presence with her in Lebanon. Proof of their communion is found in his invitation, "Come *with* me," revealing that they journey from Lebanon together.

Achievements

Journey down from the summit of Amana, from the summit of Senir and Hermon, from the dens of lions, from the mountains of leopards.

In the Bible, mountains often represent governments, meaning that the Shulammite's attainment to the summits of Amana, Senir and Hermon speak of her preparedness to assume leadership responsibilities.

Lions, a universal symbol of authority, are fearless warriors, attacking animals several times their weight and willfully putting their lives at risk to save a cub or sibling. They are family and community minded, loyal, capable, quick, powerful and resourceful. The Shulammite's time in the dens of lions signifies time spent fellowshipping with skilled and experienced leaders. As a result, she gains a fresh appreciation for church body life and humbly embraces values and skills necessary for effective leadership, such as faith, wisdom, team spirit, self-discipline, graciousness and personal sacrifice.

Leopards typify power and skill; they are swift, cunning, ruthless and dangerous. They hunt alone, not in packs, and return to kill their cubs. Significantly, the Shulammite spent time in the dens of lions, but merely traversed the mountains in which the leopards dwelled. Leopards represent the demonic forces the Shulammite has had to learn to deal with at the higher levels of spiritual

---

root word meaning *white*. The name of the mountain range of Lebanon is probably derived from snowcapped Mount Hermon.
[1] 1 John 2:15-16; 5:19

responsibility. Presumably, she has learned valuable lessons through her own personal experience in overcoming the evil one.[1]

Amana means *integrity, truth,* or *trusted* and describes the quality most valued in a leader. Powerful people will be feared, even honored, but they will not be loved if they are not trusted. People will not maintain their allegiance to someone who does not keep his word or is otherwise duplicitous. What seem to be minor or inconsequential infractions from the leader's perspective— tardiness, exaggeration, the failure to fulfill small favors as promised— can bring severe and lasting repercussions from those looking for someone worthy of their trust.

The Shulammite is willing to commit herself wholeheartedly to her beloved's loving leadership because he has proven himself worthy of trust. His love demands that he always act consistent with the truth and that his word, therefore, never be broken. Out of her commitment of obedience to him, the Shulammite is supremely committed to exemplifying the same kind of integrity in her own life.

Senir is the Amorite name for Mount Hermon and means *breastplate.* The Shulammite's obedience from a pure heart provides her with a breastplate of righteousness, faith and love that protects her from the fiery darts of the enemy.[2] As Moses and countless others have discovered, it takes great love, patience and wisdom to lead a group of people who can at times become complaining, independent and accusatory. Leaders are favorite targets of Satan, who knows that if he strikes the shepherd, the sheep can be scattered.[3] Because the failure of a leader can have far reaching ramifications, leaders must be particularly adept at guarding their hearts from every kind of spiritual attack.

Hermon means *sacred* or *devoted* and represents the degree of dedication required of every leader, especially a spiritual leader. Because of her devotion to the king, the Shulammite's life is

---

[1] 1 John 2:13-14
[2] Isaiah 59:17; Ephesians 6:14; 1 Thessalonians 5:8
[3] Zechariah 13:7

dedicated to advancing the kingdom of God upon the earth. Her life is no longer her own but has been completely set apart unto God. Due to her constant communion with the Lord, she does not view some activities as being secular and some as sacred, for even everyday affairs are lived in union with Christ and are therefore holy unto God.

Invitation

For the first time, Solomon calls the Shulammite his *bride* (using the term four times in this discourse alone). Even after revealing himself as the bridegroom-warrior-king (3:11), he did not use the bridal term of endearment. It is only now, after the Shulammite has gone to the mountain of myrrh and to the hill of frankincense (4:6) that she is called his bride. Her practice of obedient devotion provokes an implied promise from her beloved that she is a chosen one and there is nothing to hinder her from experiencing the spiritual union she so earnestly desires.

The Shulammite's unreserved devotion also prompts a second entreaty from her beloved (4:8). His first invitation found the Shulammite resting and waiting, for he beckoned her to arise and come with him into the fruitful fields of service in his vineyard (2:10-14), but now that she has gone to the mountain of myrrh and attained to the high places of leadership, he asks her to lay aside her accomplishments in order to come down to the garden of intimacy (4:12). He is not necessarily asking her to give up her responsibilities, but to count them as insignificant in her pursuit of a greater knowledge of Christ.[1]

How easy it is for God's servant to feel that he is pleasing to God because he has attained a certain level of ministry responsibility. The Shulammite must consider her achievements as worthless for establishing her personal identity or any feeling of importance or success; to enjoy greater intimacy, she must be willing to lay them all down in her heart and mind if not in actual practice.

---

[1] Philippians 3:8

Ravished Heart

The Shulammite fascinates her beloved; she makes his *heart beat faster with a single glance* of her *eyes*. Her slightest attention toward the Lord stirs him with unfathomable desire in the core of his being. The point is made even more poignantly by the alternate translation: *you have ravished my heart*,[1] implying the Shulammite's capacity to seize control and forcibly carry away the emotions of her beloved. Solomon repeats the statement for emphasis, as though acknowledging that it is too unbelievable that Christ should not remain the master over his own emotions. Finding himself in such a precariously vulnerable position, the Shulammite's beloved admits that the object loved has gained the power to plunder and devastate the heart of its lover. Amazingly, this is a peril Christ longs to endure.

It is intriguing to think that God created humans with emotional capacities modeled after his own, for he created man in his own image and likeness. The difference is that God, who is perfect love, has the capacity to deeply feel the pains and the ecstasies of what humans experience as mere fleeting sentiments. Knowing the extent to which one's slightest affections enthrall the heart of God is meant to inspire an even greater passion in one's pursuit of him.

Even a strand of the Shulammite's necklace, that is, a single act of obedience (1:10), regardless of how seemingly mundane to the believer, sets off an impassioned response in the heart of God. Having volunteered to adorn her neck with beads of silver (1:10-11), the shepherds seem to have done their job well; their timely assistance is a reminder that the Lord is faithful to supply whatever help is necessary to the process of beautifying his bride.

Desirability

How much better is her *love than wine*! For the first time, Solomon comments on the Shulammite's love.[2] He does not merely

---

[1] This is the translation found in the *King James Version*, the *New King James Version* and the *New International Version*.

[2] He repeats the Shulammite's words from 1:2.

encourage her with words that speak prophetically of what she is becoming. No, she truly loves her beloved, and he finds her love intoxicating, a welcome and soothing relief from the weariness he endures at the hands of an ungrateful and rebellious generation. It is a refined and costly love, a love that has not yet been fully tested in the fires of adversity, but is honest and heartfelt nevertheless; it is a love that flows freely to her beloved.

The fragrance of her oils is better *than all kinds of spices*! Oils, like those that exude from within her skin, represent the qualities that have been worked into the nature of the Shulammite. She has allowed her life to become intertwined with that of her beloved so that she now emits the fragrance of the very nature of Christ.[1]

Like the Savior, from whose lips pour forth gracious words,[2] the Shulammite's lips *drip honey*. There is no trace of flippancy toward the things of God,[3] no self-pity, no self-righteous diatribes and no self-exalting narratives. Her words are sweet, life-giving[4] and, like honey, brighten the eyes of the weary.[5]

Under the *tongue,* that is, in the private thoughts and meditations[6] of the Shulammite, are *honey and milk,* a phrase symbolizing the fertility and abundance of the promised land of Canaan. These meditations of love provide a seemingly endless supply of spiritual refreshment for the Shulammite and for all those who hear the gracious words that flow from her lips. Regardless of the topic of conversation, it seems always to be about love, for this is the lens through which the Shulammite views all of life— so transforming have her meditations become!

The fragrance of her garments is like the fragrance of Lebanon. The Shulammite's garments represent her acts of goodness.[7] They produce a fragrance like the balsamic aroma of Lebanon,

---

[1] 2 Corinthians 2:14
[2] Luke 4:22
[3] 1 Peter 4:11
[4] Proverbs 16:24
[5] 1 Samuel 14:27. Brightening the eyes also typifies wisdom and understanding.
[6] Psalm 10:7
[7] Philippians 4:18; Revelation 19:7-8

suggesting the fragrant cedars that represent power, wealth, strength, dignity and beauty. By implication, all these qualities are attributed to the Shulammite, making her a worthy companion for a king.

Sister

Solomon refers to the Shulammite as his *sister*, a term of endearment expressing his fondness for the woman who seems to have always been known by him, suggesting a transparency reminiscent of what Adam and Eve enjoyed in the garden of Eden.[1] The sister paradigm emphasizes Christ's identification with humans and his longing for bridal partnership. The eternal Son of God, infinite in beauty, power, wisdom and knowledge, voluntarily laid aside the wealth and privilege of Godhead, becoming a man in order that he might shed his blood in a substitutionary death, thereby enabling humans to become born again by the Spirit into the family of God,[2] coheirs together with Christ of his eternal throne. He became one of us in order that we might become one with him. Words fail.

---

[1] Genesis 2:23-25
[2] Matthew 12:49-50; Hebrews 2:11-14

THE KING'S GARDEN

Beloved: | 4:12 **A garden locked is my sister, *my* bride,**
A rock garden locked, a spring sealed up.

Having extended the invitation (4:8), her beloved now anticipates a time of intimate fellowship with the Shulammite. He revels in her chastity, her consecration to him, knowing that there are no other lovers by which he will be compared, no competitors for her passions and affections. The *garden* of her heart, the place where she shares intimate fellowship with her beloved, is *locked* and guarded, reserved solely for him.[1] Exclusiveness serves only to heighten the pleasure of their fellowship since the Shulammite's senses are not unduly stimulated by the competing sensations of the world.

The Shulammite is responsible for planting and cultivating her garden so that it provides the most enjoyable experience for her beloved. The central feature of her garden is a life-giving *spring*, representing her spirit. When a person joins himself to the Lord, he becomes one spirit with him so that the life of God flows from within the inner man. Jesus, speaking of the Holy Spirit, told his disciples that out of their innermost beings would flow rivers of living water. The Shulammite seals up this inner life spring, meaning that she keeps it from being contaminated[2] by fleshly indulgences such as anger, self-will, gossip, deceitfulness, sexual fantasies, comparisons to others, unforgiveness, greed and things like these.

Additionally, the locked garden illustrates the Shulammite's care in protecting her secret thoughts from being dispersed abroad. Secrets create a deeper sense of intimacy in a relationship. By guarding the revelations, graces and concerns meant to be kept

---

[1] Proverbs 5:15-19
[2] Numbers 19:15; Ephesians 4:30

between the Shulammite and her beloved, the Shulammite demonstrates her increasing dependency upon him alone. She is content to know that she is understood and appreciated by him and does not look for affirmation from others for her sense of well-being.

Beloved to Shulammite:

4:13 **Your shoots are an orchard of pomegranates**
With choice fruits, henna with nard plants,
4:14 **Nard and saffron, calamus and cinnamon,**
With all the trees of frankincense,
Myrrh and aloes, along with all the finest spices.
4:15 *You are* **a garden spring,**
A well of fresh water,
And streams *flowing* **from Lebanon.**

Orchard of Pomegranates

Whether by inspiration, intercession or helps, the Shulammite is a life-giver, carrying an indomitable love for the body of Christ within her heart. The church, the recipient of her labors of love, is represented here by *an orchard of pomegranates*,[1] a metaphor describing both the scope and the fruitfulness of the Shulammite's ministry. Her heart is a very large garden indeed to accommodate an entire orchard. Like Jesus, who gave his life to redeem the church from among the souls of men, the Shulammite has been willing to invest herself in those whom he loves. How could she do

---

[1] A pomegranate is a fruit composed of many juice-filled seeds. At risk of pressing the metaphor too far, each seed represents a human life. The seed's kernel represents one's physical body. (Jesus likened his own body to a kernel of wheat that must die and be planted in the ground in order to bring forth fruit, many sons and daughters to God (John 12:24)). The seed is surrounded by a transparent sack filled with sweet liquid graduating in color from clear to deep pink, representing one's spirit and soul that pervades the body. (After Jesus died on the cross and his pericardium lanced, blood and water flowed out, illustrating that Jesus had poured out his life (his spirit and soul) for the redemption of mankind.) The seeds are naturally formed together in groups (representing church congregations) separated by a pithy membrane. These natural groupings are bound together as a unified whole by a tough, red outer skin, representing all the church in a given city. (The city-church is the primary identity of churches named in the New Testament.) An entire pomegranate tree, sharing a common soil and root system, represents the church in a given nation. The orchard represents the total body of Christ upon the earth.

otherwise? For the church is the very body of Christ, and his spirit dwells within her. This explains why, when Paul the apostle was persecuting the church, Jesus, appearing to him, said, "Saul, Saul, why are you persecuting me?"[1] In Jesus' mind, the members of his body, the church, are his very own flesh, and whatever is done to them, whether good or bad, is done directly to him.[2] Therefore, the greater the Shulammite's love for her beloved, the greater will be her love for his people, the church.

Together with the pomegranate trees grow various *choice fruits* and spices, representing the many other qualities that have been developed in the life of the Shulammite. Every believer cultivates a unique mixture of fruits and spices depending on the manner in which he responds to the revelation of Jesus given him in the grace of God. In cultivating the garden of his heart, the believer becomes a fragrant aroma of Christ[3] and a source of delight to the Father, who intensely enjoys the manifestation of his Son in the lives of his children.

Henna

Earlier, the Shulammite likened her beloved to a cluster of henna blossoms (1:14), thereby highlighting his willingness to lovingly forgive, for the Hebrew word for henna is also translated *atonement, redeem* or *forgive*. Jesus, after having been falsely accused and unjustly crucified, was heard to say, "Father, forgive them; for they do not know what they are doing."[4] He now celebrates that this very same virtue of forgiveness has been worked into the heart of the Shulammite.

One day Jesus was dining at the home of a Pharisee when an uninvited prostitute entered with an alabaster vial of costly perfume. Weeping, she began to wet Jesus' feet with her tears; she kept wiping them with the hair of her head, and kissing his feet and anointing them with the perfume. Jesus took the opportunity

---

[1] Acts 9:4-5
[2] Matthew 25:40-45
[3] 2 Corinthians 2:14-15
[4] Luke 23:34

to teach that one's willingness to forgive others corresponds to his understanding of God's forgiveness toward him: " . . . her sins, which are many, have been forgiven, for she loved much; but he who is forgiven little, loves little."[1] This is not to imply that one must have committed terrible crimes in order to be able to forgive much. It means that one must recognize the serious depth of depravity within his own heart that caused him to sin against an all-benevolent and loving God. The greater one's appreciation of the severity of his sin and guilt, the greater is his appreciation of God's forgiving grace. As long as one attempts to minimize his guilt by comparing or shifting blame on others, his appreciation of God's grace is minimal.

Because the Shulammite has learned to accept the full responsibility for her sins, she rejoices greatly in the gift of God's forgiveness toward her. She is now also able to graciously forgive those who have rejected, misunderstood, abused and otherwise wounded her. Consequently, she exudes a fragrant aroma for her beloved's enjoyment in the garden of her heart.

Nard

When the king was portrayed sitting at his banqueting table (1:12), the Shulammite's immaturity at the time prevented her from partaking of its exquisite bounty. Nevertheless, her *nard* perfume, symbolizing her impassioned praise, adoration and longing for love, gave forth its spicy-sweet woody fragrance in the king's presence. It was the only fragrance emitted from the Shulammite's heart before she went to the mountain of myrrh (obedience) and the hill of frankincense (prayer). Now the nard is merely one of many fragrances in which her beloved is able to take delight.

Significantly, what was heretofore an imported perfume is now a plant rooted in the garden of the Shulammite's heart. Praise, adoration, and ineffable longing has become a permanent and sustained quality in the life of the Shulammite.

---

[1] Luke 7:47

Saffron

Saffron, the aromatic stigma of the crocus,[1] is used for coloring and flavoring foods. It is also used as perfume when mixed with oil, giving a sweet, spicy, floral scent. Taking four-thousand three hundred flowers to make an ounce of saffron, it is the world's most expensive spice, an apt illustration of *faith*, of which the apostle Peter says is more precious than gold (suggestive of the orange-yellow color of saffron).[2]

The Bible says that without faith it is impossible to please God, for he who comes to God must believe that he is and that he is a rewarder of those who seek him.[3] Faith is basic to a relationship with God and essential to accomplishing anything with God. Followers of Jesus are called *believers*. There is nothing more essential and more valuable to a relationship with God than faith.

Faith is an anchor for the soul and is necessarily based upon God's Word. Simply believing something to be true, does not imply the presence of faith as defined by the Bible. If one's confidence is based upon a concept, idea or philosophy not found in God's Word, one cannot be said to have faith. It is possible for someone to be firmly convinced in his own mind that what he believes is true, and yet be deceived with regard to what is actually true. The Shulammite's perception of her beloved is not based upon sentimental wistful longings, but is firmly rooted in what God says about himself in his Word, the Bible.

Calamus

Calamus means reed (or sweet cane) and was used for making perfume. The root word also means to *acquire* or *possess* and appears in one of God's names: God Most High, *Possessor* of Heaven and Earth. This is the name by which Abraham blessed God after returning from defeating Chedorlaomer and the kings allied with him. Abraham refused to receive any reward from the

---

[1] The crocus has funnel-shaped, purplish flowers and belongs to the iris family.
[2] 1 Peter 1:7
[3] Hebrews 11:6

king of Sodom lest he later say, "I have made Abram rich." Declaring that God is the one who owns all of heaven and earth, Abraham expressed his confidence in God's ability to prosper him. The implication is that God has the ability to control or govern that which he possesses.

As applied to the Shulammite then, calamus refers to her alacrity in governing that which she possesses. A person cannot govern anything if he cannot first govern himself. The apostle Paul admonishes every believer to possess his own vessel in sanctification and honor, not in lustful passion like those who do not know God.[1] Comparing himself to an athlete, Paul cites his own life as an example of one who restrains the natural appetites of his physical body for spiritual purposes.[2]

A calamus reed is straight and upright, a model of self-discipline and self-control.[3] No one ever accomplished anything great without discipline. The Shulammite has set her sights high— union with deity. She is counting on God's grace to do what she cannot, for mere human effort provides insufficient strength or ability for her desire for union to be fulfilled. Nevertheless, her willingness to pay the price of personal sacrifice and self-denial in cultivating the garden of her heart is a necessary prerequisite and a wonderfully sweet smelling savor to her beloved.

Cinnamon

Cinnamon is commonly sold as quills, strips of inner bark rolled one in another. Interestingly, it is harvested by splitting young cinnamon shoots with a knife and peeling away the bark, mimicking the process of cutting away the foreskin in circumcision.

Four thousand years ago, God established circumcision as a sign of the covenant he made with Abraham and his descendants. Because it was a covenant initiated by a sovereign and imposed upon his

---

1   1 Thessalonians 4:3-5
2   1 Corinthians 9:25-27
3   Acts 24:25; Galatians 5:23; 2 Peter 1:6

subjects, the terms were both disproportionate and nonnegotiable.[1] Abraham and his descendants stood to be greatly blessed, but at the same time, they were required to honor and obey the absolute authority of the Sovereign in all things. Consequently, submitting to circumcision under the Abrahamic covenant required the humbling of oneself, not only before men, but ultimately, before God.[2]

Circumcision became an external sign of an internal singularity of devotion to God and came to represent the idea of acceptability to God.[3] In the Bible the term *circumcision of the heart* implies a total consecration or devotion to God. When Israel acted unfaithfully toward the covenant, their hearts were said to be uncircumcised and in need of humbling.[4]

Ears are said to be uncircumcised when they are closed, unable to hear so as to respond to truth.[5] However, the Shulammite is eager to listen, possessing a blind affinity for truth, particularly truth concerning herself. She is not strongly opinionated, but instead, seeking to know more than to be known and to understand more than to be understood, her humble heart yields readily to reason.[6]

It has been said that humility is not a virtue, but *the* virtue, for it is foundational to all other graces one might receive.[7] It is *the* core requirement necessary for gaining access to the true knowledge of God. The value God places upon humility is appropriately typified by cinnamon; highly prized for its delightfully fragrant aroma and its warm pungent taste, cinnamon has been regarded in ancient times as a gift fit for monarchs.

---

[1] This is similar to a suzerainty covenant, common during feudal times, in which an overlord guaranteed the safety of his serfs, while all the land, crops and even the serfs themselves, remained the property of their overlord.

[2] See more on humility in the explanation of the Shulammite's hair (4:1; 6:5; 7:5).

[3] Isaiah 52:1

[4] Leviticus 26:41

[5] Jeremiah 6:10; Acts 7:51

[6] James 3:17

[7] James 4:6; 1 Peter 5:5

Frankincense

Frankincense, meaning *white* or *pure,* was one of the essential ingredients in the incense God prescribed for Israel to burn before him. When placed upon the fire, the incense produced a fragrant aroma, symbolizing the prayers of the saints. Frankincense speaks of the purity of devotion which springs from the heart of one who is wholly the Lord's.

Jesus said that the pure in heart are blessed for they shall see God.[1] This is the desire burning in the heart of the Shulammite: that she might see and know her beloved more perfectly. Her desire will be satisfied because she has fulfilled the condition of purity of heart. There are no disqualifying issues in her life. She is convinced that only her beloved holds the key to fulfilling the longing in her heart for love.

Myrrh

Myrrh is an aromatic reddish-colored resin that is released by piercing the bark of the myrrh tree; it signifies the suffering Jesus experienced and the flow of blood that was released when his body was nailed to the cross. It has already been noted (3:6; 4:6) that myrrh, meaning *bitter,* conveys the personal cost of obedience,[2] but the word also means *strong,* indicating that it is through the bitter circumstances of life that one is made strong.

The Shulammite has learned to persevere through difficult trials. She is learning to live by the life of Another, as did the apostle Paul who said, "We are afflicted in every way, but not crushed; perplexed, but not despairing; persecuted, but not forsaken; struck down, but not destroyed; always carrying about in the body the dying of Jesus, that the life of Jesus also may be manifested in our body. For we who live are constantly being delivered over to death for Jesus' sake, that the life of Jesus also may be manifested in our mortal flesh. So death works in us, but life in you."[3]

---

[1] Matthew 5:8
[2] Hebrews 5:8
[3] 2 Corinthians 4:7-12

Aloes

Aloes refers to the aromatic resin of the eaglewood tree[1] used to perfume garments,[2] beds and closets. In Hebrew, the word literally means *tents* and conveys the idea of dwelling or abiding, illustrating the Shulammite's desire to make her heart the habitation of God, a place where the Holy Spirit does not simply visit like a wayfarer at an inn, but where he feels welcome to take up permanent residence.[3] The Shulammite is relentless in her pursuit of uninterrupted intimacy with her beloved.

A harlot perfumes her bed with aloes[4] and broaches all barriers of modesty and decorum in an attempt to simulate authentic intimacy for the naive. Because she offers no commitment to love, the most the harlot can offer is a passionate moment of corporeal closeness. Feigning genuine admiration, she leaves her lover's heart empty and unsatisfied, having given nothing to sustain the life and longing of his soul.

The human heart was created with a desire to know and to be known, to love and to be loved, and to coexist in intimate union with another. Realistically, all human relationships fall vastly short of the ideal and are at best a whisper of the ultimate experience— intimacy with God. There is no love so secure, so rewarding, so warm, so tender and so thrilling as the love of God revealed in the person of Jesus. Outside of Christ, there is a continual, never to be satisfied, longing to be known and loved.

Some might protest that continual intimacy with God is unrealistic in this life, but Jesus clearly envisioned the eventuality. He promised his disciples that if they abide in him, they would experience such favor with God that they could ask for whatever they wish, and it would be done for them![5] The Shulammite has made great advancements in her ability to maintain an intimate

---

[1] The eaglewood tree was found in eastern India.
[2] Psalm 45:8
[3] John 1:32
[4] Proverbs 7:17
[5] John 15:7

walk with God since she committed herself to a life of total obedience and unceasing prayer.

Fresh Water

The Shulammite is *a garden spring,*[1] *a well of fresh*[2] *water.* No longer languishing like a thirsty soul in a desert place, she is full of the life of God. Like pure sparkling *streams* tumbling from the snow-covered peaks of Lebanon, the Shulammite has been abundantly supplied[3] with all the graces necessary for producing a luscious garden, replete with many choice fruits and exotic spices. She is full of the Holy Spirit, regularly experiencing his love, joy, peace, faith, hope, power, boldness and many other evidences of his presence.[4]

Her beloved looks expectantly at being refreshed in the Shulammite's exotic garden. It is staggering to think that a mere human can invigorate the heart of God, but her beloved finds gladness in the Shulammite's joyful obedience and heartfelt worship, solace in her entreaties of mercy,[5] and endless pleasure in the many fragrances emanating from the garden of her heart.

Shulammite: | 4:16 **Awake, O north *wind,***
And come, *wind* of the south;
Make my garden breathe out *fragrance,*
Let its spices be wafted abroad.
May my beloved come into his garden
And eat its choice fruits!

Biblically, the north is often the place from which judgment or opposition comes; therefore, the *north wind* speaks of the cold winds[6] of adversity. From the *south* comes another type of *wind* equally hostile— the siroccos, blasts of hot parched air often

---

[1] *A garden spring* is literally a *fountain of gardens* (plural), and is translated so in the New King James Version, overstating the garden metaphor to imply the lush bounty of her supply.
[2] The word translated *fresh* literally means *living.*
[3] Isaiah 41:17; 44:3; 58:11; Joel 3:18
[4] John 4:14; 7:38
[5] Ezekiel 22:30; James 2:13
[6] Job 37:9

accompanied by choking clouds of dust.[1] Although the garden of the Shulammite's heart contains many delightful fruits and fragrant spices, their aromas remain, to a great extent, locked within. With the blowing of adverse winds, the aromatic spices are stirred, causing the Shulammite's garden to exhale scents that were previously hidden and unknown.

The choice fruits and *spices* represent the various graces of the Holy Spirit that have been fashioned in the Shulammite. The release of their aromas signifies the manifestation of the Spirit's presence that can be revealed only through adversity. For example, one might be a person of great faith, but it is only when that faith is challenged that its true character becomes evident. One might be naturally kind, but it is in loving one's enemies that the true quality of the love becomes apparent. One might be typically joyful, but it is in the midst of tragically grievous circumstances that the true nature of the joy is made manifest. One might seem to be patient and peaceful, but it is when burdens become excessively stressful that the real source of one's peace becomes evident.

Normally, one would not invite adversity, but the Shulammite is so overwhelmed by the delight her beloved has expressed in her that she recklessly calls upon the winds to stir up the fragrant aromas. She hopes of making her garden even more alluring to her beloved, for adversity not only manifests the true condition of the soul, but also serves to instruct and refine it, producing an even more excellent garden.

Using another metaphor, Amos prophesied: "Moab has been at ease since his youth; he has also been undisturbed on his lees,[2] neither has he been emptied from vessel to vessel, nor has he gone into exile. Therefore, he retains his flavor, and his aroma has not changed."[3] Wine is typically poured from vessel to vessel to aid the fermentation process by oxygenating the wine and filtering out distasteful dregs. The Moabites were like wine that had not been

---

[1] Tenney, *The Zondervan Pictorial Encyclopedia of the Bible, Volume Four* (Grand Rapids, MI: Zondervan, 1980) 576-577. See also Luke 12:55.
[2] *Lees* are dregs of wine that settle during fermentation.
[3] Jeremiah 48:11

poured from vessel to vessel, meaning that, because they had not known adversity, they had become complacent; they needed to be stirred in order for their flavor to be enhanced.

The Shulammite awakens the winds, hoping to attract her beloved, not primarily for the pleasure she will receive, but in hopes of enhancing the pleasure he will receive. Consequently, after calling upon the winds, she no longer refers to *her* garden but invites her beloved to *come into his garden* and *eat its choice fruits*. The Shulammite has totally yielded her mind, will and emotions to her beloved, realizing that she exists for his pleasure;[1] he does not exist for hers.

It seems that the Shulammite understands (if not fully, she is soon to discover) that union requires participation with her beloved, not only in blissful times of prayer, but in the full range of divine experiences. The Shulammite joyfully embraces the afflictions that accompany righteousness, and in this she agrees with the apostle Paul when he longed pensively, " . . . that I may know Him, and the power of His resurrection and the fellowship of His sufferings."[2]

The Shulammite is asking for a baptism of fire. It will come, but not before this Act closes with an intimate encounter with her beloved.

---

[1] The word translated *garden,* a metaphor for the soul or inner life, literally means *enclosure.* Although the Shulammite's garden is maintained strictly for the enjoyment of her beloved, in having the fragrance wafted abroad, she undoubtedly realizes that others will also be made aware of the presence of Christ in her life. For some, it will provide encouragement and inspiration, giving them reason to hope; for others, it will remind them of their own condemnation. This is what the apostle Paul had in mind when he said that God "manifests through us the sweet aroma of the knowledge of him [Christ] in every place. For we are a fragrance of Christ to God among those who are being saved and among those who are perishing; to the one an aroma from death to death, to the other an aroma from life to life" (2 Corinthians 2:14-16).

[2] Philippians 3:10-11

Beloved to Shulammite:	5:1 **I have come into my garden, my sister, *my* bride;**
	I have gathered my myrrh along with my balsam.
	I have eaten my honeycomb and my honey;
	I have drunk my wine and my milk.

Having graphically illustrated the beauty and desirability of the Shulammite (4:1-15), her beloved now moves decisively to satisfy his ravenous longing for intimacy. The Shulammite has matured significantly, and her garden provides him with a uniquely gratifying experience.

Eight times[1] in this passage the Shulammite's beloved uses the possessive *my*, establishing his claim to her garden and all it contains, reveling in the fact that her heart is completely his. All her affections, all her experiences and all her understanding are assimilated by him in intimate union. He accepts the Shulammite's judgment and declaration that her spiritual development has not been for herself, nor for ministry, but for him.

Gathering the *myrrh, along with* all the other spices,[2] the Shulammite's beloved savors the various graces that have been worked into the life of the Shulammite by the Holy Spirit. *Myrrh,* representing the fragrant aroma of persevering obedience,[3] is particularly celebrated as a source of special delight. The Shulammite would have made no progress at all if it had not been for her willingness to embrace the cross of Christ, taking up her own cross and following him in total obedience.

Eating *the honeycomb and* the *honey*, Solomon is strengthened and his eyes are brightened,[4] indulging himself in the pleasure of assimilating the wisdom and understanding the Shulammite has gained through her many life experiences and meditations of love. She has advanced well beyond the naiveté of her youth and provides her beloved with a depth and quality of fellowship he finds only in mature saints.

---

[1] The *my* preceding *bride* does not actually appear in the original.

[2] *Balsam* can also be translated *spices*.

[3] Song 3:6; 4:6; 4:14; 5:5

[4] 1 Samuel 14:27

Milk represents the childlike innocence that has been restored to the Shulammite through her obedience and constant meditations. The milk that her beloved once found to be under her tongue (4:11), now flows freely. He drinks of this spiritual abundance from one whose words are filled with life, life that overflows from a heart totally absorbed with him.

Wine is for celebration and speaks of the intoxicating joy that Christ experiences in his communion with one in whom the divine nature is formed.

CLOSING

Solomon, the | 5:1b **Eat, friends;**
poet-author: | **Drink and imbibe deeply, O lovers.**

An Undisclosed Author

Three times the poet-author clearly indicates the end of a major segment of the song with nearly identical closings (2:7; 3:5; 8:4). However, here appears a major transition, but the writer does not present the usual closing. Instead, he interjects a statement made by an unidentified speaker. The uniqueness of this closing is for emphasis.

"Eat, friends! Drink and imbibe deeply, O lovers!" To whom shall these words be credited? They cannot be ascribed to either the Shulammite or her beloved, for they themselves are the lovers here addressed. The daughters of Jerusalem do not yet understand mature love and look upon it more with wonderment than enthusiasm. All the other characters appearing to this point are too far removed from the setting to be presumed to be speaking now. It seems most likely that this is an interjection by the poet-author (Solomon) in order to underscore the significance of this transition.

If the poet-author had ended here, the reader would have no reason to think that there was any more to the narrative, for at this point the story line is complete.

In Act I the Shulammite feels the emptiness of her own soul and pleads with her beloved to draw her after him. Moving from being a mere spectator at his table to actually enjoying his presence, the experience is fleeting, so she asks the shepherds who have helped her get this far if they might further strengthen her heart, for she is lovesick.

In Act II her beloved invites the Shulammite to overcome her fears and join him in fruitful fields of service. Recoiling from his offer, she loses the sense of his presence, driving her to fervently seek and again find her beloved.

In Act III the Shulammite receives a revelation of the bridal company and commits herself to the development of her own spiritual life. The king, impressed by the Shulammite's new level of dedication, is effusive in his acclamation of her beauty. Eager to please her beloved, she goes to the mountain of myrrh and the hill of frankincense; she also calls to awaken the winds, taking great pains to maximize his present and ensuing pleasure in the garden of her heart. Her beloved drinks his wine and his milk, filling himself with joy over the life that has been yielded to him. Now the two lovers are encouraged to eat and drink, and their union is blessed forever.

Feeding Upon Christ

As noted in the previous verse, the Shulammite's beloved feasts upon the divine life he finds in her, but of what will the Shulammite eat and drink? She feasts upon the life that resides in her beloved. In this, she represents the believer who longs to spend time in the presence of God, meditating upon his beauty, power and love, for it is in beholding the Lord that one becomes a partaker of his divine nature.[1]

King David's foremost desire was that he might dwell in the presence of God all the days of his life, beholding the beauty of the Lord and meditating in his temple.[2] He maintained that the presence of God is a source of joy and pleasure from which one never tires.[3] David sought God in great earnest, hungering with all his heart to know God more fully. Such longing resulted in revelations of God's power and glory that, paradoxically, never satisfied, but only fueled, his desire for an even greater knowledge of God.[4]

---

[1] 2 Corinthians 3:18
[2] Psalm 27:4
[3] Psalm 16:11; 36:8
[4] Psalm 63:1-2

Lamentably, not every soul shares David's desire for the presence of God. Adam and Eve, after eating the forbidden fruit, hid themselves from the presence of God.[1] Israel rebelled against the presence of God,[2] and Jonah fled from the presence of God.[3] However, there have been others, like Moses, who have treasured the presence of God.[4]

Moses had seen God do many miracles in the process of delivering the nation of Israel out of Egypt and in caring for them in the wilderness. Although he had talked with God face to face, just as a man talks to another man, Moses wanted more. Desiring to know God more perfectly, he boldly asked that he might see God's glory. It was then that the Lord revealed himself to Moses as "the Lord God, compassionate and gracious, slow to anger, and abounding in lovingkindness and truth."[5]

By this revelation Moses received more than mere information; he was given opportunity to drink of the divine nature. When Moses asked to see God's glory, the Lord responded with a revelation of his character and nature. When one beholds the glory of the Lord by divine revelation, there is an impartation of the divine nature, for one becomes like that which he beholds. Being conformed to Christ's image, one's capacity to receive increasingly greater revelation is enlarged.

Through prayer

The person seeking to know God invests time in meditation, study, prayer, fasting and waiting upon God.

His meditations are generally most fruitful when centered in God's Word, for the Scriptures are the clearest revelation of God to the human race. Only through the Word of God can one's soul be anchored in the truth. The world is constantly working to conform one's mind to its values,[6] but by meditating upon God's Word, one

---

[1] Genesis 3:8
[2] Psalm 78:56, 60
[3] Jonah 1:3
[4] Exodus 33:15
[5] Exodus 34:6
[6] Romans 12:2

aligns himself with the truth. His soul becomes acclimated to the temperament of heaven and is cleansed of the little doubts, fears and questions that accumulate from his daily treading in the world.

One can also learn about God by meditating upon his character as revealed in his creation or by fellowshipping with him in a manner that transcends human words or thoughts, for there are times when words, even one's own thoughts, are limited. Since God is spirit, he must be spiritually perceived in the tranquility of one's own spirit.[1] It is not necessary to travel far to meet with God; one needs only to look within himself, for there lies the garden in which he and the Beloved will meet.

Through obedience

Growing in the knowledge of God is something that takes place not only in the prayer closet or in study, but in everyday life experiences. To know Christ is to live in his presence. It is to share his thoughts, his feelings and his very life. This is the kind of relationship Jesus shared with his Father. Jesus learned to draw upon the life that is in the Father. He tells his disciples that in like manner, whoever eats him (Christ), will also live because of him (Christ): "He who eats my flesh and drinks my blood abides in me, and I in him. As the living Father sent me, and I live because of the Father, so he who eats me, he also shall live because of me. This is the bread which came down out of heaven; not as the fathers ate, and died, he who eats this bread shall live forever."[2]

Jesus is the magnificent tree of life that was in the Garden of Eden; he is the bread that fell from heaven to feed the Israelites during their wanderings in the wilderness. He is the Way, the Truth and the Life— a life-giving spirit who imparts life to all those who come to him. Jesus is the resurrection and the life, and whoever believes in him will have life and have it abundantly. It was by him, through him and for him that all things have been created,

---

[1] John 4:24; 1 Corinthians 14:15-17
[2] John 6:56-58

and it is in him that all things hold together. Eating Jesus' flesh and drinking his blood has all to do with receiving his life.

Jesus told his disciples that he had food about which they knew nothing. His food was to do the will of the Father.[1] In other words, Jesus received life and sustenance through his obedience to the Father. In like manner, the believer drinks deeply of Jesus when he walks in obedience to him, drawing upon the strength of the spirit of Christ within.[2] Drinking of Jesus involves living by the strength of Another. It requires that the believer be willing to give up his own life in order that the life of Christ be fully formed in him.[3]

The Father's Blessing

Eat, friends; drink and imbibe deeply, O lovers.

The exhortation to eat and drink is given to two who are as much friends as they are lovers.[4] It would make an appropriate toast to a bridal couple at their wedding feast, a blessing that might well linger in their minds as they find themselves wholly engaged in rapturous love.

Initially, the Shulammite did not know how to eat at the table of her beloved (1:12); later, her experience was fleeting (2:4). She has now matured to the place where her beloved takes particular delight in visiting her garden.

Solomon, as the poet-author of the song, symbolizes the Father in heaven, blessing the union between his Son and his Son's bride. The Father receives no greater joy than to see his children joined in intimate union with the Son of God so that the life of the Son is seen in them. For this reason, the Father says, *"Drink and imbibe deeply, O lovers!"* The Father gave his Son to the world through a supreme act of selfless love and is overjoyed when human souls gratefully draw upon the life made available to them in Christ.

---

[1] John 4:32-34
[2] Galatians 2:20
[3] Philippians 3:10-11
[4] The Shulammite uses the same language in reference to her beloved in 5:16.

Although this song is about the relationship between Christ and his bride, the believer's fellowship is with both the Father and the Son. The Father blesses this union not only for the sake of his Son, but also because it is only through this union that his desire to share his unfathomable love with his children can be realized. No man can come to the Father except through Christ. In this verse (5:1) is found a minuscule glimpse into the heart of the Father, who longs for his children to know his love.

So climactic is this closing that it could easily be the end of the song. However, it does not signal the end, but merely an intermission, appearing nearly in the middle of the song. This crowning moment of intimacy granted the Shulammite is in preparation for the severe testings that are about to follow, testings that will deepen love in order that the relationship be more enjoyable for both the Shulammite and her beloved. For although this scene portrays the Shulammite experiencing an intimate and wonderful experience with Christ, she is not yet fully abiding in him.

Act IV

Love Tested

Open to me, my sister, my darling . . . !

This Act describes two severe tests:

1. *A Night Visit* (5:2-5:8) tests the Shulammite's commitment to her beloved, and

2. *A Holy Distraction* (6:11-13a) tests her commitment to his people.

Each test is followed by an affirmation of the Shulammite's beauty and desirability (6:4-9; 7:6-9a), as well as a redefinition of the love relationship with her beloved (6:3; 7:10). The Shulammite is about to learn the degree of discipline and personal sacrifice required of the soul desiring complete union with the Beloved.

A NIGHT VISIT

Shulammite: 5:2   I was asleep, but my heart was awake.
A voice! My beloved was knocking:
'Open to me, my sister, my darling,
My dove, my perfect one!
For my head is drenched with dew,
My locks with the damp of the night.'

5:3   I have taken off my dress,
How can I put it on *again?*
I have washed my feet,
How can I dirty them *again?*

5:4   My beloved extended his hand through the
opening,
And my feelings were aroused for him.

5:5   I arose to open to my beloved;
And my hands dripped with myrrh,
And my fingers with liquid myrrh,
On the handles of the bolt.

5:6   I opened to my beloved,
But my beloved had turned away *and* had
gone!
My heart went out *to him* as he spoke.
I searched for him, but I did not find him;
I called him, but he did not answer me.

5:7   The watchmen who make the rounds in the
city found me,
They struck me *and* wounded me;
The guardsmen of the walls took away my
shawl from me.

A Dream

The Shulammite is asleep in bed, but her heart is awake. In other words, she is dreaming: her beloved is knocking for her to open the door, for he has been out in the damp of the night. The Shulammite hesitates but quickly relents, only to find that her beloved has disappeared into the night.

It seems odd that the Shulammite would hesitate to open the door when visited by her beloved, for how could any believer deny such a request from the Lord? It is inconceivable that if the Lord Jesus knocked on the door of one's house (and it was readily apparent that it was in fact the Lord), the believer would not (after recovering from the initial shock and amazement) immediately rise and let him in. How is it then that the Shulammite, who truly loves her beloved, does not immediately throw open the door and gladly fly into his embrace? The answer is that she is dreaming, and in her dream she responds in ways quite different from how she would act in her waking moments. The dream has come to test and reveal underlying heart attitudes, helping the Shulammite discover things she might not otherwise know about herself.

He Knocks

"Open to me," he pleads. The Shulammite's beloved has been in the darkness outside, unsheltered, and his head is now *drenched with the dew of the night.*[1] The darkness and the afflictions of the night represent the sufferings that Christ endures.[2]

Of course, Christ suffered during his life on earth, being rejected, falsely accused, mocked, tortured and finally subjected to a cruel death on a cross, but what goes unnoticed by many is that he continues to suffer pain and sorrow even now. For although his sacrificial work of atonement is complete, he still grieves over those who reject the gospel, blaspheming his name and the name of his holy and gracious Father and the name of the blessed Holy Spirit, who has come to convince those in the world of their lost condition, their impending doom and their responsibility to live

---

[1] Daniel 4:15, 23, 25; 4:33; 5:21

[2] The picture is reminiscent of the Lord Jesus when he was in the garden of Gethsemane. There he labored under the knowledge of the suffering that he was about to endure. He cried out to the Father that if possible he might be delivered from the coming ordeal of physical and emotional torment, praying so fervently that drops of blood oozed from the pores of his skin (Luke 22:44). Jesus suffered acutely because he was about to experience the pain of rejection, false accusation and betrayal by those he loved most dearly, but even more significantly, he would feel abandoned by his Father, prompting him to cry out on the cross, "My God, my God, why have you forsaken me?" Yet, Jesus remained faithful. He learned the cost of obedience through the things he suffered.

righteously before God.[1] Jesus grieves over those who have never heard the wonderful gospel of the kingdom, languishing in darkness, their minds held captive by Satan to do his will.

In addition, Christ endures rejection from within his own house— the church. He is greatly pained by those who cannot freely worship him because their minds are preoccupied with the things of the world. Although they deceive themselves to think they are very zealous for God, they are in reality lukewarm in their attendance of those things that are most important to him. He experiences acute sorrow over others who, although aware of their divided hearts, are yet unwilling to rouse themselves from their lethargy. He has unceasing grief over still others who live in open sin, defiance and rebellion, and he is brokenhearted over those who have been given many gifts and blessings, but show little gratitude or fervor in their return to him.

Seeking shelter from the discomforting *damp of the night*, the Shulammite's beloved hopes to find in her a place of rest from all the indifference of the world and anxieties of the church. He anticipates consoling himself in her singular love and affection.

Her beloved stands knocking at the door of the Shulammite's heart, calling out in terms familiar to her: *my sister*, my intimate friend; *my darling*, object of my affection; *my dove*, my devoted one. Then, with genuine admiration, he calls her by a new name, *my perfect one*, recognizing the advances in her spiritual development since she went to the mountain of myrrh (obedience) and the hill of frankincense (prayer). He deems the Shulammite ready to encounter him in new realms of intimacy.

She Hesitates

Inconvenienced

The Shulammite's life makes sense. It is ordered. There is a place for everything, and everything is in its place. Having overcome her previous fears, she is now committed to a life of voluntary service (4:6). She has grown in character and wisdom (4:7-13), and she has

---

[1] John 16:8

experienced times of deep intimacy with her beloved (5:1). But now he comes at an inappropriate time. She has retired for the night, enjoying a well-deserved rest,[1] and does not wish to be inconvenienced.

The Shulammite has laid aside her robe, which speaks of her acts of righteousness or good works. She has taken off her shoes, which represent her labors in proclaiming the gospel.[2] These things are important, to be sure, but in her way of thinking, everything has its time and place. She was willing to give her daylight hours (4:6), not considering that the night might also be required of her. She is typical of so many believers who reason that serving God should be just as controllable as any other activity. They are quite happy to teach, pray, give, build, help, preach, comfort, encourage, admonish, even fast periodically, as long as it is convenient, as long as it fits into their chosen lifestyle, allowing sufficient time for them to still have a life of their own.

In her own mind, the Shulammite feels justified in questioning her beloved's request. She has been faithful in ministry without neglecting her prayer life. "Why is it so important that I respond to him *now*? I have finished my work and I am retired for the night. What more could he reasonably expect? If there is something else that he wants from me," she imagines, "certainly it could wait until morning."

She misunderstands

Unfortunately, the Shulammite misunderstands the purpose of her beloved's visit because she views their relationship too much through the eyes of service. He has come not to call her to greater service, but to a new dimension of intimacy. He has come that she might know him more fully by understanding the sorrow he feels over sinners and the depth of pain caused by their rejection of him. The revelation of his suffering is a precursor and an invitation for her to feel the pain of his heart: to participate with him as he weeps

---

[1] Washing of the feet and putting off clothes implies rest (Genesis 19:2; Nehemiah 4:23).

[2] Isaiah 52:7; Ephesians 6:15

over the condition of lost souls with cries of intercession, to share with him the insults and innuendoes, the misunderstandings, rejections and persecutions, and to fellowship with him in his sufferings.[1]

Suffering was unknown in the Garden of Eden, home to the first man and woman, Adam and Eve. From that beautiful playland, they were to govern the earth and all it contained. The whole of physical creation was in harmony with the plan and purpose of God until Adam and Eve determined to set their wills against God by eating the forbidden fruit of the tree of the knowledge of good and evil. As a result, all of creation was separated from God and plunged into spiritual darkness. Because all men are born into this darkness, it is natural for them to love the darkness and resist the light of the knowledge of God. For this reason, the Lord Jesus, the perfect representation of the Father, was rejected by the world and condemned to die by crucifixion. Jesus said that the servant is not greater than the master; if the world hates him, the master, it will hate his disciples also.[2] Thus, every follower of Jesus can expect to experience the inevitable suffering that accompanies the clash between two opposing worlds: this present darkness and the invading kingdom of light.[3]

Every soul who desires the depths of God must be perfected through suffering.[4] It is in the crucible of affliction that a soul discovers its true purpose. The vanities of the world are exposed as impostors and the reality of the blessedness of the Savior and of his kingdom is impressed upon the heart. It is through suffering that the Father extricates the soul from the love of this world so that the soul's capacity for loving him might be enlarged.

The present difficulty for the Shulammite is that she has never seen her beloved as he comes to her now, covered with the dew of the night. She has seen him beautiful and exalted, a powerful, wise and majestic warrior-king, and a tenderhearted and compassionate

---

[1] Philippians 3:10
[2] John 15:18-20
[3] Acts 14:22
[4] Hebrews 5:8; 1 Peter 5:10

lover of her soul. To see him afflicted or sorrowful, this is new.[1] To think that her beloved is calling her to participate with him in his suffering, this is startling.

Like so many believers, the Shulammite is thankful that Jesus became her substitute, suffering a cruel and horrible death on the cross so that she might be reconciled to God. That was a price that he paid *for* her so that she might experience forgiveness, peace, joy and an abundantly blessed life. She understands in a vague sort of way that there is a cost to following Christ, but she thinks of the cost in terms of things she must give up, things that are displeasing to God and harmful to her relationship with him. She has not fully comprehended the extent to which her desire for a shared life would intrude upon her own physical and emotional comforts. Faced with this new understanding, she hesitates.

He Persists

Actually, it was the Shulammite who initiated the process that has led to this bedtime encounter. In a moment of spiritual courage, she invited the winds of adversity to blow in order to intensify the fragrance emitted from the garden of her heart (4:16), hoping to make herself even more alluring to her beloved.

Remembering the sincerity and depth of desire in the heart of the Shulammite, her beloved is not easily dissuaded by her rebuff. He pushes past her momentary dawdling and reaches *his hand* through the peephole, as though he was attempting to unbolt the door from the inside. Revealing his arm, her beloved tantalizes the Shulammite, showing himself more compelling in hopes that she will be shaken out of her complacency. If he so desired, he could forcibly open the door, but he restrains himself, allowing the Shulammite the opportunity to willingly open this door to her heart.

Witnessing the tangible evidence of her beloved's persistent love, the Shulammite's *feelings* are *aroused*. Torn between a feeling of

---

[1] Of course, she is aware that he suffered on the cross, but that was finished two thousand years ago.

shame and rekindled desire, she humbly rises to open the door. The proud will never know God. Only the humble are willing to deny their physical passions and desires in order to obey God in all things large and small. For the Shulammite to experience greater intimacy with her beloved, she must mortify every self-indulgence: self-absorption, self-applause, and those ever so subtle demands that her opinions and feelings be known and understood by others.

Unwilling to be inconvenienced, the Shulammite violates humility's prime directive: to regard others as more important than oneself.[1] But because of his unfathomable love, her beloved does not take offense, nor does he give up on the Shulammite. Thanks be to God for his mercy and his unfailing love! He faithfully persists in enticing her to come after him.

She Pursues

Placing her *hands* and *fingers* on the *bolt* of the door, the Shulammite finds it dripping with *liquid myrrh*, the telltale evidence of the abundance of myrrh that presumably flowed from her beloved as he attempted to unfasten the bolt. The copious flow of myrrh, representing perfected obedience,[2] speaks of the excellence of her beloved's submission to the Father. Her beloved is well qualified to lead the Shulammite through the refining fires designed to perfect obedience in her. Significantly, some of the myrrh is now transferred to the Shulammite, an indication that her decision to rise and open the door has already helped to produce in her the graces of a responsive and obedient spirit.

Nearing the myrrh, the Shulammite realizes her beloved had come with romantic intentions, for in those days it was not uncommon for a man to perfume himself with myrrh in preparation for a romantic encounter. It now begins to dawn on the Shulammite that her beloved's visit was not ministry-related, but had all to do with drawing her into greater realms of intimacy. With sheepish excitement, she pushes open the door, but it is too late. Her beloved has gone.

---

[1] Philippians 2:3
[2] Song 3:6; 4:6; 4:14; 5:1

Hearing his distant voice, the Shulammite's heart sinks. Panic overtakes her as she runs through the streets searching for her beloved. While having to contend with violent spasms of remorse, she calls out to her beloved, but he does not answer. Like a cruel fleeting echo, she can almost hear her own voice: "Draw me after you, and let us run together" (1:4). To be sure, he is drawing her, but in a fashion she had not anticipated.[1]

In the frantic search for her beloved, the Shulammite encounters unexpected opposition from the watchmen and the guardsmen. Feeling a sense of guilt, the Shulammite's dream becomes the arena in which she punishes herself for having acted carelessly toward her beloved. The watchmen, intercessors who should be a source of healing and restoration, become a source of wounding. The guardsmen, shepherds who should be a source of comfort and protection, take away her shawl, the little comfort and protection she has. The removing of the shawl, a representation of her authority, hints at a stripping away of the Shulammite's ministry responsibilities, adding further insult to injury.

A believer often finds himself feeling distant from God. Desperate to sense God's nearness, he sometimes looks to spiritual leaders, only to find them inaccessible, unapproachable or otherwise insensitive to his plight. Oftentimes, this seeming failure on the part of leadership is part of a divinely orchestrated plan in which God weans the believer from his dependency upon others, teaching him that ultimately he must count on God as his only source.

Occasionally, because of their own immaturity, church leaders simply lack the experience base to adequately empathize with the distraught believer. They can be like unsympathetic young eagles happening upon a fellow eagle in the process of molting his feathers. During these times, the molting eagle appears to be weak

---

[1] Withdrawal of the conscious awareness of God's presence is often disconnected from any form of disobedience but is simply God's initiation of a process in which one learns to trust him without any comforting reassurances of his presence. The prophet Isaiah notes this process when he asks, "Who is among you that fears the Lord, that obeys the voice of his servant, that walks in darkness and has no light? Let him trust in the name of the Lord and rely on his God" (Isaiah 50:10).

and sickly, prompting the eagle onlookers to hasten his apparent demise. Older eagles, those who have gone through the process themselves, seem to treat the developing eagle with a knowing respect and will even bring food and chase away the young contemptuous birds.

In the Shulammite's case, however, there are no such knowing eagles coming to her rescue.

<table>
<tr><td>Shulammite to the
daughters of
Jerusalem:</td><td>5:8</td><td>**I adjure you, O daughters of Jerusalem,
If you find my beloved,
As to what you will tell him:
For I am lovesick.**</td></tr>
</table>

Out of desperation, the Shulammite attempts to enlist the aid of anyone who might be able to help. She pleads with the daughters of Jerusalem that, if they should *find* her *beloved*, they are to *tell him* she is *lovesick*. Thus, in spite of the harsh treatment she has received from the watchmen and guardsmen, the Shulammite is not offended by the body of Christ. She humbly asks the daughters of Jerusalem to pray for her. Here is evidence that the Shulammite is maturing, for the last time she was lovesick, she asked the shepherds to relieve her distress by feeding her fresh revelation (2:5); now she simply asks the maidens to aid her with their prayers.

THE KING'S BEAUTY

daughters of
Jerusalem to
Shulammite: 5:9 **What kind of beloved is your beloved,**
O most beautiful among women?
What kind of beloved is your beloved,
That thus you adjure us?

Inspired by the Shulammite's devotion, the daughters of Jerusalem believe that she must know her beloved in a way that they do not yet know him. They are particularly intrigued as they observe her dogged loyalty even in spite of the mistreatment she has received from spiritual leaders. Concluding that her beloved must surely be outstanding to elicit such devotion, they ask the Shulammite to further enlighten them.

After having been mistreated by the watchmen and guardsmen, the Shulammite is somewhat vindicated, at least in the minds of the daughters of Jerusalem, evidenced by the appellation: *most beautiful among women*. The daughters of Jerusalem recognize her spiritual maturity, and they have no knowledge of her most recent failure. Although devastating to the Shulammite, her failure was an issue entirely between her and her beloved. How merciful the Lord is to cover the shame of the Shulammite when she so easily could have been exposed!

At the outset of this song, the daughters of Jerusalem rejoiced in their king and extolled his love (1:4), but their understanding of him was shallow. Later, they began to notice a difference between the Shulammite and themselves and asked for her help in overcoming the spiritual oppression in their lives (2:15). Now it is the Shulammite's knowledge of God, evidenced in her maturity, that has awakened a hunger within their own hearts to know the Beloved more fully. They beg to know what she sees in him.

5:10 **My beloved is dazzling and ruddy,**
    Outstanding among ten thousand.
5:11 **His head is** *like* **gold, pure gold;**
    His locks are *like* **clusters of dates,**
    And **black as a raven.**
5:12 **His eyes are like doves,**
    Beside streams of water,
    Bathed in milk,
    And **reposed in** *their* **setting.**
5:13 **His cheeks are like a bed of balsam,**
    Banks of sweet-scented herbs;
    His lips are lilies,
    Dripping with liquid myrrh.
5:14 **His hands are rods of gold**
    Set with beryl;
    His abdomen is carved ivory
    Inlaid with sapphires.
5:15 **His legs are pillars of alabaster**
    Set on pedestals of pure gold;
    His appearance is like Lebanon,
    Choice as the cedars.
5:16 **His mouth is** *full of* **sweetness.**
    And he is wholly desirable.
    This is my beloved and this is my friend,
    O daughters of Jerusalem.

The Shulammite is quick to respond to the daughters of Jerusalem, for there is no conversation that delights her so much as that which extols the beauty of her beloved. She has grown much in her knowledge of God since she last spoke to the daughters of Jerusalem, urging them to gaze upon her glorious king and his bridal company (3:11). The Shulammite has been to the mountain of myrrh (obedience) and the hill of frankincense (prayer). She has been to Lebanon, to the summits of Amana and Hermon where she learned to assume the responsibilities of leadership. She has enjoyed sweet fellowship with her beloved in the Edenic garden of her heart (5:1). What a joy it is for the Shulammite to extol the beauty, wisdom, power and love of the one who has become more than a lover, but her most cherished friend, her very life!

It is helpful to pause for a moment and consider what events may have influenced Solomon's desire to pen the most evocative love story in the Bible. It was Solomon's father, King David, who introduced intimate worship to the nation of Israel, declaring that his single and utmost desire was that he might gaze upon the beauty of the Lord all the days of his life.[1] David's reign marked the beginning of an era in Jerusalem of impassioned worship, punctuated with vehement longings and permeated with an abundance of fresh revelation concerning the passions of God's heart.

Although the biblical record is not conclusive as to what extent Solomon consciously applied this song to the divine romance, the vocabulary and the sentiments were in the air.[2] It is no wonder that from this period of Jerusalem's history would spring the most comprehensive portrait of the beauty of the Lord Jesus Christ ever written. Other biblical passages are more explicit, but they are mere snapshots, revealing usually one or two of his attributes at a time. Although more complete, the symbolic nature of Solomon's portrayal here requires that it be carefully unpacked to be appreciated.

Where does the Shulammite begin? How does she describe the one who is the image of the invisible God,[3] eternally radiating incomprehensible and unspeakable glory? One might expect the Shulammite to stumble over her opening lines in attempting to justly respond to such a lofty theme, but unhesitatingly and skillfully, she releases a torrent of verbal images that graphically portray the one who has become her shameless obsession.

Dazzling

Radiant in splendor, majestic in holiness, awesome in glory, the Shulammite's beloved is, first of all, *dazzling*. His hair is brilliant as snow; his eyes are like flames of fire, and his face shines brighter

---

[1] Psalm 27:4
[2] See Psalm 45.
[3] Colossians 1:15

than the noonday sun,[1] illuminating the whole of the New Jerusalem.[2] He is absolutely stunning, the focus of heaven! Wherever he goes, every head turns; every eye is luxuriously fixed on him, gazing intently upon his endless beauty.[3] There is none like him, the only one worthy to receive all power and riches and wisdom and might and honor and glory and blessing and dominion forever and ever![4] The angels and all of creation unceasingly praise him, for he is the King of kings and Lord of lords, the First and the Last, the Beginning and the End. He is the Lamb slain from the foundation of the world, now exalted in glory, giving life[5] to all those who come to him! He is the quintessence of love, compassion, mercy and grace. To see Christ is to be filled with rapturous praise and irresistible adoration!

Ruddy

The Shulammite's beloved is also *ruddy*,[6] indicating that, notwithstanding all his dazzling glory, he is also very human. In the days of his flesh, the Son of God was tempted at all points, yet without sin. Being intimately acquainted with human weakness, he has therefore become a compassionate and faithful High Priest,[7] continually making intercession on behalf of his saints.

Because of his obedience and overcoming faith, Jesus became the display model of a new order of beings destined to experience a marriage between the physical and the supernatural: humans in which the spirit of God dwells and through whom the glory of God is manifest.[8] It is insufficient to view Jesus as merely a prototype, however, for he is also the life-giving spirit who animates and indwells all who come after him. Jesus is an omnipresent spirit manifest in a human body, the God-man, the heart of God made

---

[1] Matthew 17:2; Acts 9:3; 22:6; 26:13; Revelation 1:14-16; 19:12
[2] Revelation 21:23
[3] Psalm 27:4
[4] Revelation 5:12-13
[5] John 5:21, 26; 10:10; 1 Corinthians 15:45
[6] *Ruddy* is translated from the Hebrew *admoni* (also translated *red*), derived from the same root word used for the name of the first man *Adam*.
[7] Hebrews 4:15
[8] 1 Corinthians 15:45-49

flesh, a perfect man, uniquely wonderful; there is none like him, nor will there ever be. He is the centerpiece of all of creation. Words are inadequate to describe his beauty. An unending recital of superlatives fails to exhaust his grandeur. He is *outstanding among ten thousand*, singularly magnificent among ten billion times ten billion.

Head like Gold

Nothing can be added to the Lord Jesus that is not already in him in its totality, for in him is an infinite array of divine perfections. The excellency and the majesty of such perfection is represented by pure *gold*.

The golden *head* speaks of Christ's divine authority, his throne having been established from before the world began.[1] God sits in the heavens and laughs at the wicked, while declaring the installation of his king upon his holy mountain.[2] Kings and judges of the earth are warned: "Humbly cast your affections upon him now in fear and trembling lest you experience his anger when he comes!"[3] Jesus is "the image of the invisible God, the first-born of all creation, for by him all things were created, both in the heavens and on earth, visible and invisible, whether thrones or dominions or rulers or authorities— all things have been created by him and for him. He is before all things, and in him all things hold together."[4] God has "highly exalted Him, and bestowed on Him the name which is above every name, that at the name of Jesus every knee should bow, of those who are in heaven, and on earth, and under the earth, and that every tongue should confess that Jesus Christ is Lord, to the glory of God the Father."[5]

A head of pure gold speaks pointedly of the perfect justice with which the Lord Jesus rules, for the spirit of wisdom rests upon him. He does not judge by mere appearances, nor does he make decisions based upon what others say, but his judgments are

---

[1] John 1:1-3; 17:5; Philippians 2:6-7
[2] Psalm 2:4-6
[3] Psalm 2:10-12
[4] Colossians 1:15-17
[5] Philippians 2:9-11

thoroughly righteous, bringing deliverance to the poor and the afflicted as he removes the wicked man from among them.[1] For this cause the nations rejoice.[2]

Raven-black Hair

His locks are clusters of dates, black as a raven.

Hair represents the divine empowerment that rests upon the Beloved for leadership. The Lord Jesus exemplifies every quality one would hope to find in a competent leader: trustworthy, capable, confident, creative and inspiring.

Jesus is a good leader because he was first a good follower. As a young man on the earth, he became a master carpenter and faithfully served his stepfather Joseph,[3] but this was a mere enactment of a role he shared with his heavenly Father from eternity past. Creation was a Father-Son partnership, one in which Jesus, a master workman full of wisdom, lovingly honored his Father with faithful and zealous service.[4] As they artfully fashioned stars, planets, the earth and all it contains, Jesus was daily his Father's delight, playfully rejoicing before him always.[5]

Coming to earth as a man, Jesus remained obedient, even unto death. For this reason, the Father loves and trusts the Son and has highly exalted him, bestowing "on him the name which is above every name, so that at the name of Jesus every knee will bow, of those who are in heaven and on the earth and under the earth, and that every tongue will confess that Jesus Christ is Lord, to the glory of God the Father."[6] Jesus, seated at the right hand of the Father, rules with absolute authority, power and wisdom. His work is finished; his throne is secure, and his oneness with the Father is absolute.

---

[1] Isaiah 11:3-4
[2] Deuteronomy 32:43; 1 Chronicles 16:31
[3] The virgin Mary miraculously conceived when the Holy Spirit came upon her and she gave birth to Jesus, the Son of God. She then had relations with Joseph who helped Mary parent the child Jesus.
[4] John 2:17
[5] Proverbs 8:30; Hebrews 1:9
[6] Philippians 2:9-11

Raven-black hair intimates the strength and vitality of a young man, suggesting that Jesus is no stale or somber autocrat, but an inspiring and energetic older brother, champion and friend. Like clusters of dates,[1] his able leadership is inviting, full of sweetness and life-giving. The one who knows Christ Jesus, feels inexplicably compelled to follow after him with the hope of becoming a partaker of his marvelous divine life.

Eyes like Doves

His eyes are like doves beside streams of water, bathed in milk and reposed in their setting.

Immeasurably deep, transparent, searching, like prismatic crystals neatly set, breathtakingly beautiful, the eyes of her beloved captivate the Shulammite. Each eye is surrounded by a sea of white, reminiscent of unblemished doves bathing calmly in a pool of milk.

Nearby streams of water complete the image of tranquility amidst turbulent movement, portraying the steady focus and emotional intensity of her beloved's tender gaze. The Shulammite is completely transfixed, feeling transparent, vulnerable, fully known yet fully accepted. Nowhere else can she experience such peace and overwhelming love as when she looks into the eyes of her beloved.

To gaze into the incomparable eyes of Jesus, the loveliest of all eyes, is to drink of the serenity of heaven. The measure and strength of Jesus' peace, rooted in his divinity, is beyond human comprehension. To know the depth of this peace is to plumb the depths of the Godhead, and yet, almost unbelievably, Jesus utters by inspiration of the Holy Spirit, an eternal promise: "Peace I leave with you; *my* peace I give to you; not as the world gives, do I give to you. Let not your heart be troubled, nor let it be fearful."[2] Jesus does not offer conventional peace, but *his* peace, a heavenly peace of which the world knows absolutely nothing.

---

[1] The meaning of the Hebrew word is uncertain; it appears only here and may have the meaning of *hills*.
[2] John 14:27

Cheeks like Balsam

His cheeks are like a bed of balsam, banks of sweet-scented herbs.

The cheeks of the Shulammite's beloved are a metaphor for the many and varied emotional qualities manifest in the face of Christ. Like banks of sweet-scented herbs and spices,[1] his expressions are pleasant, inviting, alluring and refreshing. They are not calculated illusions designed to benefit the wearer, but spontaneous actions springing from a tender and guileless heart overflowing with love.

How wonderful is this God-man who responds with just the right word, the perfect inflection, the perfect gesture and the perfect expression in every situation! However, Christ's actions are far from being mere responses to the actions of others, for every discernible expression of Christ defines the moment. That is to say, the face of Christ accurately reveals the heart, mind and purpose of God in any given situation.

Never has there been a man like Jesus, one who possesses and is able to express an innumerable array of excellencies. In Christ is combined both the eternal wisdom of the ages[2] and the meekness of a child,[3] the strength of a warrior and the gentleness of a nursing mother, the righteousness of a judge and the mercy of an intercessor, the majesty of a king and the humility of a servant. He can express the deepest of pain[4] or unbridled joy.[5] He is awesome in holiness yet full of compassion, unwavering in truth yet patient with all men, the Lion from the tribe of Judah yet the Lamb slain from the foundation of the world. There is none like Jesus. He is the fullness of the Godhead in bodily form, the exact representation of the Father, the perfect embodiment of love. Eternity provides insufficient time for one to tire of marveling at the beauty, wisdom and grace that is to be found in Christ Jesus.

---

[1] The sweet-scented herbs possibly allude to his scented beard.
[2] 1 Corinthians 1:24
[3] Matthew 11:29
[4] Matthew 23:37; Hebrews 5:7
[5] Hebrews 1:9

Lips like Lilies[1]

Liquid myrrh drips from the lily-like lips of the Shulammite's beloved. Significantly, the Hebrew word translated *dripping* (5:13) can also be translated *speaking*. Clearly, the liquid myrrh refers to the sweet nectar that flows abundantly from the lips of Jesus. From the very outset of his ministry, people wondered at the gracious words that were falling from his lips,[2] prompting amazed observers to remark, "No one ever spoke as this man."[3]

It has already been noted that myrrh represents the fragrant aroma of persevering obedience.[4] Because of his submissiveness to the Father, Jesus experienced a richness of the life of the Spirit such that his words became life-giving, reproducing his humble and loving nature in those who would receive the words he spoke.

Myrrh can also have romantic overtones (5:5). Here (5:13) the Shulammite revels in the desirability of her beloved's words, no doubt considering the extreme pleasure of contemplating his words of love. The Scriptures are variously, often narrowly, understood depending upon the paradigm through which one views God and his creation. The bride of Christ receives all of God's Word as an expression of ardent love, enticing the heart, renewing the mind and transforming the soul.

Hands like Rods of Gold

His hands are rods of gold set with beryl.

Precious gemstones[5] adorn the golden hands[6] of the Shulammite's beloved, meaning that his actions are not haphazard, but divinely

---

[1] The *lilies* referenced here are probably the red-flowered "lily" such as the scarlet tulip or anemone. See note on 2:1.
[2] Luke 4:22
[3] John 7:46
[4] Song 3:6; 4:6, 14; 5:1, 5
[5] The Hebrew word *tarshish*, variously translated (here as *beryl*, in the *New International Version* as *chrysolite*, and in the *New English Bible* as *topaz*), also refers to the gem's provenance, an area known for supplying *gold topaz*.
[6] The word can also include the forearm.

ordained, purposeful and masterfully executed. He does all things well.

Brilliant jewels of beryl, the color of fire, allude to the purity of divine justice with which Jesus executes his power. He can be trusted to have the best interest of his bride at heart. Together with the Holy Spirit, he is her protector, avenger, provider, comforter, caregiver, life-giver, trainer, teacher and friend. As the divine Husbandman, he tills the fallow field of her heart; as the careful Vinedresser, he prunes distracting branches from her life; as the Good Shepherd, he guides her into lush feeding grounds; as the Great Physician, he heals her wounded soul,[1] and as the Resurrection and the Life, he renews her physical body. Divine healings are mere tokens of resurrection life, for ultimately he will transform the body of his bride's humble state into complete conformity with the body of his glory by the exertion of the power that he has to subject all things to himself.[2]

Abdomen like Ivory

His abdomen is carved ivory inlaid with sapphires.

Figuratively, the abdomen[3] refers to the seat of the emotions, particularly, feelings of compassion. The abdomen of the Shulammite's beloved is composed of exquisitely *carved ivory*: beautifully alluring, costly and pure. Likewise, the intensity and sincerity of Jesus' compassion is incomparably attractive.

People often stop themselves from feeling genuine compassion, afraid of what such vulnerability might cost them. Wounded, hurting and self-justified, they anesthetize themselves from the possibility of further pain by isolating themselves from potential sources of conflict.

When disappointed and offended, many try to minimize their pain by convincing themselves that the pain *doesn't matter*. Instead of forgiving and attempting to rebuild the injured relationship, their

---

[1] 1 Peter 2:24
[2] Philippians 3:21
[3] The Hebrew word *meeh*, translated here as *abdomen*, also means *internal organs* or *bowels*.

hearts become increasingly callous until the relationship too *doesn't matter*. Thus, no longer plagued by disturbing memories of the offense, they conclude that they are now walking in forgiveness.

Jesus, on the other hand, is always fully engaged, a life-giving spirit, never detached or withdrawn. His abdomen of ivory (a biotic substance) represents that which is alive. Far from shutting down emotionally, Jesus remains very much alive within. He has the capacity to experience ecstatic joy, biting grief, roaring laughter, vehement wrath and passionate love.

Deeply moved with compassion and unfulfilled longings for intimacy, Jesus was willing to endure the pain of human rejection. For the joy of redeeming his bride and reconciling her to the Father, he did not shrink from suffering the agony of the cross. His love is pure, selfless, long-suffering and sacrificial. For two thousand years, he has continued to hold out his arms of salvation to a stiff-necked and rebellious people.

The abdomen of the Shulammite's beloved is inlaid with rich azure-blue sapphires, representing the presence of divine revelation. Jesus is moved by that which moves the Father; he is the Father's heart made manifest. Jesus does not even speak of his own accord, but lives to glorify the Father. To see Jesus is to know the Father.[1]

Legs like Alabaster

His legs are pillars of alabaster set on pedestals of pure gold.

Stately pillars of alabaster describe the legs of the Shulammite's beloved. Pillars provide support and strength; they represent the administration of the kingdom of God.

Alabaster, a relatively weak building material, alludes to the inclusion of the bride of Christ in the government of Jesus' empire.[2] The humanness of Christ's administration should not cause one to conclude that the administration itself is weak, for it is the very

---

[1] John 14:9

[2] Additionally, alabaster is made of calcium, the very substance of which human bones are formed.

spirit of Christ dwelling within his bride, represented by the pedestals of pure gold upon which the pillars are set, that gives her strength. This marvelous truth of oneness with deity was not understood by the early prophets, nor even by angels, but has now been made known to the church.[1] Oh, the wonderful mercy and grace of God that the bride should share Christ's throne with him as he has promised: "He who overcomes, I will grant to him to sit down with me on my throne, as I also overcame and sat down with my Father on his throne."[2]

Two pillars are reminiscent of the two pillars in front of the temple of Solomon, a portrayal of the coming kingdom of God. One pillar was named Jachin (literally, *he will establish*) and other Boaz (literally, *quickness*). In these names are revealed the certitude that God's kingdom will be established on the earth and that its establishment will come about quickly. God is extremely patient, but when the time to act is fully come, he often moves very swiftly.[3] Now, in the fullness of time,[4] God will be moving very quickly in the establishment of his kingdom upon the earth.

Appearance like Lebanon

The overall *appearance* of the Beloved is like the venerable mountains of *Lebanon*, a symbol representing majesty, power and grandeur. He is *choice* as the stately *cedars* of Lebanon which, growing to an imposing one hundred feet in height, represent nobility and strength. Having a non-assuming and yet commanding presence,[5] he is an unassailable fortress, an impregnable rock. The Lord Jesus delivers the poor who cry for help and the orphan who has no helper.[6] He is a father to the needy[7] and a husband to the widow. He is clothed in righteousness

---

[1] 1 Corinthians 6:17; Ephesians 5:31-32; Colossians 1:26-27; 1 Peter 1:10-12
[2] Revelation 3:21
[3] Exodus 12:11; Malachi 3:1; Luke 18:7
[4] Ephesians 1:10
[5] Job 29:7-10
[6] Job 29:12-13
[7] Job 29:16

and justice,[1] and he makes the widow's heart sing for joy.[2] He is a buckler and a shield, an ever-present help in the time of trouble.

Full of Sweetness

After systematically describing the features of her beloved from head to foot, culminating with a description of his overall appearance, the Shulammite makes mention of his *mouth*, literally, the palate or roof of his mouth. By restraining her words concerning his palate until last, she discloses the value she places upon the intimacy she shares with her beloved.

Having already described those characteristics that are visible and readily apparent, the Shulammite now moves to that which lies hidden, revealed only to those who draw near. Spiritually, the palate speaks of wisdom and understanding.[3] Her beloved's palate is sweet (literally, *sweetnesses*), meaning his manifold ways are pleasant and wholly desirable.[4]

Who is like the Lord Jesus? Consider his ways. He who created the earth, stars and galaxies also keeps them each suspended in their proper place. He establishes the boundaries of the sky, the spinning of the earth and the temperature of its core. By his word, every atom holds together, every heart beats and every soul finds its next breath. He teaches the deer to calf, the spider to spin and the eagle to fly. He determines the courses of nations, civilizations and kings, raising up one and putting down another. He knows the end from the beginning; eternity is within his grasp. He beautifies every flower, inspires every artist and causes every soul to dream. All his ways are sweet; there is none like him! The depth of God's wisdom is beyond knowing.[5] The apostle Paul agrees: "Oh, the depth of the riches both of the wisdom and knowledge of God! How unsearchable are His judgments and unfathomable His ways!"[6]

---

[1] Job 29:14
[2] Job 29:13
[3] Job 6:30; 12:11-12; Psalm 119:103
[4] Psalm 34:8; 119:97-103
[5] Job 28:12, 20-23
[6] Romans 11:33

Many are those who love the attributes of God— his mercy, his justice, his life— but how many love his ways? For the ways of God consist of more than mere qualities to be admired from a distance. God's ways are as intrusive and inescapable as gravity, always engaging man's reluctant participation.

The ways of God are very different from the ways of man. The human heart values euphoric mountaintop experiences, whereas the Lord also values the valleys. The human heart imagines spiritual growth as a buoyant continuum, whereas in actuality, the Lord refines the soul by adding to and taking away. The human heart looks for the quick fix, the easy win, the permanent solution, whereas the Lord has chosen to grant victory little by little, requiring the development of perseverance, wisdom and love.[1] The human heart considers itself as the most significant soul, whereas the Lord's way is for one to consider others as more important than oneself.[2] The Lord's way is to bring life out of death, the greatest out of the least and glory out of shame.

Audaciously, some complain, "God is basically good, but there are some things I just don't like about what he does." The Shulammite would never speak so, for she loves not only his attributes, but also his ways. She desires to know what motivates his actions, rejoicing in all his ways even when she does not fully understand them. To the Shulammite, her beloved is wholly desirable; there is nothing about him she does not enjoy.

Especially when going through difficult times, the wisdom of God's ways often lies hidden from the uninitiated and is frustrating to those who are wise in their own eyes, but the Lord promises untold riches, glory, power and joy to those who silently endure suffering and tribulation,[3] allowing the nature of Christ to be perfected within.

---

[1] Deuteronomy 7:22
[2] Philippians 2:3
[3] Acts 14:22

Beloved and Friend

This is my beloved and this is my friend. The Shulammite has pursued a relationship with her beloved, not merely for the pleasure of an intimate relationship at the physical and emotional levels. She wants more than a lover. She wants a friend, a trusted companion, one with whom she can enjoy a shared set of values, one who is capable of providing full-orbed intimate fellowship at all levels: physical, emotional, intellectual and spiritual.

Believers are in danger of seeking supernatural manifestations of the Lord's presence merely for the sensual experience of the moment, while the Lord intends his visits to be so much more. For the express manifestation of his Spirit contains within it the kernel of a deeper revelation of his nature. Moses understood, for he cried, "Show me your glory,"[1] only after he had prayed, "Let me know your ways."[2] The Lord responded by causing his glory to pass by while he proclaimed, "The Lord, the Lord God, compassionate and gracious, slow to anger, and abounding in lovingkindness and truth; who keeps lovingkindness for thousands, who forgives iniquity, transgression and sin."[3] Within the manifestation of God's glory was cloaked a revelation of his nature. It was this greater understanding of God's person that Moses was seeking and was granted.

The Shulammite will never be content with less than constant intimate communion at all levels. She does not wish to live in a house separate from the king, like Queen Esther who knew the king occasionally, sharing his company only when invited. No, the Shulammite longs to be the king's companion as well as his wife,[4] not only his lover but also his friend. She fully expects to attain to the epithets of Enoch and Noah, who walked with God,[5] as well as Abraham's appellation, friend of God.[6]

---

[1] Exodus 33:18
[2] Exodus 33:13
[3] Exodus 34:6-7
[4] Malachi 2:14
[5] Genesis 5:22, 24; 6:9
[6] Exodus 33:11; James 2:23

6:1 **Where has your beloved gone,**
O most beautiful among women?
Where has your beloved turned,
That we may seek him with you?

Throughout the song it has been apparent that, although the daughters of Jerusalem have a measure of love for the Lord, they have at the same time had other loves more important than him. At the outset of the song (1:4) they found his love more exhilarating than wine, but they were unable to deal with the little foxes that hindered their relationship with him (2:15). Even after receiving a revelation of the bridal company (3:11), they showed no interest in pursuing the overcoming bridegroom-king at a deeper level of intimacy. It was only after the Shulammite asked them to pray for her (5:8) that they expressed a desire to know her beloved more fully. Intrigued by the dedicated passion they witnessed during the testing of her faith, the daughters of Jerusalem then asked the Shulammite to describe the nature of her beloved (5:9).

Now, convinced and overwhelmed by the Shulammite's characterization of her beloved, the daughters of Jerusalem ask a second question. Instead of, "*What* is he?" they ask, "*Where* is he?" for they too now want him. In asking where he has gone, they reveal their desire to learn more deeply of his ways. He is not yet *their* beloved for they humbly ask the Shulammite, "Where has *your* beloved gone?" In earnest they repeat the question: "*Where has your beloved turned?*"

Just as the Shulammite had to go to the shepherd's tents to learn of her beloved's ways, the daughters of Jerusalem now look to the Shulammite to instruct them. They do not want to attempt to find him alone, but they prefer to go with a trusted guide. The Shulammite is well qualified in their eyes to help them for she is, after all, the *most beautiful among women*.

6:2 **My beloved has gone down to his garden,**
To the beds of balsam,
To pasture *his flock* **in the gardens**
And gather lilies.

6:3 **I am my beloved's and my beloved is**
mine,
He who pastures *his flock* **among the lilies.**

His Garden

As though jarred back to reality, the Shulammite ponders the question: "Yes, indeed, where has my beloved gone?" Gradually, the truth dawns upon her: "Of course, *my beloved has gone down to his garden, to the beds of balsam.*"

By directing them to the *gardens*,[1] the Shulammite calls the daughters of Jerusalem to the development of their inner life. If they want to find the Beloved, they must look deep within and give themselves to the tending of their gardens. A fruitful garden is attractive to the Beloved; it is to there that he has *gone down*, and it is there that they will find him.

Having not experienced her beloved's presence since she rejected his night visit (5:3-8), how is it that the Shulammite is suddenly able to instruct others about where he is to be found? The Shulammite's confidence is rooted in her knowledge of what her beloved values; he enjoys the fragrant spices of his garden, the life of the Spirit, his very own nature, cultivated in the souls of men (4:16-5:1).

There are some whose gardens are quite lush. They are the *lilies*, precious souls who have found their rest in the quiet waters of God's Spirit.[2] Their simplicity, inner nakedness, submissiveness and continual self-sacrifice are a source of special delight to the Beloved, who gives them particular attention, gathering them to himself. How blessed is the one whom the Lord chooses and brings

---

[1] *His garden* is a general reference to the church; *the gardens* refers to the souls of specific individuals.
[2] The meaning of lilies is explained in 2:16.

near to himself to dwell in the courts of the Lord and behold his beauty![1]

Compassionate Counsel

Last time the daughters of Jerusalem asked for help, when their vineyards (a metaphor for their souls) were being spoiled by little foxes, the Shulammite carelessly dismissed their plea (2:15-16). She was neither willing nor prepared to take the time to deliver them from their spiritual woes. Although willing to inform them of her beloved's presence by the still waters where the lilies grow, the Shulammite lacked the personal experience and spiritual understanding necessary to guide them there.

However, since that time, the Shulammite has grown immensely, and compassion now marks her response. Instead of an offhanded reply, the Shulammite gives practical help about how the daughters of Jerusalem might find her beloved.

First, as already mentioned, they must develop the gardens of their hearts.

Second, they must let the Beloved *pasture* them in the *gardens* where the *lilies* grow. In other words, if they want to know him more deeply, they must learn to glean from mature saints, those who have gone before them. This is not to say that they should look to others to solve their problems, but that they should seek to learn from the example of others' lives.

The advice the Shulammite now gives the daughters of Jerusalem is similar to the counsel she had received from her beloved early in her quest. Hoping to be guided to the place of healing and restoration, the Shulammite asked the Good Shepherd where he pastures his sheep. In response, he directed her to the tents of the shepherds (1:7-8), for they had already learned what she was longing to discover. Similarly, the Shulammite directs the daughters of Jerusalem to seek out the gardens of the lilies, for it is among them that they will find the Beloved.

---

[1] Psalm 27:4; 65:4

A Soul at Rest

Gone is the anxious insecurity of immature love (3:1-4) and the frantic disquiet of apparent estrangement (5:6-8). Instead, the Shulammite exudes confidence even in her seeming separation: *"My beloved has gone down to his garden."* Her soul is at rest. How is it that the Shulammite has been able to come to this place of quiet assurance?

It was the maidens' question, "What kind of beloved is your beloved?" (5:9) that prompted the Shulammite to recount his many excellencies. Meditating upon the beauty of her beloved (5:10-16) has brought healing and refreshment to her soul. She is confident that he loves and cherishes her, confident that, even though she has lost the sense of his presence, she has not lost *him*, confident that the fire of love burning in his bosom has not subsided.

The Shulammite no longer demands continual reassurances of his love, but is learning to rest in the knowledge that she and her beloved are one. If they are truly one, she need not frantically search for him, but by faith she merely rests in the oneness he has already provided. Instead of crying out for intimacy, she rejoices that he is with her, continually binding her to himself.

Herein lies one of the secrets of the *lilies*, that company of saints who continually abide in his love. They realize that God's presence is not defined by one's subjective sensory awareness, but by the constancy of his love. For if God's love is constant, then he is necessarily intimately involved in every circumstance of every moment. The lilies have learned to apprehend by faith the reality of his abiding love.

A Defining Moment

After telling the daughters of Jerusalem they can find her beloved in the gardens of the lilies, the Shulammite has no need of speaking further. She has answered their question well enough.

Why then does the Shulammite find it necessary to explain her relationship with her beloved? Humbled by her hesitation at his night visit and by the fact that she has only recently learned to rest in his seeming absence, the Shulammite has been pondering the issue of her identity as one of his lilies.[1] Feeling the need to clarify some things in her own mind, she makes a declaration: *I am my beloved's and my beloved is mine*. With these words the Shulammite redefines her relationship with her beloved.

This is the third such defining moment up to this point. A brief summary follows:

1. *My beloved is to me* . . . (1:13-14). Here, although the Shulammite longs for intimacy with her beloved, she views the relationship only in terms of the pleasure *she* will receive. She does not yet appreciate his desire to enjoy her.

2. *My beloved is mine, and I am his* (2:16). Acknowledging that she belongs to him, the Shulammite's identity is firmly rooted in her love for God. However, even though she has had wonderful experiences in his presence, she has not yet embraced the call to selfless service in loving others. She has deepened her level of consecration to her beloved, but still views the relationship primarily as an opportunity for her own enjoyment.

3. *I am my beloved's, and my beloved is mine* (6:3). Now, instead of emphasizing that her beloved belongs to her, the order is reversed, and the Shulammite focuses on the fact that she belongs to her beloved. She now understands that the relationship does not exist primarily to satisfy her desires, but his.

Although the Shulammite hesitated to open the midnight door to her beloved, she ultimately arose and embraced the invitation to join him in his suffering (5:2-6). Life is now first of all about him, her beloved.

---

[1] The focus of her thoughts is also evidenced by the fact that lilies are mentioned twice in this brief discourse.

Thus, the Shulammite demonstrates her agreement with the words of Jesus: "Whoever wishes to save his life[1] shall lose it; but whoever loses his life for my sake shall find it."[2] She gives up her life (that is, her affections and her self-will) in a deeper way than she has ever understood before, knowing that in so doing she will gain his life. The exchanged life is becoming a reality, and the Shulammite begins to experience the words of the apostle Paul when he said, "I have been crucified with Christ; and it is no longer I who live, but Christ lives in me; and the life which I now live in the flesh I live by faith in the Son of God, who loved me, and delivered himself up for me."[3]

Although the Shulammite panicked at the loss of her beloved's presence, her soul is now at rest. Having joined herself to her beloved by faith, she is profoundly united to him in a way she never understood before. Now fully assured of his love, she gladly exclaims that she is wholly his.

A Willing Guide

The Shulammite frames the redefinition of her relationship with her beloved in such a way as to draw immediate attention to her previous rebuff to the daughters of Jerusalem, when they pleaded for her help with the little foxes (2:16). For then she said,

> "My beloved is mine, and I am his;
> he pastures his flock among the lilies,"

and now in similar form, she says,

> "I am my beloved's and my beloved is mine,
> he who[4] pastures his flock among the lilies."

The Shulammite appears to be correcting her previous statement, as though wanting the maidens to understand that because her

---

[1] The Greek word *psuche*, here translated as *life*, is literally *soul*.
[2] Matthew 16:25
[3] Galatians 2:20
[4] The addition of the word *who* changes the meaning slightly. In the first instance, the Shulammite merely tells the location of her beloved. In the second instance, she uses the same phrase to define his nature, implying her advancement in the knowledge of him.

relationship with her beloved has changed, her attitude toward them will also be different. She does not intend to again dismiss their request for help.

However, the maidens' present plea is of a different sort altogether. In the first instance, harassed by enemy assaults, they merely required love, encouragement and prayer. Now they are asking to be led into deeper levels of intimacy with God.

Though willing to serve, the Shulammite makes a modest assessment of her qualifications. After pondering her own identity as one of the lilies,[1] she is still unwilling to say precisely that she is one. Although prudence demands her silence on this point, it is not unreasonable to assume that she is also somewhat reluctant to present herself as an authority on knowing God.

Pausing to reflect on her present spiritual state, the Shulammite likely considers how she has changed since the last time she was approached by the daughters of Jerusalem. Since then she has embraced the vision of her own spiritual maturity (3:6-11), pledging herself to a life of obedience and prayer (4:6), and she has been granted a rare experience of unbounded divine love (5:1). However, in spite of her insights and ecstasies, it is her unwavering devotion to her beloved since his most recent departure that serves to assure the Shulammite of her own spiritual development. Now, willing to suffer the cost of personal inconvenience, she tepidly offers to guide the daughters of Jerusalem into the deeper realms of knowing God.

This venture is going to require a new level of transparency on the part of the Shulammite, for she cannot help others develop their devotional lives without also sharing with them some of the secrets of her own personal relationship with God. To be an example of faith and endurance is one thing, but to be an example of a burning heart makes one vulnerable at a deeper level. Stirring up all the spiritual courage she can, she might be heard quoting the words of the apostle Paul: "Be imitators of me, just as I also am of Christ."[2]

---

[1] See the previous subsection: *A Defining Moment.*
[2] 1 Corinthians 11:1

Her willingness to hold herself out as an example in all areas of her life marks a significant transition in the life of the Shulammite, having huge implications with regard to her ministry style. She will become less dependent on her leadership skills and more reliant upon her ability to inspire passion for God through love and godliness. She will depend less on her personal productivity quotient and more on her effectiveness at healing, restoring and empowering others. She will be more focused on being a source of pleasure to God than about obtaining visible results. Even her preaching and teaching will take on a new light as she learns to trust more in the Holy Spirit's ability to illuminate, convince and transform than in her own ability to inform, impress, motivate and enlist.

The Shulammite is acutely aware that the most precious commodity she has to give is the life she possesses in God.[1] Her willingness to dispense herself as broken bread to others is a monumental step in the development of the Shulammite's inner life, a step that her beloved has been anticipating for some time.

---

[1] 1 Thessalonians. 2:8; 1 John 3:16

THE SHULAMMITE'S BEAUTY

<table>
<tr><td>Beloved to
Shulammite:</td><td>6:4</td><td>You are as beautiful as Tirzah, my darling,
As lovely as Jerusalem,
As awesome as an army with banners.</td></tr>
<tr><td></td><td>6:5</td><td>Turn your eyes away from me,
For they have confused me;
Your hair is like a flock of goats
That have descended from Gilead.</td></tr>
<tr><td></td><td>6:6</td><td>Your teeth are like a flock of ewes
Which have come up from *their* washing,
All of which bear twins,
And not one among them has lost her young.</td></tr>
<tr><td></td><td>6:7</td><td>Your temples are like a slice of a pomegranate
Behind your veil.</td></tr>
</table>

Excited by the Shulammite's deepened level of consecration, trust, and willingness to serve, her beloved contemplates her beauty. Impulsively, he applauds the Shulammite's freshly heightened power of allurement.

Noticeably absent is any rebuke for the Shulammite's earlier hesitation in responding to her beloved (5:3). The simple withdrawal of his presence was enough to secure her undivided attention, resulting in more fervent love and greater submissiveness.

Beautiful, Lovely and Awesome

Tirzah, meaning *pleasantness* or *delight,* was a luxuriant imperial city[1] with massive walls and elegant stone architecture. Nestled in an elevated fertile valley surrounded by salient limestone hills, it becomes an emblem for the Shulammite's striking beauty, now accentuated by her willingness to deny herself by loving and serving others.

---

[1] Tirzah, a Canaanite royal city, was conquered by Israel under Joshua four hundred years prior to Solomon. King Jeroboam, successor to Solomon over the northern part of Israel, makes Tirzah his capital.

Throughout her recent ordeal, the Shulammite's unswerving loyalty evidenced a dignity, strength and stability that reminds her beloved of yet another majestic city, the Israeli capital city of *Jerusalem*. Situated on a high mountain plateau protected by deep precipitous ravines and surrounded by mountains, Jerusalem bears a secure regal quality befitting her name: *foundation of peace*. To her belong the prophets and a kingdom, the promise of an eternal throne from where Messiah, the Son of God will rule the earth with absolute authority and justice.

Like Jerusalem, the Shulammite is *lovely*. The word translated *lovely* can also mean *suitable* or *befitting*, but befitting of what? In her beloved's eyes, the Shulammite's noble bearing makes her suitable to wed a king, and not just any king, but the sovereign Lord of all creation, Jesus the Christ.

Never has there been, nor will there ever be, an army capable of prevailing against this glorious king, yet her beloved admits to trembling before the Shulammite, whom he describes as *awesome as an army with banners* upraised. Like a child awed and transfixed at the terrifying sight and thunderous sound of a military parade, so the king's heart is impaled, smitten with a deep-felt admiration of the Shulammite's overpowering beauty.

Paralyzing Eyes

Confused (literally, *paralyzed*), by the Shulammite's eyes, her beloved begs that she look away from him. Like a deer caught in the headlights of an approaching vehicle, he is incapacitated by the Shulammite's gaze.

The secret to the Shulammite's power lies not only in her striking beauty which, as just noted, has the power of an *army with banners*, but also in the intensity of her gaze, a gaze of ardent love so fiercely focused as to paralyze its subject. Her concentrated attention is evidenced by her recent description of her beloved (5:10-16). Lacking in her portrayal is any mention of her beloved in relation to others (as in 2:3), for he is incomparably beautiful, singularly loving and infinitely powerful.[1] Her eyes see only him.

Initially likened to peaceful doves (1:15; 4:1), the Shulammite's eyes have progressively gained mastery over her beloved. Although once cherished for even a single heart-throbbing glance (4:9), her eyes now threaten to do what a thousand armies could never have accomplished— to subdue the will of this unconquerable king! Thus, he portrays the Shulammite's gaze as dangerous, begging that she look away. Of course, for all his pleading, he does not actually want her to look away from him, for it is the very mystery and danger of this gaze, producing a feeling of vulnerability shared only by lovers, that he longs to experience.

Poetic imagery becomes the means by which the Shulammite's beloved exaggerates his plight, tempting the reader to automatically soften the import of his words. But one is reluctant to trifle with Scripture, for it is intriguing to consider the extent to which the Lord Jesus is fascinated by the worshipful devotion of his bride. Undoubtedly, he is moved with a raging love and desire unfathomable to the human heart.

Expectant Contemplation

The Shulammite's beloved repeats the praises he lavished upon her earlier (4:1-5) regarding her shimmering black *hair*, sparkling milk-white *teeth* and demurely blushing *temples*. Lurking is the question of why he mentions only these three features and not also her lips, mouth, neck, and breasts, features that he had mentioned in his previous description.

Key to understanding the answer to this question is the Shulammite's steady gaze, an allusion to the many meditations of her heart that have been firmly set upon her beloved. No longer content with mere glimpses of his glory (4:9), she quiets her soul,

---

[1] The three qualities are more fully explained under 1:3. Correspondingly, the Shulammite is beautiful as Tirzah, lovely as Jerusalem and awesome (powerful) as an army (6:4).

waiting upon God[1] with a confident expectation of receiving a more clear and constant revelation of his face.[2]

The Shulammite has moved past asking others for help in finding her beloved (5:8), for she knows where he is and how to find him. He has gone down to the gardens (6:2). It is in the tranquility of her own spirit that she will meet with him and, beholding him, be transformed into his image,[3] thus enlarging her capacity to know him even more.

Therefore, her beloved extols the three primary qualities that have helped bring the Shulammite this far in her spiritual quest, qualities that have allowed her to experience moments of oneness and supernatural bliss, qualities absolutely essential for her continued growth in the revelatory realm.

Hair

As explained earlier, the Shulammite's cascading *hair* highlights her humble and submissive nature.[4] It is her humility that allows the Shulammite to appreciate the greatness of God and the tremendous need that she has of him. This awareness of her own lack gives her the courage to live with continual longing.

However, she waits patiently for greater unveilings of the glories of Christ, anticipating but not demanding,[5] for the Shulammite is looking neither for spiritual revelations to validate her worth in the eyes of others, nor for supernatural experiences to validate her own sense of self-worth and acceptability to God. She is confident of her beloved's love and humbles herself with prayer and fasting, not as a method of persuading God, but as a means of preparing her heart for what he already yearns to give— union with the Divine.

---

[1] Psalm 46:10; 123:2; Isaiah 8:17; 40:31
[2] Exodus 24:9-11; Numbers 12:8
[3] Numbers 12:8; Ephesians 1:17; 2 Corinthians 3:18
[4] See 4:1 for a further explanation of the Shulammite's hair and 4:14 (cinnamon) for more on her humility.
[5] Psalm 123:2

Teeth

The Shulammite's *teeth* signify her propensity for meditating upon God and his Word. This practice is indispensable, not only for continuing to grow in the knowledge of God, but also for maintaining one's constant focus on God's presence, helping the soul to be aware of and to obey the voice of the Holy Spirit throughout the day.

Although the Shulammite's teeth are again likened to *a flock of ewes* (as in 4:2), they are not *newly shorn* ewes here, indicating that the Shulammite has long since put off the burden of earthly cares and affections that so easily rob the soul of precious moments in God's presence. She has remained firm in her devotion to her beloved, investing many hours in seeking his face.

Temples

The Shulammite's blushing *temples* speak again (as in 4:3) of her tender conscience before God. Purity of heart is a quality absolutely indispensable for one desiring intimacy with the eternal Godhead, for without holiness no one will see the Lord.[1] Jesus said clearly that it is the pure in heart who shall see God.[2]

Beloved: | 6:8 | **There are sixty queens and eighty concubines,**
And maidens without number;
| 6:9 | ***But* my dove, my perfect one, is unique:**
She is her mother's only *daughter*;
She is the pure *child* of the one who bore her.
The maidens saw her and called her blessed,
The queens and the concubines *also*, and they
  praised her, *saying*,
| 6:10 | **'Who is this that grows like the dawn,**
As beautiful as the full moon,
As pure as the sun,
As awesome as an army with banners?'

---

[1] Hebrews 12:14
[2] Matthew 5:8

Queens, Concubines and Maidens

King Solomon had two classes of wives: free-wives and slave-wives. A free wife, sharing the social status of her husband, received the title and prestige of a queen. A slave-wife was called a concubine. The difference between a queen and a concubine in marriage is the rights and privileges granted the former. Queens ruled, whereas concubines served. Although a concubine might enjoy conjugal intimacy, she exercised no authority over the family; her children had no right of inheritance, and she did not own private property, but was herself the property of her husband.

Queens

Sixty queens of Solomon's household typify mature saints,[1] those who grew completely into what God had created them to be. They are those in heaven who enjoy the highest degrees of intimacy and authority with God, for not everyone in the heavenly realm enjoys the same function, revelatory experiences or reward,[2] the greatest of all rewards being an increased revelation in the knowledge of God.[3] Therefore, it behooves every believer to graciously submit to the purifying process granted during his life on earth by the Father of mercies,[4] for it is through this refining process, conforming the believer to the image and likeness of Christ, that his capacity for ever-increasing revelation is enlarged.[5]

Concubines

Eighty concubines represent those who did not make use of the opportunities given them during their life on earth to grow in the knowledge of God. They did not pursue intimacy with God and, therefore, did not attain to the higher realms of glory in heaven.

---

[1] As noted concerning the sixty mighty men (3:7), six is the number representing man; ten represents completeness. Sixty (6x10) represents completed or mature man.

[2] Luke 19:17-19; 1 Corinthians 3:13-15; Revelation 14:4

[3] Genesis 15:1; Ephesians 1:17; Philippians 3:10

[4] 2 Corinthians 1:3

[5] Matthew 5:8

Some, like the dying thief who was crucified beside the Lord Jesus, waste their lives in all manner of wanton sin but at the last, by the mercies of God, repent and are received into paradise.[1]

Others spend much of their lives as believers but, having received many graces, they do little with what they have been given.[2] Guided mostly by convenience, they squander their many opportunities for deepening their relationship with God. Entertainments and preoccupations, though not necessarily sinful in themselves, become a substitute for prayer and meditation for these poor souls attempting to find personal satisfaction in things other than God himself.

They are like the prodigal son who, through wasteful living, squandered all that his father had given him. Propitiously, the son eventually regained his senses and, though his inheritance was lost, was himself welcomed back into his father's house.[3] Likewise, the concubines' celestial identities are not defined by their losses, but by the mercy of God, for there are *eighty concubines*, eight being the biblical number to represent new beginnings.[4] Out of God's mercy, he gives these immature believers fresh opportunities to experience his life and glory in eternity, albeit, to a lesser degree than they might have otherwise known if they had better prepared themselves for their heavenly state.

Maidens

Maidens without number are the daughters of Jerusalem, the main body of Christ's church upon the earth (1:3; 2:2). Every one of the maidens has the potential of becoming a queen if she so desires. Sadly, too many see themselves as mere servants of Christ. They rejoice in their salvation and in the goodness of God (1:4) but lack the motivation to pursue deep and profound intimacy with the Beloved. Nonetheless, others, like the Shulammite, will respond to

---

[1] Luke 23:43
[2] Luke 12:48
[3] Luke 15:11-32
[4] In the Bible, seven often represents a complete cycle; the next number, eight, therefore represents a new beginning.

the gentle wooing of the Holy Spirit and cry, "Draw me after you and let us run together" (1:4).

Unique and Pure

Of all the queens, concubines and maidens, the Shulammite, her beloved's *perfect one, is unique: she is her mother's only daughter*.[1] Amazingly, the Lord Jesus is able to give himself fully to each member of his corporate bride as though that one member was the most precious of them all.

Yet, a deeper meaning is to be found here, for the Shulammite's uniqueness is evident not only at the individual level, but also at the corporate level. In other words, the bridal company that begins to arise in preparation for the closing of this age and the dawning of another is unique in all the history of the church (symbolized here as *the one who bore her*).[2] The Shulammite represents not the whole church, for then there would be no *maidens without number* (6:8) with whom to interact (6:13; 7:1-5); at this stage, she is merely a portion of the church. The Shulammite is an incomplete prefigurement of the mature church for which the Lord returns at the end of the age.[3]

Although still developing, the Shulammite is *pure* or clean, meaning that she has rid herself of the inner defilement of her own self-will. She has patiently endured the involuntary trials of false accusations, misunderstandings and betrayals. She has also given herself to the voluntary disciplines of fasting, servanthood, worship, meditation, diligent study and fervent prayer. Her willingness to embrace inconvenience and suffering has worked to purge the selfish motivations from her heart. The steadfast faith she evidenced during her most recent test (5:6-7) has worked to cleanse the Shulammite from the enemies of self-absorption,

---

[1] When God referred to Isaac as Abraham's *only son* (Genesis 22:2, 12, 16) God was highlighting the fact that Isaac was the fulfillment of God's promise to Abraham. God also had regard for Abraham's son Ishmael and promised he would become a great nation. The Shulammite is *her mother's only daughter*, meaning that she is the fulfillment of the bride promised to Jesus.

[2] The *mother*-church typology is explained under 3:4.

[3] Ephesians 4:13

self-determination and self-indulgence. All her so-called personal rights have been relinquished to her beloved in an act of selfless love.

Praised by Saints

Who is this that grows like the dawn, as beautiful as the full moon, as pure as the sun, as awesome as an army with banners?

Saints of every age applaud the unveiling of this glorious troop, ordained by God to lead the church into her marvelous destiny at a time when deep darkness covers the earth. Like the dawning of the sun, the overcoming end-time church, represented by this advance troop, begins to come forth out of the historical darkness of her immaturity, manifesting the brilliance of the glory of God. Nations come to her light and kings to the brightness of her rising.[1]

> Envisioned in the heart and mind of God,
> foretold by the prophets, anticipated by all of
> creation, she was birthed in obscurity yet
> universally celebrated. Her beauty, wisdom,
> power and love gained both the admiration
> and the envy of kings. She nurtured saints and
> dispelled demons. She dressed the wounds of
> the afflicted, cared for the poor and the needy
> and contended for the rights of the oppressed.
> Cynics tried to discourage her; heretics tried to
> divide her; Satan tried to pollute her, and
> tyrants tried to kill her. After two thousand
> years of being misunderstood, maligned,
> mocked and mistreated, she remains—
> invincible, incorruptible—
> the Church.

Reflecting the light of the sun against a silent darkened sky, the *full moon* graphically portrays the Shulammite as she radiates the glory of God in the midst of a deaf and dying world. Just as the moon

---

[1] Isaiah 60:1-3

has no light of itself, but merely reflects the light of the sun, the Shulammite has no light but that of Christ.[1] Proclaiming the good news of the kingdom of God, she expressly and naturally manifests the character of Jesus, showing forth the kingdom's cardinal virtues of humility, love, peace and joy.

Pure, or unsullied, *as the sun*, the Shulammite exhibits the righteousness and perfect justice of the coming kingdom age. The thought of righteous judgment is good news for the humble and a warning to the proud, just as the sun is both a blessing to some and a curse to others. For, while many are warmed and invigorated by its rays, others are withered and remembered no more.

An awesome victorious *army*, the end-time bride liberates the weak and downtrodden while striking terror in the hearts of God's enemies, for this glorious bride will yet execute God's authority and justice upon the earth[2] by virtue of the spiritual authority granted her as the wife of the Lamb.[3]

Maturing unto the measure of the stature which belongs to the fullness of Christ,[4] the church prepares herself for union with the Divine. The implications of these words present the judicious mind with an almost unbelievable reality that staggers the imagination! Nevertheless, no longer relegated to the back seat of irrelevancy, the church here begins to move into her eternal destiny, manifesting the reality of Christ and his kingdom in the earth. Full of love and power, the Shulammite is a formidable force, treading upon serpents and scorpions without being harmed.[5] With seeming unlimited power, whatever she asks is granted, for she abides in God and his Word abides in her.[6]

---

[1] The moon typology breaks down somewhat since the glory of God actually radiates from within the Shulammite.
[2] 2 Corinthians 10:6; Revelation 19:14
[3] Psalm 110:2-3; Revelation 21:9
[4] Ephesians 4:13
[5] Luke 10:19
[6] John 15:7

A HOLY DISTRACTION

Shulammite: 6:11 **I went down to the orchard of nut trees
To see the blossoms of the valley,
To see whether the vine had budded
Or the pomegranates had bloomed.**
6:12 **Before I was aware, my soul set me
Over the chariots of my noble people.**

A brief review of the Shulammite's experience in regard to her beloved's presence is helpful here.

In Act I, although she longs intensely for her beloved, the Shulammite does not know how to feed from his table and is unable to enjoy the manifestation of his presence. After hearing his comforting words of love, she is taken into his banqueting hall where she experiences moments of joy and rest in his love. But the banquet hall is still not the bridal chamber, and her lovesick soul cries for more, begging the shepherds for supplemental feeding.

In Act II the Shulammite resists her beloved's initial invitation to service (2:10-13), but because of her immaturity, the consequences are slight. She suffers a momentary loss of his presence from which she quickly recovers.

In Act III the Shulammite receives a marvelous revelation of the bridal company and commits to the process of developing her inner life. Feeding among the lilies (4:5), she learns to abide in the peace and love of God, inspiring her to a life of prayer, obedience and responsible leadership. She then enters into a profound experience with her beloved in the garden of her heart (4:16-5:1), but her commitment to sacrificial service had yet to be tested.

Act IV opens with her beloved knocking on the door of the Shulammite's heart, this time to invite her to share with him in a life of self-sacrifice (5:2-7). When she balks, the Shulammite once again experiences the withdrawal of his presence. She panics, searching wildly for her beloved and finally asking the daughters of Jerusalem for help. This leads to an opportunity for the Shulammite to reaffirm her love for her beloved (5:10), resulting in a reciprocal reaffirmation from her beloved (6:4-10).

Having thus been tested with regard to her commitment to her beloved, the Shulammite is now tested regarding her commitment to the precious souls whom he loves.

Orchard

Aware of her growing stature, both in the eyes of her beloved and in the eyes of the church, the Shulammite recognizes her responsibility to give her life in sacrificial service to others. Still bereft of her beloved's presence, the Shulammite listlessly ventures out among the souls of men, represented by an *orchard of nut trees* or, more precisely, a walnut grove.

Nuts still clinging to the trees represent souls who have not yet abandoned themselves to God. Jesus said that unless a seed falls to the ground and dies, it abides alone; but if it dies, it bears much fruit.[1] His message was threefold.

First, the seed falling to the ground represents Jesus' own physical life that he would sacrifice for the salvation of mankind, resulting in a harvest of many sons and daughters unto God.

Second, Jesus' fruitfulness was predicated upon his willingness to set aside his heavenly glory and come down to earth as a man, continually yielding his soul life (his mind, affections and self-determinate processes) to the Father in sweet abandonment and trust.

Third, every believer must likewise die to his own self-will in order to experience the life of Christ abiding in him,[2] for one's self-will is an enemy of God. It wars against the Spirit of God as he attempts to prepare the human heart for complete union with Christ.[3]

---

[1] John 12:24
[2] John 12:25; Galatians 2:20
[3] Romans 5:10

Relinquishing one's will to God can be an extremely painful process and is unnecessarily prolonged by most. Having such a fond attachment to their own life, they are loath to abandon it. The story of a young boy who acquired a boxer puppy illustrates the point. The boy's father explained that it was time to pin up the puppy's ears and cut its tail so that it would look like other boxers. Taping the ears did not present a problem, but having such a fond affection for his pup, the little boy hated to think of the pain the puppy would experience if he were to cut off its tail. So the young boy decided that, out of compassion for the pup, he would cut off a little bit of its tail each day. Clearly, one's willingness to sever all earthly attachments early in his Christian life is most conducive to a joyful, faith-filled, overcoming walk with God.

Humans were created to experience the glory of the exchanged life, a partnership with the Divine whereby the human provides the vessel and Christ supplies the life that indwells and animates the human vessel. Habitual yielding to the indwelling Spirit transforms this new creation until Christ is fully formed in it. This is God's eternal purpose for man, a marriage between the supernatural and the natural such that the glory of Christ is manifest in humans throughout his creation forever.

Blossoms

Purposefully, the Shulammite continues through the orchard of nut trees *to see the blossoms of the valley, to see whether the vine had budded or the pomegranates had bloomed.* The budding vines and pomegranates refer to believers who are just coming forth into fruitfulness in their lives and ministries.

Her beloved had tried to coax the Shulammite into these very fields of service early in the song (2:10-14), but at that time, still reeling from her period of lethargy and spiritual neglect, she was unwilling to risk losing the sense of his presence by which she was comforted in the cleft of the rock. So determined was the Shulammite to protect the sense of his presence, that she ignored the daughters of Jerusalem, even in their pleas for help (2:15). Ultimately, her inaction cost her the very presence she was trying to preserve, but after having been equipped with new leadership skills learned during her time among the lions and leopards (4:8), she enjoyed a blissful reunion with her beloved.

Now once again the Shulammite is seemingly alone. How she longs to be with her beloved! Nevertheless, she is well advanced in love and willing to accept the responsibility of ministering to young budding saints. Instant obedience and faithful perseverance, even without the sense of her beloved's nearness, is a lesson the Shulammite learned well during her recent night visit. She now fully embraces the call to sacrificial service.

Chariots

Surveying the valley, wondering how she might help the blossoming believers, the Shulammite's mind begins to wander. For although her obsessive gaze has captivated the heart of her beloved (6:5), it has not yet satiated the longings within her own heart for a more intimate knowledge of him. Unintentionally, her thoughts drift.

Before she is *aware* of what is happening, the Shulammite is daydreaming about what it would be like to be among the *chariots of* her *noble people.* Chariots, vehicles of transport, signify the soul's rapturous journeys into heavenly places. Like King David, the Shulammite has one desire, that she might dwell in the house of the Lord and behold his beauty all the days of her life.[1] Desire for revelatory encounters has become the Shulammite's holy preoccupation.

She is betwixt and between; for although the Shulammite is more willing to serve than ever before, her aspirations for heavenly encounters are also greater than ever before. She loves her beloved and gallantly accepts the invitation to minister in his fields of service, but at the same time, she longs to commune with him in prayer and meditation, preferring to be locked away with her beloved in their garden of love (5:1).

---

[1] Psalm 27:4

When the Shulammite considers the cost of ministry, she does not think so much in terms of physical stress or financial sacrifice, for she is both industrious and generous. The main issue for the Shulammite is the sacrifice of time that she might have otherwise spent with her beloved in meditation upon his Word and contemplation of his glory. Unconsciously, she weighs two alternatives: mounting the chariot (of bliss) or surveying the valley (of need).

Chariots are vehicles familiar to nobility, people of power and rank. The Shulammite's *noble people* are mature saints, overcomers, the bridal company, the aristocracy of heaven,[1] believers who have been perfected in love.[2] She imagines herself being among heaven's most privileged class, capable of enjoying transportations, revelations and a myriad of spiritual delights.[3]

Seemingly distant from her beloved, the Shulammite is tempted to withdraw from public ministry and devote herself solely to prayer and meditation. Yet in her heart, she knows that God is to be found among his people as well. Jesus made it plain, "To the extent that you did it to one of these brothers of mine, even the least of them, you did it to me."[4] Will the Shulammite allow herself to be distracted (albeit, by holy ambitions) from following her beloved in humble obedience, the pain of which seems particularly acute since she does not now sense his presence?

An important lesson can be drawn from the life of the prophet Elisha when he asked for a double portion of the spirit of Elijah, his master. As they were talking, a chariot and horses of fire separated the two of them, but Elisha's gaze would not be turned aside. Because he remained focused upon his master, his request was granted.[5] Likewise, the Shulammite must remain focused on the person of Jesus through humble service and not be distracted by her desire for personal supernatural experiences.

---

[1] Members of this aristocracy have been referred to as *queens*, as opposed to *concubines* (6:8-9).
[2] Matthew 5:44-48; Philippians 3:12-14
[3] Psalm 16:11
[4] Matthew 25:40
[5] 2 Kings 2:9-12

Probing the Shulammite's thoughts, one would likely find times when she fancied passing through death and waking in the very presence of God, so superior it is to be with him than to be in this world. Who can fathom the ecstasy of open-eyed wonderment in steadily beholding the face of the Father of lights?[1]

Expressing similar sentiments, the apostle Paul confessed that he had a strong desire to depart and be with Christ, while at the same time realizing that to live on in the flesh was necessary for the sake of the church. Ultimately, he chose to forgo personal gain, opting for fruitful labor among God's people. Forging a timeless model of selfless dedication, the apostle succinctly states, "To live is Christ."[2] In other words, to remain on the earth, involved in ministry to others, is to live out the reality of the exchanged life, manifesting Christ to the world. Paul understood fellowship and true intimacy with God.

Alternate Interpretation

Some may identify more readily with the Shulammite in this passage if they interpret her daydreaming as reflections upon what her life could be like if she were back home among her own people.[3]

Undoubtedly, her life in the country was much simpler relative to palace life, which represents the complexities, isolation and weariness that often accompany public ministry. Albeit, there are rewards built into Christian ministry: the satisfaction of selfless giving, the power of the Holy Spirit's manifestations, the experience of God's faithfulness and the revelation of Christ's love being enlarged within. Joyful experiences abound: a glimmer of hope seen rising upon the face of the oppressed, tears of remorse seen pouring forth from a broken and a contrite heart, songs of praise and thanksgiving heard from the lips of one in the fire of affliction, and opportunities for telling of the goodness of God and

---

[1] James 1:17
[2] Philippians 1:21
[3] This is not the preferred interpretation because it does not flow with the Shulammite's progress to this point.

the matchless beauty of his Christ. However, ministry to immature believers can become quite taxing. There are long hours, needless disappointments, misunderstandings with disproportionate consequences, sleep-stealing perplexities and humiliating improprieties to be endured.

As a result of her pursuit after God and her involvement in ministry, the Shulammite has matured significantly. Because of what she has become, this once-darkened shepherdess reasons (in this scenario) that she probably would be well-accepted back home, even amongst the royalty of her people. The Shulammite thinks they are likely to honor her.

Here, the Shulammite resembles the believer who is actively engaged in ministry, but for an instant allows his mind to wonder what it would be like to live as an ordinary person, having no concern over other people's problems, no late-night phone calls, no interpersonal conflicts to have to work through, no responsibility for other peoples' lives. She reasons, "I could still be zealous for God, but without the pressures of the ministry. I could probably do well financially and still have plenty of free time with which to just enjoy God."

For others, the temptation may be more subtle. They are content to remain involved in the work, but they settle for a life of mediocrity, enjoying the comfort and honor the ministry affords, but no longer on the cutting edge of the kingdom's advance.

In either case, they are tempted to believe that it is possible to enjoy the fruit of salvation and at the same time find relief, satisfaction and fulfillment in the pleasures of the world.

However, the apostle John teaches that all that is in the world, the love of wealth, the desire for sensual pleasure and the arrogance of a self-determined life, are not from the Father, but from a world opposed to God.[1] To yield to such a temptation is to resurrect the self-life, bringing darkness to the soul and immeasurable grief to the heart of God. It is to follow after the example of Israel when

---

[1] 1 John 2:16

they had rejected God, who in response said, "My people have committed two evils: they have forsaken me, the fountain of living waters, to hew for themselves cisterns, broken cisterns, that can hold no water."[1] Searching for one's own source of fulfillment apart from the abiding presence of Christ is akin to trusting in a cracked cistern to provide refreshment while rejecting the life-giving spring.

In this case, it behooves the reader to heed the admonition of the psalmist: "Listen, O daughter, give attention and incline your ear; forget your people and your father's house; then the King will desire your beauty; because he is your Lord, bow down to him."[2]

| daughters of Jerusalem to Shulammite: | 6:13a **Come back, come back, O Shulammite; Come back, come back, that we may gaze at you!** |

Dismayed by the Shulammite's inattention, the daughters of Jerusalem urgently call out, attempting to bring her *back* from her distant thoughts. Because she so radiates the beauty of her beloved, walking in love, power and wisdom, the daughters of Jerusalem importune the Shulammite that they might *gaze* upon her beauty. She has become valuable to them, not for what she does, but for what she has become.

Notably, though the daughters of Jerusalem had been cautioned twice already to not awaken the Shulammite, they receive no rebuke for attempting to rouse her from her daydreaming, for the Shulammite is not experiencing a mystical sleep inspired by her beloved, but merely a lapse in her attention to the task at hand. Indeed, her beloved has been trying to involve the Shulammite in ministry to others as a gift to facilitate the enlargement of her heart so as to increase her capacity to enjoy him more.

The daughters of Jerusalem introduce here the name *Shulammite*. Although the derivation is uncertain, it can be understood as a

---

[1] Jeremiah 2:13
[2] Psalm 45:10-11

female form of *Solomon*,[1] implying that in their eyes the Shulammite has attained a spiritual and physical maturity, making her a suitable counterpart for her beloved Solomon, just as Eve was made to be a suitable companion for Adam in the garden of Eden.[2] There is no higher praise they could afford her.

Shulammite to the
daughters of
Jerusalem:

6:13b **Why should you gaze at the Shulammite,**
As at the dance of the two companies?

Two companies is literally *Mahanaim*, the name of the place where Jacob was visited by two hosts of angels that had come to comfort and strengthen him on his way to a dreaded encounter with his brother Esau.[3] Apparently, the Israelites had composed a *dance* to memorialize the guardianship of these angels. Observing such a dance would likely stir feelings of joy and peace over the watchfulness of God; it might also provoke wonder at the beauty, goodness and strength of the splendid heavenly messengers.

The Shulammite is incredulous. She seems to be asking the daughters of Jerusalem, "Why do you clamor for my presence as though I were some sort of heavenly being? Am I really that important to you?" Unaccustomed to having such demands placed upon her life, the Shulammite is surprised by the attention she now receives.

Working to perfect his nature in her, the Holy Spirit has been keeping the Shulammite from premature exposure in ministry lest she be carried away by the temptations accompanying fame. Although she has been aware of the spiritual development taking

---

[1] *Solomon* is derived from a root meaning *completion* and *fulfillment*, implying a state of wholeness or perfection with regard to oneself and relationship with others. See Song 8:10.

[2] The naming of the Shulammite is reminiscent of the naming of the first woman. After God created the first man, placing him in a garden, there was found no partner suitable for the man. So God caused a deep sleep to fall upon him and took one of his ribs from which God fashioned a woman. When the woman was presented to the man, he said, "She shall be called *ishshah* (woman) because she was taken out of *ish* (man)." The man had found his counterpart (Genesis 2:18-23).

[3] Genesis 32:2-8

place within her, the true depth of grace in her life has been hidden both from her and from others. Now, in this unveiling of the Shulammite, she is unable to appreciate the extent to which she is truly valued by others and questions whether it is misplaced admiration.

daughters of
Jerusalem to
Shulammite:

7:1 **How beautiful are your feet in sandals,**
O prince's daughter!
The curves of your hips are like jewels,
The work of the hands of an artist.
7:2 **Your navel is** *like* **a round goblet**
Which never lacks mixed wine;
Your belly is like a heap of wheat
Fenced about with lilies.
7:3 **Your two breasts are like two fawns,**
Twins of a gazelle.
7:4 **Your neck is like a tower of ivory,**
Your eyes *like* **the pools in Heshbon**
By the gate of Bath-rabbim;
Your nose is like the tower of Lebanon,
Which faces toward Damascus.
7:5 **Your head crowns you like Carmel,**
And the flowing locks of your head are like
purple threads;
The **king is captivated by** *your* **tresses.**

Humility is not evidenced by the belittling of oneself, but by having a modest and circumspect appraisal of reality. The Shulammite endeavors to know what prompts the daughters of Jerusalem to value her presence among them, not that she might glory in their praise, but that she might be encouraged to give herself more fully to them. Gladly obliging, the maidens detail nine of the Shulammite's most outstanding characteristics— from the ground up. As will be seen later, this makes a profound impact upon the Shulammite, resulting in her willingness to assume a greater responsibility in ministering to the daughters of Jerusalem.

Liberating

Beautiful feet symbolize the evangelistic efforts of the Shulammite, as explained by the prophet Isaiah: "How lovely on the mountains are the feet of him who brings good news, who announces peace and brings good news of happiness, who announces salvation, and says to Zion, 'Your God reigns!'"[1] The daughters of Jerusalem thrill to see God's delivering power and hear of his faithfulness and his tender mercies. The Shulammite's message is with authority, for she comes not with enticing words of man's wisdom, but with demonstration of power and of the spirit.[2] She speaks as one who has had a personal encounter with God, one who knows God intimately.[3]

Her feet *in sandals,* the Shulammite is willing to go long distances, enduring rocks, thistle, inclement weather and many oppositions to bring the gospel to others. Her efforts are not limited to what is safe or convenient, but with great love and zeal, she carries the good news of the kingdom to the nations.

She is a *prince's daughter,* meaning that the Shulammite's august spirit and royal bearing qualify her to capably represent the church as a bearer of good news to the world.

Skillful

The Shulammite's *hips are like jewels,* exquisitely formed; her movements are graceful and agile, like Adino, captain of the captains of King David's mighty men. The mind can only imagine the elegance and dexterity exhibited by Adino when he slew eight hundred men in one battle, earning him the nickname *voluptuous.*[4] Likewise, the Shulammite is impressively effective and productive when tackling the work of the kingdom.

Hips also allude to the Shulammite's strength; she is industrious, a tireless worker for her beloved and quite competent. Her life and

---

[1] Isaiah 52:7; Nahum 1:15: Ephesians 6:15
[2] 1 Corinthians 2:4
[3] 1 John 1:1-3
[4] *Adino* literally means *voluptuous* (2 Samuel 23:8).

ministry is proof that more can be accomplished in one minute operating under the power and anointing of the Holy Spirit than hours of laborious struggling without him.

Joyful

Overflowing with joy, the Shulammite's *navel*, that is, her emotions, are said to be *like a round goblet which never lacks mixed wine*. She radiates the life of Jesus, the one whom the Bible declares was anointed with the oil of gladness above all his fellows.[1] Having learned to rejoice in all things, the Shulammite never lacks this *mixed wine*. Always finding something to be thankful about,[2] she is a continual source of joy and encouragement to those around her.

Her navel is said to be like a *round goblet*, indicating the availability of this joy to others; the Shulammite's joy is contagious, a continual source of refreshment to the daughters of Jerusalem.

Nourishing

Having devoted herself to careful study and meditation upon the Scriptures, the Shulammite's *belly is like a heap of wheat*. There is no famine for the Word of God, for the Shulammite is a silo of grain, a ready supply of nourishment to the daughters of Jerusalem. A heap of wheat does not imply that she has become bloated by feeding only herself, for the Shulammite maintains her shapeliness through the habitual exercise of dispensing the Word of God to others.

In the Hebrew language, the word for *belly* can also be translated *womb*, suggesting that the Word within the Shulammite is alive and therefore life-giving. The fruitfulness of the Shulammite, impregnated by the Word of God, is portrayed by the flowering *lilies* surrounding the wheat.

Tenderhearted

As previously attested by her beloved (4:5), the Shulammite's *breasts are like two fawns*, a portrayal of her gentle manner. Having a

---

[1] Hebrews 1:9
[2] Philippians 4:4; 1 Thessalonians 5:16;

well-developed sensitivity to the feelings of others, she is both disarming and inviting. Although careful to never cause pain or injury to another, the Shulammite remains vulnerable to the possibility of others' carelessness in human relationships. Her example of expressing genuine affection, even to those who remain unmoved, is a constant source of healing and comfort to the daughters of Jerusalem.

Like *fawns of a gazelle*, the Shulammite's heart is responsive. She will not let anger or unforgiveness brew, but she is alert to the slightest activity of the enemy in her own heart. Unwilling to jeopardize her own peace or that of another, she is quick to ask forgiveness for the slightest infraction.

Resolute

Like a *tower* beautifully inlaid with polished *ivory*, the Shulammite's *neck* is both strong and virtuous. Her excellent spirit displays uncommon courage in the face of adversity, as Solomon elsewhere observes, "The righteous are as bold as a lion."[1]

Having secured a lengthy history of right choices, the Shulammite's steadfast leadership and royal bearing bring a sense of stability and security to the daughters of Jerusalem. However, though uncompromising with regard to biblical values, she fails to display any air of condescension. The Shulammite is not compelled by stubbornness or self-righteousness, but the purity of an indomitable will absolutely surrendered and consecrated to God.

Peaceful

Peering into the *eyes* of the Shulammite, clear and undisturbed as the glistening *pools* of *Heshbon*, the daughters of Jerusalem find a soul at rest. Never seeming to be anxious or upset, the Shulammite's eyes communicate the warm inner glow of a spirit at peace with herself and with God. Absent are the fearful flitting glances, the invasive calculating stare, the perfunctory twinkle and the withering scowl. Instead, the maidens find affability,

---

[1] Proverbs 28:1

attentiveness and empathy— a wellspring of the Beloved's calm and reassuring love.

Heshbon, meaning *to think*, alludes to the source of the Shulammite's peace. She has learned to set her mind upon that which is good, edifying, pure and lovely— things worthy of praise.[1] Careful to maintain an unpolluted mind, her vision of the transcendent kingdom of God is not easily obstructed by worldly prognostics. The Shulammite looks confidently at the future, imparting peace and hope to the daughters of Jerusalem.

Protective

Solomon's empire was opposed by the kings of Syria, whose capital was Damascus. A watch *tower* perched upon the mountains *of Lebanon* and facing north *toward Damascus* serves to stand guard against any enemy activity that might threaten the peace of Israel.

Likewise, the Shulammite's *nose*, symbolizing her keen spiritual discernment and parental instinct, alerts her to subtle intrusions of the enemy that threaten the peace and well-being of the daughters of Jerusalem. Through prayer and by speaking the truth in love,[2] she helps others mature in the knowledge of God and overcome personal weaknesses that jeopardize their own well-being and that of the church.

Being fiercely committed to preserving the unity of the Spirit[3] among the members of Christ's body, the Shulammite is quick to silence gossip, defuse fear and mitigate evil suspicions. The first sign of division, discord, compromise or a host of other spiritual enemies is an instant call to intercession, often accompanied by gentle correction of those in opposition.

Sensitive to the leading of the Holy Spirit, the Shulammite addresses most spiritual problems before they manifest by teaching the church how to rightly apply the Word of God to their lives. In this way she helps build up a wall[4] of righteousness

---

[1] Philippians 4:8
[2] Ephesians 4:15
[3] Ephesians 4:3
[4] Ezekiel 22:30

around the Christian community, forestalling many potential setbacks.

Life-giving

The Shulammite's *head crowns* her *like Carmel*, a place associated with great beauty and fertility, crowning the north of Israel with its verdant hills.

According to Hebrew thought, the life of the human body flows from the head; thus, the daughters of Jerusalem here acclaim the Shulammite as a source of life to the Christian community, the body of Christ. Radiating the life of Christ, she imparts this divine life to others through loving, servant-style leadership. She does not lord it over those allotted to her charge but leads by example, so when the Chief Shepherd appears, she will receive the unfading crown of glory.[1]

Her beloved had earlier likened the Shulammite's cascading hair to a flock of goats, representing her humble and submissive nature (4:1; 6:5). Here the daughters of Jerusalem note that the *flowing locks of* her *head are like purple threads*. Purple, symbolizing royalty, intimates the Shulammite's royal bearing. Thus, not demanding or authoritarian, but with gentleness and humility does the Shulammite represent the authority of the divine family.

The maidens knowingly tell that *the king is captivated* (literally, *bound*, *caught* or *imprisoned*) *by* her *tresses*, that is, by her noble and gracious spirit. Similarly, the all-powerful Christ Jesus, although subject to no man, is overwhelmed and transfixed, a prisoner of his own fascination, over the excellent spirit cultivated in this mature bride.

---

[1] 1 Peter 5:3-4

7:6 **How beautiful and how delightful you are,**
My **love, with** *all* **your charms!**

7:7 **Your stature is like a palm tree,**
And your breasts are *like its* **clusters.**

7:8 **I said, 'I will climb the palm tree,**
I will take hold of its fruit stalks.'
Oh, may your breasts be like clusters of the
vine,
And the fragrance of your breath like apples,

7:9a **And your mouth like the best wine!**

Observing the *tête-à-tête* between the daughters of Jerusalem and the Shulammite, her beloved is confident that the maidens will sufficiently encourage the Shulammite to refocus her attention upon the ministry at hand. Nevertheless, he leaves nothing to chance. He is well aware that the praises of the daughters of Jerusalem, however encouraging they may be, will not sustain the Shulammite who, although pleased to obey the call to service, ultimately requires complete union with her beloved. She will never be satisfied with anything less.

Therefore, her beloved affirms the maidens' estimation of his fascination with the Shulammite: *"How beautiful and how delightful you are, my love, with all your charms!"* His opening line does little to prepare the reader for the most intimate longings of Christ recorded in the entire song, if not all of Scripture.

Stature

Her beloved begins by likening the Shulammite's noble *stature* to that of the stately date *palm*— tall, upright and fruitful— a picture of perfection. Astonishingly, the bride of Christ will attain to a stature commensurate with *the fullness of Christ* before he returns to receive her unto himself.[1] One can only try to imagine a mature bride, filled with divine life, made suitable for one who is more than a king, the very Lord of all creation, the only begotten of the Father, love incarnate. Oh, the mercy and the wisdom of God, that the human heart should be fashioned by the Holy Spirit so as to

---

[1] Ephesians 4:13

entice the Son of God until he is seized with unrelenting longing for union!

Breasts

Not since their garden tryst (5:1), has her beloved feasted on the virtuous fruit of divine love produced in the life of the Shulammite. Having exhausted the pleasure of mere admiration, he is no longer content to merely look upon the beauty of his most cherished love. Longing for greater intimacy, he vows determinedly: *"I will climb the palm tree; I will take hold of its fruit stalks."*

The Shulammite has matured since her beloved last likened her youthful breasts to the gentle and responsive fawns of a gazelle (4:5). Now, like unvented wine, the intoxicating fruit of mature love residing in her bosom promises to be a source of comfort and spiritual refreshment to her beloved.

How is it that the God of heaven can find comfort in the breast of a mere mortal? Certainly, this tries the limits of all human sensibilities. Is not the eternal God of all creation completely content within himself? Does he require human consolation?

It may be helpful to consider the father of several children. He may at one moment be saddened or distressed by an errant child, but is at once refreshed by thoughts of another more obedient and cheerful child.

Similarly, God is grieved at man's unending wickedness (5:1), but as the Shulammite intercedes on their behalf, reminding God of the sacrifice of Christ and of his promises to forgive, heal, deliver and establish, her deliberate prayers and impassioned pleas for mercy assuage his righteous wrath and awaken divine compassions, leading to a greater outpouring of his grace.

Additionally, through many other good works, the Shulammite helps to relieve the groans of human suffering, mitigating the cause of man's unthankful and blasphemous accusations against God. Her labors also work to prepare the soil of men's hearts that they might joyfully receive the implanted Word of God. In all these things, the heart of her beloved is soothed of the vexatious willfulness of sinful man.

Breath

As her beloved climbs the date palm still further, he anticipates inhaling the Shulammite's *breath*[1] (a symbol for her inner life[2]). Although the price has been at times exceedingly great, the Shulammite's obedience has resulted in a heart that exudes a fragrant aroma,[3] like the sweetness of *apples*,[4] a source of eternal delight for her beloved. This is not an achievement for which the Shulammite can claim credit, for it was God who gave her life, and it was God who has been at work in her both to will and to work for his good pleasure.[5] The Shulammite's part simply has been to diligently and continually yield to the power of the Holy Spirit at work within her.

Mouth

The Shulammite's *mouth* (literally, *palate*) represents wisdom and spiritual understanding.[6] Her beloved imagines it to be *like the best wine*, as intoxicating as it is pleasant. The greatest expression of her wisdom is the tenacity with which she has persevered in her lifelong quest to know her beloved more perfectly. She realizes how foolish it is to squander one's life in the pursuit of those things that will shortly perish and at the same time forsake the knowledge of the one who is eternal.

Having excelled at learning the ways of God, the Shulammite is able to cooperate with the formative winds of the Holy Spirit. She has learned the joys of contentment, always giving thanks for all things. She has learned that love is more influential than wealth. She has learned the advantage of weakness and how to live by the strength of another, her self-sufficiency having yielded to

---

[1] The word translated *breath* is literally *nose*.
[2] Genesis 2:7
[3] 2 Corinthians 2:16
[4] An interesting play on words, the Hebrew for apples, *tappuach*, comes from *naphach*, meaning *breathe* or *blow*.
[5] Philippians 2:13
[6] Job 6:30; 12:11-12; Psalm 119:103

God-dependency. She has learned the wisdom, patience and grace of making knowledge acceptable to others. Gone are the impetuosity and naiveté of youth; the Shulammite has aged like a fine wine, having become increasingly desirable to her beloved.

AN AFFECTIONATE CO-LABORER

Shulammite to Beloved:	7:9b	**It goes *down* smoothly for my beloved, Flowing gently *through* the lips of those who fall asleep.**

Choice wine, a mature and impassioned knowledge of God, proceeds[1] *smoothly* from the Shulammite's mouth toward[2] her beloved. But he is not the only beneficiary of this fine wine, for it flows gently over *the lips of* all *those who fall asleep*, those who are, like the Shulammite, detached from the cares of this life, dead to the world but alive unto God.[3] Here is evidence that the Shulammite is no longer reluctant to give herself to the members of Christ's body, the church. She will dispense her wine, and it will glide gently through the lips all those who share her lovesickness for her beloved.

The wine flows *gently* because the Shulammite has ceased from self-striving. She has abandoned all hope of forcing others into conformity with her personal brand of holiness.[4] As naturally as water courses to the lowest point, this wine gravitates toward spiritual hunger. She knows that sated souls loathe even honey,[5] and unless the Spirit draw them, they will not have the capacity to enjoy, let alone contain, this new wine. But it will stream softly through the lips of the soul obsessed with a thirst for the Ultimate Reality. The knowledge of God finds its true home in the heart of the one whose life is destitute apart from him.

---

[1] The word *down* does not appear in the Hebrew. The word translated *goes* can also be translated *departs* or *proceeds*.
[2] The word translated *for* is literally *toward*.
[3] See notes on 2:7.
[4] Galatians 6:12
[5] Proverbs 27:7

| 7:10 **I am my beloved's,**
And his desire is for me.

Moved by her beloved's longing for union (7:6-9a), the Shulammite demurely concedes his estimation of her spiritual worth, acknowledging a flow of life that touches her beloved as well as choice saints (7:9b). Now a yielded vessel, dedicated unreservedly to the purposes of her owner, the Shulammite again redefines her relationship with her beloved. This is the final of four such definitions,[1] the first three having been already explained (6:3).

1. *My beloved is to me* . . . (1:13-14).
2. *My beloved is mine, and I am his* (2:16).
3. *I am my beloved's, and my beloved is mine* (6:3).
4. *I am my beloved's, and his desire[2] is for me* (7:10).

In her third defining statement (6:3), the Shulammite recognized that the relationship does not exist primarily to satisfy her needs and desires, but it exists primarily to satisfy her beloved. Only secondarily does it exist to satisfy her. Yet now, the Shulammite abandons even this subordinate claim.

In so doing, the Shulammite experiences the momentary bliss of yielding herself unreservedly to a relationship that exists solely to satisfy her beloved. It is momentary because she can never totally extricate herself from her own desire for love (8:3). However, paradoxically, it is her willingness to release her claims upon love that brings the greatest revelation and experience of love and union. These moments of rapturous yielding are possible because the Shulammite is secure in the knowledge that her beloved is consumed with desire for her.

This final redefining of the relationship does not prompt a response from her beloved, nor is the Shulammite looking for one,

---

[1] This is also the fifth and final *I am* statement made by the Shulammite (1:5; 2:1, 16; 6:3; 7:10).

[2] The Hebrew word translated *desire* is found in only two other places in the Bible where, in both cases, it seems to suggest a desire to possess or take captive (Genesis 3:16; 4:7).

for she requires no further reassurances of his love. She has ceased from seeking her own pleasure, even in spiritual things.

No longer living for the enjoyment of love, but simply for love itself, the Shulammite is eager to labor together with her beloved. Immediately, she initiates the following invitation.

Shulammite to Beloved:	7:11	**Come, my beloved, let us go out into the country,** **Let us spend the night in the villages.**
	7:12	**Let us rise early** *and go* **to the vineyards;** **Let us see whether the vine has budded** **And** *its* **blossoms have opened,** **And** *whether* **the pomegranates have bloomed.** **There I will give you my love.**
	7:13	**The mandrakes have given forth fragrance;** **And over our doors are all choice** *fruits,* **Both new and old,** **Which I have saved up for you, my beloved.**
	8:1	**Oh that you were like a brother to me** **Who nursed at my mother's breasts.** *If* **I found you outdoors, I would kiss you;** **No one would despise me, either.**
	8:2	**I would lead you** *and* **bring you** **Into the house of my mother, who used to** **instruct me;** **I would give you spiced wine to drink from the** **juice of my pomegranates.**

Seizing the Initiative

"Come, my beloved, let us go," entreats the Shulammite. The significance of this invitation cannot be overstated, for the Shulammite has now come to the fourth and climactic phase of her relationship with her beloved.

In the first phase, the Shulammite works hard, but enjoys little or no relationship with her beloved, her darkened soul evidencing this period of spiritual neglect (1:5-7).

In the second phase, the Shulammite enjoys relationship with her beloved (1:12-2:6), but, fearful of neglecting her inner life, she declines her beloved's invitation to arise and join him in his vineyards (2:10-13).

Eventually, after a period of considerable spiritual growth, the Shulammite learns how to make time for both work (6:11) and relationship with her beloved. However, her life remains somewhat compartmentalized. She has time for everything, but everything must wait until its time, meaning that even her beloved, when drawing near at an inconvenient time, is forced to experience her momentary rebuff (6:12).

In this fourth phase, the Shulammite attempts to combine spiritual intimacy *with* her work. Seizing the initiative, she invites her beloved to join her on a trip *into the country*, where they will inspect the *vineyards* and *pomegranates*. Like the bridal company she eyed earlier (3:6), the Shulammite's heart has become something of a spiritual palanquin ready to carry the presence of the Lord into the fields he so loves to visit. The Shulammite is beginning to experience the answer to her prayer: *"Draw me after you and let us run together"* (1:4). Her beloved has drawn her, and now they will run.

Having matured in love, the Shulammite embraces her mission with a newfound zeal. Whereas, at one time the Shulammite hesitated at being roused from her bed (5:3), she now proposes rising *early* to see if *the vine has budded* or the *blossoms have opened*. The bud and flower refer to believers who are just coming forth into fruitfulness in their lives and ministries. Previously, the Shulammite could not be bothered by their pleas for help (2:15), but now she eagerly anticipates the opportunity to investigate their progress and help wherever possible.

Partnering with God

Discovering and doing the will of God is often a source of great perplexity for believers. They generally find themselves somewhere between two extremes. On the one hand, they can be virtually self-directed, seldom waiting for the Holy Spirit's direction in their decision-making processes, or they can be unwilling to make any forward motion without first feeling that they have received a specific command from the Lord.

Paradoxically, as one matures in his relationship with the Lord, there is an increasing sense of restriction and, at the same time, a greater sense of liberty in the decision-making process. The sense of restriction comes from no longer feeling the freedom to do those things that are not profitable either in helping to advance the Lord's purposes in the earth or in enhancing one's own love relationship with him. This feeling of confinement is not burdensome, however, but joyfully embraced as an expression of one's love for the Beloved. The increasing sense of liberty stems from having increased responsibility in the decision-making process, the Lord seeming to give opportunities and options where there were once only directives.[1]

The Shulammite is learning to operate in the context of a divine-human partnership in which her choices are often governed by her knowledge of the heart of God, without having a clearly identifiable directive from God. The relationship is beginning to look more like a marriage than a master-servant relationship.

Oftentimes, a young bride, although eager to please her husband, is unsure of his wishes and needs specific instruction in every matter. However, as a wife learns the likes and dislikes of her husband, she no longer finds it necessary to ask his opinion on every issue, for she has studied him long enough to know what would please him in most situations. Over time, as each party attempts to act in a way that would please the other, the two wills become one. At this point, the wife, still eager to please her husband, might have occasion to initiate some action. Her desire is not to act independently, but to please her husband by acting with what might be termed *submissive initiative*.

---

[1] The apostle Paul appears to have experienced this kind of liberty, for there were times when the Holy Spirit interrupted the apostle's plans and redirected his steps as he went (Acts 16:6-10). Moses too felt the liberty to heed Jethro's counsel concerning the appointment of leaders (Exodus 18:14-27); immediately following, Moses received a divine visitation during which God did not object.

Applied to one's spiritual life, such submissive initiate is accompanied by a sense of peace and joy through which the Holy Spirit bears witness that the decision has not only the Lord's approval, but also his active participation.

Far from being presumptuous,[1] the Shulammite is not quick to assume that her desire is always God's desire, but maintains an extreme sensitivity to anything that might be contrary to the will of God. She does not wish to do those things which are merely acceptable, but those things which are profitable,[2] life-giving[3] to herself and to others. Applying this principle of submissive initiative, the Shulammite invites her beloved to go with her into the countryside. Not surprisingly, the invitation is to nothing more than what her beloved has wanted her to do for quite some time.[4]

Unremitting Intimacy

"There I will give you my love." The Shulammite pledges that in the fields of service, she will lavish her love upon her beloved. She has found that she does not need to be isolated from the needs of humanity to experience intimacy with her beloved. On the contrary, it is often in the midst of the work that one is most finely in tune with the heartbeat of the Beloved Savior, who came not to be served, but to serve and to give his life a ransom for many.[5] The Shulammite has entered into a union with her beloved that enables her to bring him with her as she labors. Living by the strength that he supplies, she enjoys a greater rest and fruitfulness than ever before. She knows that her beloved greatly enjoys laboring in his vineyards, and as they share a common yoke by co-laboring together, their friendship will enjoy a heightened state of understanding and intimacy.

When one keeps his heart fixed upon the Lord, each moment of the day becomes an opportunity to grow in the knowledge of God, for

---

[1] Psalm 19:13
[2] 1 Corinthians 6:12; 10:23
[3] 1 Corinthians 15:45
[4] He makes the initial invitation (2:13); later, she attempts to go, but without him (6:11).
[5] Matthew 20:28

the Lord reveals himself to the believer in many ways and through varied activities. For example, in the process of building an ark that would contain at least two of every animal from upon the face of the earth, Noah undoubtedly pondered, not only the righteousness and mercy of God, but also his resourcefulness. Joseph, who was given authority to govern all of Egypt, the most powerful nation on the earth in his time, learned to appropriate God's wisdom as it relates to administration. Nehemiah, while equipping his workers with both tools and weapons, gained understanding of God's vigilance. Plowing with twelve yoke of oxen before him, and he with the twelfth, Elisha had opportunity to appreciate God's strength of endurance.

With practice, a believer can cultivate a conscious awareness of God's presence throughout the day, even while performing normal activities. This requires diligence in maintaining one's heart in a state of love, peace and joy, and walking in the light, never hiding from the truth. It involves frequent meditation upon the Word of God and impulsive yielding to moments of quiet, intimate discourse with the Father and with his Son.[1]

Such constancy cannot be accomplished by self-discipline alone, for one's mind naturally gravitates toward the object of its affections. Unless the heart is stirred with passionate desire for intimacy with God, the soul will experience constant defeat and self-recrimination in its attempt to focus upon him.

Therefore, the Shulammite does not intend to neglect her private times with her beloved. In fact, she anticipates their village retreats being even more especial as they punctuate expanding fields of service. *Mandrakes*, also called love-apples, and other fruits adorn the doorway of a room prepared by the Shulammite in which she anticipates stoking the fires of love through impassioned praise, worship, meditation, supplication and earnest waiting upon God in his presence.

---

[1] 1 John 1:3

Unfulfilled Familiarity

Although she enjoys relating to her beloved as a mature adult, there is no part of the Shulammite's life that she wishes to remain hidden or apart from him. She fantasizes what her childhood might have been like if they had grown up as *brother* and sister in the same household together.

For one thing, she would not have wasted any opportunity to express her affections toward her childhood friend. As siblings she would have had the freedom to *kiss* him, even in public, without any fear of reproach. How she loathes the self-imposed repression of her affections that appears masquerading as decorum.

Secondly, the Shulammite is so transparent and vulnerable when alone with her beloved that she is confident she would not have been embarrassed for him to be present during her awkward years of instruction. She wills him the freedom to know her past. Totally secure in his love and acceptance, the Shulammite feels no need to hide anything from him. Their relationship is reminiscent of Adam and Eve in the garden of Eden, where they were naked and not ashamed.[1] She longs for her beloved to intrude upon every relationship; even her irreplaceable mother-daughter relationship is subjected to him.

Thirdly, the Shulammite imagines having the opportunity to share her maidenhood blend of *spiced wine* with her beloved. The familial context of this passage veils the romanticism associated with the Shulammite's memories of producing her own choice wine. As she gathered and juiced the pomegranates, cleaned and prepared the vats, added carefully selected spices and thoughtfully monitored the fermentation process, the Shulammite undoubtedly had occasion to consider the man to whom she would one day serve her special blend.

The juice of the *pomegranates*, refined and aged, represents the Shulammite's life: her dreams, hopes and ambitions. For her to dispense this wine speaks of her desire to pour out her life and her

---

[1] Genesis 2:25

love for her beloved.[1] The Shulammite has exhausted her skill at verbalizing the depth of her love; simply put, she belongs entirely to him.

> Shulammite: | 8:3 **Let his left hand be under my head,**
> **And his right hand embrace me.**

At the end of Act III (immediately prior to the intermission in this song), the Shulammite invites her beloved to come into his garden and eat its choice fruits (4:16). He responds eagerly, and the two of them enjoy a moment of blissful union. Then Act IV presents the Shulammite with two trials that work to refine the depth of her dedication and love. Now, having come to the end of Act IV, she again offers herself to her beloved. However, this time the Shulammite begins by inviting him to join her in the fields of faithful service (7:11), something her beloved has been desiring almost from the beginning of the song (2:10); she promises that there she will give him her love (7:12). Now she sighs her innermost thoughts.

The Shulammite sees herself totally given to the embrace of her beloved. With his *left hand* supporting her *head* (which represents the fountain of all her life forces), her neck is laid bare. She would instinctively guard her neck if it were not for the vulnerability and trust that she feels toward her beloved. Her entire soul, with all its faculties of imagination, reason, understanding, memory, conscience, senses and will, are unreservedly yielded to him. She has uttered the words of this passage before (2:6),[2] but the intervening experiences have produced a level of maturity and trust that adds a new depth of meaning to them.

Applied figuratively, the Shulammite is here describing a type of contemplative prayer in which one's soul is profoundly yielded to the movements of the Holy Spirit. As one grows in the art of prayer, he adds new dimensions to his experience, without

---

[1] Wine, which often symbolizes joy, also communicates the Shulammite's desire to bring joy to her beloved.
[2] This sentence appears twice, both times before the same adjuration.

discarding the old (7:13), which then provide a great degree of versatility, enabling him to readily adapt to the mood of the Holy Spirit and enjoy greater depths in God. To be more specific, people generally think of prayer as active speaking or possibly singing to God, but one can add to this experience active listening, watching and waiting on God.

At this stage, the Holy Spirit communicates by impressing words, images or thoughts upon one's mind or spirit. Then, as the soul quiets itself still further, until all self-generated activity ceases, one can experience what is often described simply as oneness with God. Such momentary experiences of mystical embrace are expressions of God's love, token gifts from the Beloved for his bride. These sublime experiences into the depths of God are extremely satisfying, yet at the same time tantalizing, stirring longings for still greater intimacy with the Beloved.

CLOSING

Beloved to the daughters of Jerusalem: 8:4 **I want you to swear, O daughters of Jerusalem,
Do not arouse or awaken *my* love,
Until she pleases.**

Lacking the experience base to understand the Shulammite's uncontrolled surges of longing, the *daughters of Jerusalem* are still apt to misinterpret her lack of enthusiasm for trivial social activities, her fastings from food and her disdain for earthly pleasures, as religious extremism. Like Job's comforters, they easily conclude that the Shulammite's listlessness can be corrected by helping her see the error of her ways.

Her beloved preempts any potential interference. Wishing the Shulammite to enjoy all that her soul is willing and able to absorb at this level of intimate communion without any distraction, he warns the daughters of Jerusalem to not disturb her until she is ready to be awakened from her dreamy state.

Actually, this third adjuration is much more severe than the previous two (2:7; 3:5), for this time the Shulammite's beloved asks the daughters of Jerusalem to *swear* that they will not interfere. His gravity illustrates the seriousness with which the Lord watches over and protects his elect in their journey toward spiritual maturity. As her mortal existence fully flowers into conformity with the image and likeness of Christ, she becomes indescribably desirable to her beloved, causing him to become increasingly jealous over her.

So incomparably beautiful has the Shulammite become in the eyes of her beloved that he fails this time to adjure the daughters of Jerusalem by the strong and graceful *gazelles or the hinds of the field*. For no longer does he see the Shulammite in light of what she is becoming, but he sees her as she is.

Act V

—

Mature Love

Love . . . its flashes are flashes of fire, the very flame of the Lord.

POWER OF LOVE

8:5 **Who is this coming up from the wilderness, Leaning on her beloved?**

The question is rhetorical; it is plain that the one *leaning on her beloved* is the Shulammite. She is seen coming up from the wilderness, a biblical metaphor for the place of testing, a divine anvil upon which God hammers out his very nature in the souls of his elect. All who heed the call to become part of Christ's eternal bride unavoidably find themselves enmeshed in seasons of intense wilderness testing.

In the Shulammite's case, two fiery trials tested her commitment to love her beloved and his people.[1] In total abandonment of soul, she successfully relinquished her rights to enjoy rest independently from her beloved and to indulge in spiritual delights at the expense of ministry to others.

Having learned to yield herself totally to her beloved, the Shulammite has now entered into a new dimension of spiritual rest, evidenced by the change in her demeanor— leaning on her beloved. She trusts in him implicitly for her protection, provision, vindication,[2] understanding[3] and comfort.

In leaning upon her beloved, the Shulammite resembles Jacob of the Old Testament. Hoping to receive a blessing, Jacob wrestled through the night with the angel of the Lord and was afterward struck in the hip, causing him to walk with a permanent limp. A significant aspect to Jacob's blessing was in learning to value weakness, a key to the appropriation of divine power. Weakness in one's natural strength and abilities provides opportunity to draw

---

[1] These were the two test in Act IV: A Night Visit (5:2-8) and A Holy Distraction (6:11-7:9).
[2] Psalm 26:1; Isaiah 54:17; Joel 2:23
[3] Proverbs 3:5

upon the strength of the Holy Spirit resident within. The apostle Paul acknowledged how his weakness enabled the power of Christ to be perfected in him: "Therefore I am well content with weaknesses, with insults, with distresses, with persecutions, with difficulties, for Christ's sake; for when I am weak, then I am strong."[1]

"*Who is this*?" exclaim the daughters of Jerusalem in astonishment. Few souls display the degree of purity, tenderheartedness and leadership acumen for which the Shulammite has already been praised (6:10; 7:1-5); even fewer exhibit the brokenness formed only in the furnace of wilderness testings. The daughters of Jerusalem are in awe of the humility of Christ that has been worked into the Shulammite.

Earlier, the Shulammite was impressed by the bridal company she witnessed coming up from the wilderness (3:6) and her beloved with them as a conquering warrior. But here it is the Shulammite whose soul has been conquered and, now part of the bridal company, comes up out of the wilderness with her beloved.

It should not go unnoticed that it is the Lord Jesus who is typified here as the one coming up from the wilderness together with his bride. Jesus spent forty days being tested in the desert wilderness in preparation for his ministry on earth, but in a greater sense, Jesus' entire life on earth was a wilderness testing in relation to his eternal reign. He who had formed the worlds, who had no beginning of days, who enjoyed infinite glory in the bosom of the Father and dwelt in unapproachable and glorious light, voluntarily laid aside his power and glory in order to come down to earth as a man.

There Christ suffered rejection and humiliation at the hands of ungrateful men, ultimately enduring the horrors of a hideous and painful crucifixion. Because he had been made sin (necessary for him to fully atone for the sins of all mankind), he also experienced the darkness of apparent abandonment by his eternal Father. Nevertheless, through all his trials and tribulations, Jesus

---

[1] 2 Corinthians 12:10

gloriously triumphed over sin and death, securing for himself his eternal bride.

Beneath the apple tree I awakened you;
There your mother was in labor with you,
There she was in labor *and* gave you birth.
8:6 **Put me like a seal over your heart,**
Like a seal on your arm.
For love is as strong as death,
Jealousy is as severe as Sheol;
Its flashes are flashes of fire,
The *very* flame of the LORD.
8:7 **Many waters cannot quench love,**
Nor will rivers overflow it;
If a man were to give all the riches of his
house for love,
It would be utterly despised.

Apple Tree

Dismissing the maidens' astonishment, the Shulammite shifts the focus to her beloved, whispering, *"Beneath the apple tree I awakened you."*[1] This seems a curious reaction to the wonderment and awe she just heard from the daughters of Jerusalem. What could have been going on in her mind?

It is apparent that the Shulammite is aware of her power of allurement, not only as it affects the daughters of Jerusalem, but also as it affects her beloved, for she claims to have *awakened* or roused[2] his desires for her. By this she broaches the subject of the power of her love, a theme she will develop in the two verses that follow. At the same time, it seems she wants to credit her beloved as the reason why she loves him so, as evidenced by her leaning upon him. Her reasoning goes something like this:

---

[1] At first glance, it would seem that it is the Beloved who awakens the Shulammite to spiritual realities. However, the masculine pronoun suffixes in the Hebrew tend toward a female speaker, to which the *New American Standard Bible* and the *New International Version* agree.

[2] The Hebrew word *ur*, translated here as *awakened*, is used when urging God to arouse himself (Psalm 44:23; 59:4), stir up his power (Psalm 80:2) or awake (Isaiah 51:9).

"The daughters of Jerusalem esteem me greatly as they see me leaning upon you, thereby demonstrating that I am totally yielded and obedient to you from my heart. It is true that I am, but only because you pursued me, worked with me and taught me to trust you. It is also true that you did all of this for me because I desired to know you and because I loved you with total abandonment, for you do not bring every soul into this kind of union. However, I cannot claim credit for loving you, since it was actually you who first loved me. It was *beneath the* overarching branches of the *apple tree* (2:3-4), the canopy of the revelation of your love, that my response roused you to aggressively and passionately, yet tenderly, pursue me.[1] All that I am and all that I have in my relationship with you has been given me by grace."

There your mother was in labor . . . and gave you birth. In addition, the Shulammite recognizes that it was under the canopy of God's love that humankind (specifically, Israel) gave birth to the precious Savior, for it was love that moved the Father to send his Son into the world. Jesus came to make known the Father's heart of love, but was rejected. Israel struggled; she travailed, yet did not recognize the time of her visitation. She did not even realize that she was giving birth.[2]

Signet

The Shulammite assures her beloved that, regardless of the many rejections he has suffered from others, she will remain unswervingly devoted. *"Put me like a seal* or signet *over your heart,"* she importunes.

In Solomon's day, kings (and others of influence) would commonly engrave a stone signet with a distinctive mark that would

---

[1] The Shulammite's initial experience under the apple tree (2:3) was pivotal, for prior to that time, her beloved directs her to "go forth" (1:8), but afterward he becomes proactive: he "brought" her into his banqueting hall (2:4) and then is seen "coming . . . climbing . . . leaping" (2:8).

[2] It must be remembered that the early church was primarily Jewish, yet as a whole, Israel rejected their Messiah. However, eventually there will come a change of heart and all of Israel will be saved (Romans 11, especially verse 26).

represent their name.[1] The signet was then either suspended from the neck on a string[2] or worn on one's finger.

In the Bible, when God referred to someone as his signet ring, he was signifying that the person was his chosen representative.[3] Therefore, the Shulammite asks her beloved to seal the fact that she is his. She promises that, like a signet carried over the heart of her beloved,[4] she will be a faithful representation of his name and a faithful extension of his authority in the earth. Realizing her divine purpose, she does not shrink from the implications of union with her beloved; she is his eternal partner. However, far from making a plea for power, the Shulammite is simply and forcefully attempting to gladden her beloved with pledges of fidelity.

Put me like a seal . . . on your arm. Since a signet was not typically secured to the arm itself, but to an appendage of the arm, a finger, why does not the Shulammite simply ask to be put like a seal or signet on her beloved's finger? In choosing the word *arm*, she conjures up a more robust image, for she uses a word that is more commonly used metaphorically to symbolize *power* or *strength* (often God's strength). In this way, the Shulammite completes the analogy. As a signet over his heart, she faithfully represents his nature in all that she thinks and feels; as a signet upon his arm, or finger, she faithfully represents his character in all she does.

Death

In this climactic point of the entire song, the Shulammite reaches for the pinnacle of expression in her attempt to describe the nature of true love. She contends that *love is as strong as death.* Just as nothing can escape death's inevitable dominance and permanency, so nothing can ever dissuade true love. It is relentless in holding its prisoner captive.

---

[1] The signet was often pressed into clay or wax to authenticate a document.
[2] Genesis 38:18
[3] Jeremiah 22:24; Haggai 2:23
[4] She conjures imagery of the stones upon the breastplate of Israel's High Priest, engraved with the names of the tribes of Israel (Exodus 28:11, 21; 39:6, 14). A reference to her beloved's affections being set upon the signet carried close to his heart is not lost in this illustration.

Further, *jealousy is as severe as Sheol* (the grave or the afterlife).[1] The grave, intolerant of any compromise, violently strips its guests of all other means of comfort or life support. Likewise, jealous love, intensely asserting its right of possession, mercilessly assails any obstacle to union with the one so loved. True love will never compromise singlehearted devotion, not for wealth, not for fame and not for pleasure.

Thus, the Shulammite paints a picture of idyllic love, the kind of love that she has for her beloved, but how can she be so bold, so confident in her assessment of the quality of her love? Is it really possible for one to love so perfectly, so unfailingly? Certainly, the Shulammite is no more confident of her love than any young sincere romantic and cannot be faulted with overstating her case. Still, the Shulammite is not immature; her conviction cannot so easily be attributed to youthful bravado. She well knows that humans are subject to weakness and even their best efforts to love seem always to be tainted by some degree of selfishness. Her confidence here is derived from a profound truth she readies herself to reveal.

Fire and Water

This love relationship, an inseparable union between the human and the divine, is no ordinary love affair, for one of the parties is God, the quintessential of love. How can his love ever be reciprocated with the purity and fierceness with which he loves?

Certainly, this unusual quality of love exists between the members of the Godhead, the Father, Son and Holy Spirit, but will humans swagger to the table of divine fellowship and presume equal participation with this unimaginably glorious club of three? Conversely, how could a bride be denied the most intimate of fellowship with her husband, though he be divine? Understanding the dilemma, Jesus, the beloved and only begotten Son of God, prayed and asked his Father (the progenitor of love) to put *his* love

---

[1] Sheol, the resting place for departed souls prior to the New Covenant, consisted of two areas separated by an impassable chasm: an area of torment for the wicked and an area of bliss for the righteousness (Luke 16:22-31).

in the heart of his bride, the very same love with which the Father loves the Son.[1] Thus, the Shulammite's love is not kindled and inflamed by a woman's passion, but by God. Incomprehensible.

Furthermore, Jesus becomes the answer to his own prayer as he comes to live inside his bride by the power of the Holy Spirit. Joining himself together with her spirit, he makes her a new creature[2] with a new nature in which his divine love is the defining characteristic. This marvelous miracle, the melding of divine life with human, prepares the bride to become a suitable eternal companion for her beloved, and yet, she is more than a companion. She becomes a bearer of his unspeakable glory: his transcendent power, unfathomable beauty and indomitable love being made manifest through her. Oh, the unspeakable glories of divine love!

True love is of divine origin, for *its flashes are flashes of fire, the very flame of the Lord*. According to the vision of the prophet Ezekiel, the appearance of God resembles a man seated upon a throne, having his being filled with what appears to be blazing fire.[3] The prophet Daniel saw a river of fire, presumably a portrayal of the Holy Spirit, proceeding from this throne,[4] and the apostle John, in three separate revelations, beheld the eyes of Jesus alive with flaming fire.[5]

An apt portrayal of love, fire is all-consuming and transforming, relentlessly devouring anything that stands in its way. Strong and intractable as love may be, however, it is not staid. It can be illustrated by the earth's sun which, although constant, is also fluid, a dynamic furnace from which leap violent solar flares. Likewise, the soul feels love as an ardent amorous burning with periodic upsurges of divine life, inflaming desire, refreshing and bathing the soul in divine glory.

---

[1] John 17:26
[2] 2 Corinthians 5:17
[3] Ezekiel 1:26-28; 8:2
[4] Daniel 7:10
[5] Revelation 1:14; 2:18; 19:12

Life is often bombarded with disappointing events: sickness, betrayal, failure, persecution[1] or other losses. Like chaotic floodwaters surging over the soul, these events can attempt to extinguish the fires of love. However, divine love, true love, burns so fiercely that even *many waters cannot quench it, nor will rivers overflow it.*

Just as circumstances cannot drown love, so the promise of wealth cannot endear it. The Shulammite makes it plain: *"If a man were to give all the riches of his house for love, it would be utterly despised."* There is a transcendent quality about love that sets it apart from mere outward affection. Whereas some might feign affection and even marry for money, true love can never be bribed, for true love emanates from the heart and must be freely given.

How many believers look forward to heaven with its lush gardens, luxurious mansions, beautiful music, sensational colors and supernatural ecstasies, but presently pursue the pleasures of the world? They do not yet know true love, for it is impossible to love the world or the things of the world and have true love, the love of God, within.[2]

The Shulammite loves her beloved, not for what he gives, but for who he is. Because there is none who can ever compare with her beloved, and because her love can never be given in exchange for wealth, hers is an everlasting love, indeed, a divine love.

---

[1] Revelation 12:7-17
[2] 1 John 2:15

LOVE FOR OTHERS

Shulammite to | 8:8 | **We have a little sister,**
Beloved: | | **And she has no breasts;**
| | **What shall we do for our sister**
| | **On the day when she is spoken for?**

Having pledged absolute fidelity to her beloved, the Shulammite is aware of the fact that she has not always loved him so perfectly. During her early years of womanhood, her love was embryonic: sincere, zealous, but somewhat self-serving. Although she has grown immensely since those days, she wonders if others will fare so well.

The Shulammite and her beloved *have a little sister*[1] with undeveloped *breasts*,[2] meaning she is not yet mature enough for betrothal.[3] The little sister represents future members of the bridal company, those who are still unconverted: not yet involved in a covenantal relationship with Christ.[4]

Full of love and compassion, a mature vanguard of the church for which the Lord returns at the end of the age, the Shulammite's attention turns toward the souls who will be brought to Christ during the final moments of the last days. She wonders what will happen when the little sister is eventually betrothed to Christ. How can she be protected so that she is not carried away by the deceitfulness of the world, so that she does not settle for less than total union with the Beloved?

---

[1] Jesus referred to the unconverted as children of God (John 11:52) and sheep not of this fold (John 10:16); it should not seem strange that the Shulammite calls them her little sister.

[2] Lack of breasts also signify that she has not yet begun to develop tenderhearted love (4:5; 7:3).

[3] Ezekiel 16:8

[4] Believers are already betrothed to Christ (2 Corinthians 11:2), awaiting his return, when they will experience the finalization of union. However, it does not violate the story to understand the *little sister* to include immature believers, those whose commitment to Christ is still being tested.

Here the Shulammite expresses the same concerns as did Christ when he prayed for those who would yet believe. He asked that they be kept from the evil one and sanctified in the truth, in other words, that they be conformed to the Word of God, becoming one with the corporate bride and also with the Godhead.[1] The Shulammite has learned from experience that union with Christ involves more than desire, more than passionate praise, and more than fulfilling moments in his presence. Intimacy with God also involves a walk of holiness, so she asks, *"What shall we do for our sister on the day when she is spoken for?"*

Beloved to	8:9	**If she is a wall,**
Shulammite:		**We will build on her a battlement of silver;**
		But if she is a door,
		We will barricade her with planks of cedar.

Delighted to have the Shulammite as a full partner, her beloved lovingly instructs her on the strategy for protecting their little sister. *If she is a wall*, that is, strongly devoted and already providing a great defense against the enemy, they will *build on her a battlement[2] of silver*, meaning they will make her even stronger by imparting redemptive truths that will help establish her in the faith.

However, if the little sister is a door, providing the enemy easy access, they will *barricade her with planks of cedar*. In the Bible, cedar often represents humanity, a reference here to believers whom God will use to protect and strengthen the little sister. Through prayers of intercession and by speaking the truth in love, they block the enemy's attempts at penetrating her life and leading her astray.

Jesus is the great High Priest, who continually makes intercession for the saints so that they stand holy and blameless on the day of judgment. An important task of the Shulammite at the end of the age is to stand with her beloved in offering intercession on behalf of the little sister until she also becomes mature or complete.

---

[1] John 17:15, 17, 20-21, 23
[2] A *battlement* is a reinforced tier or wall.

The maturing of the saints should be the primary objective of all church leaders, as writes the apostle Paul: "[Jesus] gave some as apostles, and some as prophets, and some as evangelists, and some as pastors and teachers, for the equipping of the saints for the work of service, to the building up of the body of Christ; until we all attain to the unity of the faith, and of the knowledge of the Son of God, to a mature man, to the measure of the stature which belongs to the fullness of Christ."[1]

According to this passage of Scripture, the ministries of apostle, prophet, evangelist, pastor and teacher will continue to function until something is achieved. What is this fateful event? Without question, the church must become *a mature man*. Since maturity is a relative term, there remains another question: just how mature will the church become? Again, the apostle Paul is unequivocal: she will attain *to the measure of the stature which belongs to the fullness of Christ*. The profundity of this statement cannot be overlooked. Before Jesus returns, the church will walk in the fullness of mature love,[2] joy, peace, power[3] and wisdom as did the Master when he was on the earth.

---

[1] Ephesians 4:11-13
[2] Matthew 5:48; 1 John 4:17
[3] John 14:12

LOVE FOR HER BELOVED

Shulammite: | 8:10 **I was a wall, and my breasts were like towers;**
Then I became in his eyes as one who finds
peace.

A Wall with Towers

Pausing to reflect upon her own experience, the Shulammite summarizes the process that led to her eventual transformation.

In Act I the Shulammite's life was out of control. Working in the vineyards, her blackened condition reveals the relative ease with which the enemy had been able to run roughshod over her life.

Then, in pursuing an intimate relationship with her beloved, the Shulammite began to develop a history of hiddenness. At times, tainted by fear and self-centeredness, her seclusion interfered somewhat with her pursuit of intimacy,[1] but essentially it served to separate the Shulammite from the things of the world, intensifying her devotion to her beloved. This hiddenness precipitated the formation of her identity described here as *a wall*, invoking the imagery of an enclosure inaccessible to all but her beloved.[2]

This enclosure is fortified by the impregnability of *breasts like towers*, an allusion to her inflexible strength in withstanding all other lovers, illustrating that the key to the Shulammite's spiritual development was her singlehearted devotion, fortified by an intensely affectionate love burning within her heart.[3]

One Who Finds Peace

In her opening lines, the Shulammite cries out to her beloved, "Let us run together," but now she finishes by saying, "*I became in his*

---

[1] Examples of her early seclusion are when she was behind a lattice (2:9), in the cleft of the rock (2:14) and behind a door in the night (5:2-5).
[2] See also Song 4:12.
[3] See Song 4:5; 7:3, 7-9 for a description of the analogy between breasts and love.

eyes as one who finds peace." She has reached the end of her journey. She has found her completeness in him and her soul is at rest.

It bears repeating that the Shulammite found this rest only after, and as a result of, maintaining singlehearted love and devotion for her beloved, for she says, "I was a wall, and my breasts were like towers; *then* I became . . . as one who finds peace." The mental picture of an undisturbed walled city with towers is inescapable. The peace enjoyed within such a city is obtained only after its walls are in place, meaning that the Shulammite experienced peace only after her heart was made inaccessible to all other lovers and burned with a love only for her beloved.

The words *Solomon, Shulammite,* and *peace* are all formed from the same Hebrew root word: *shalom.* Its meaning is much broader than the mere absence of war or strife. *Shalom* also means a state of fullness, completeness and wholeness, implying prosperity, health, safety and unimpaired relationship with others. It describes a state of fulfillment resulting from being in the presence of God.

In retrospect, it seems that the Shulammite's quest for intimacy with her beloved has also been a quest for *shalom,* for he is her rest. Her search begins with her asking, "Where do you pasture your flock, where do you make it lie down at noon?" (1:7) She then tastes of that rest as she sits under the shade of the apple tree, a representation of her beloved (2:3). Later she receives a revelation of the attainability of complete and confident rest, seeing it in the lives of sixty mighty men who bear her beloved, having their swords at their sides (3:7-8).

Rest is illustrated also by the Sabbath day observance required of Israel, a time when every man ceased from doing all his own works, demonstrating his trust in *God who Provides.* Essentially, the Sabbath illustrated the rest God intends every believer to experience when he ceases from seeking his own pleasure and speaking his own word.[1]

---

[1] Isaiah 58:13

Every believer is joined with Christ in his death, burial and resurrection. Knowing that his old self-life is dead, having been crucified with Christ,[1] the believer then lives by the strength that Christ supplies.[2] The Shulammite too, having allowed the resurrected Christ to become her life, has ceased from doing her own works and has entered into rest.[3] She is able to say with the apostle Paul, "I have been crucified with Christ; and it is no longer I who live, but Christ lives in me; and the life which I now live in the flesh *I live by faith in the Son of God*, who loved me, and delivered Himself up for me."[4] A portion of this verse can be also translated, "I live by the faith *of* the Son of God," meaning that the apostle is animated and sustained by the life, as well as by the very faith, of the Lord Jesus. That is rest.

King David tasted something of this rest, musing, "My heart is not proud, nor my eyes haughty; nor do I involve myself in great matters, or in things too difficult for me. Surely I have composed and quieted my soul; like a weaned child rests against his mother, my soul is like a weaned child within me."[5] When hungry, a nursing child is unable to rest in the embrace of its mother, for it will be anxiously searching for food. However, a weaned child has learned to wait until feeding time and thus is able to enjoy a sense of calm in the embrace of its mother. David likens his own soul to that of a weaned child in describing his heart attitude in the embrace of God. He is content to know that he is loved by the Lord. Not constantly looking to be fed, he waits for the appropriate feeding times according to the wisdom of the Father.

Immature believers are unable to rest in God. They are constantly looking for a fresh word, revelation, feeling or confirmation of his love; they are anxious, fretful souls. When they lack understanding, they question God's veracity; when disappointed, they question his faithfulness. Though they desire peace, they seem never to be able to find it. Conversely, it is as the Shulammite fixes

---

[1] Romans 6:4-6
[2] Philippians 4:13
[3] Hebrews 4:9-10
[4] Galatians 2:20
[5] Psalm 131:1-2

her affections with unswerving loyalty upon her beloved, she finds that elusive validation so anxiously sought by many. *"In his eyes,"* she says, "I became as one who finds peace."

Though conscious of the value her well-fortified soul affords others, her identity is derived from what she has become for her beloved. Having entered into rest, her soul becomes an eternal resting place for the Godhead.

The Lord asked this question of the nation of Israel through the prophet Isaiah: "Heaven is my throne and the earth is my footstool, where then is a house you could build for me? And where is a place that I may rest? For my hand made all these things."[1] He then answers his own question, saying, "But to this one I will look, to him who is humble and contrite of spirit, and who trembles at my word." In other words, the place in which God is looking to dwell is the hearts of believers who are of a humble and contrite spirit, for in them only will God find rest.

The Shulammite has secured her new identity; she is the dwelling place of God, the temple of the Holy Spirit, the new creation, the new man, the body of Christ, the bride of Christ and a joint-heir together with him. She has entered into what was promised by Jesus: "If anyone loves me, he will keep my word; and my Father will love him, and we will come to him, and make our abode with him."[2]

Solomon's reign of peace foreshadowed the coming reign[3] of Christ when all the earth will experience *shalom*. Christ's kingdom was also foreshadowed in the seventh day of creation, the day on which God rested from all his works. The first man, Adam, was created on the sixth day, a day when God worked, but the Shulammite has become with Christ the man of the seventh day, for she has already entered into God's rest. Having overcome all her enemies, the Shulammite walks in perfect love, joy and peace,[4] and has become a harbinger of the coming kingdom age.

---

[1] Isaiah 66:1-2
[2] John 14:23
[3] Revelation 20:4-7
[4] Matthew 5:48; James 1:4

Shulammite: 8:11 **Solomon had a vineyard at Baal-hamon;**
He entrusted the vineyard to caretakers;
Each one was to bring a thousand *shekels* **of**
silver for its fruit.

Solomon's *vineyard* is a reference to the church which the Lord Jesus[1] entrusts *to caretakers*, ministers who teach and otherwise care for the people of God. A *thousand shekels* rent is paid by the caretakers in exchange for the privilege of working in their master's vineyard. This rent represents the fruit of righteousness the Lord expects to be returned to him in the lives of his people.

Two truths are illustrated here: first, as the owner of the vineyard, Jesus has a right to require a specific return, and second, the return he requires is the fruit of righteousness.

During the time Jesus walked the earth, it was the leaders of Israel who had been entrusted with the Word of God and given the responsibility of caring for the souls of men. Jesus used the vineyard-owner paradigm to explain how the kingdom would be taken away from them and given to another people who would produce the fruit of the kingdom.[2]

Since that time, the responsibility of caring for the souls of men has been entrusted to thousands of church leaders. Although history testifies against many, the Shulammite is among those who have faithfully labored in the Lord's vineyard, bringing forth the desired fruit.

Shulammite to 8:12 **My very own vineyard is at my disposal;**
Beloved: **The thousand** *shekels* **are for you, Solomon,**
And two hundred are for those who take care
of its fruit.

---

[1] Christ is portrayed in the name *Baal-hamon,* meaning *possessor of abundance* or *lord of a multitude.*

[2] Matthew 21:33-43

1000 Shekels

Though she labors faithfully in the Lord's vineyard, the Shulammite has a *vineyard* of her *very own*; that vineyard is her own soul (1:6). She points out that it is at her *disposal*, meaning that she has a right to do with it as she will, establishing her right of self-determination. That is to say, the life given her by God is really hers. If she chooses to surrender it back to him, it is by an act of her own free will, making the gift extremely precious to her beloved, for it is given voluntarily, not out of coercion, fear or duty, but out of love.

Because she is the owner of her vineyard, the Shulammite is not obligated to pay rent to Solomon. Her willingness to give him a *thousand shekels* rent is an acknowledgment that all she owns and all she has become belongs to him; she does not claim any rights of possession independent of her beloved.

Not only is the garden of her soul (her mind, will and affections) his (4:16), but the fruit of maturity is also his. The maturity developed in the Shulammite's life was not her own doing, but was accomplished by the grace of God working in her; nor has the fruit been produced for her own enjoyment, but only for the pleasure of her beloved. Her soul is his garden, to delight in as he will.

During the seventy or so years of life given each man on earth, God tests his heart to find out what he values, what he really desires. These desires (and corresponding actions) form the basis for his eternal reward. In the Shulammite's case, all she wants is her beloved, and she has spent a lifetime in the pursuit of knowing him and loving him. Forever he will be her incomparable reward. Eternity will provide insufficient time in which to fully comprehend the immensity of such a reward.

200 Shekels

Although the Shulammite claims nothing for herself, there is remuneration for those who ministered to the Shulammite, helping her in the process of bearing fruit. Grateful for their help, she pays them out of her own funds so that they might be compensated without diminishing the thousand shekels Solomon is to receive.

In this, the Shulammite accepts full responsibility for the development of her own soul. She acknowledges that the help she received was required because of her own weakness, not because of any inadequacy in her beloved's provision. If she was in any way deficient, it was not because of a lack of grace on his part, for she is fully aware of the many occasions on which she failed to trust him totally.

Oftentimes, those sent to help mature the believer are not viewed as a blessing at the time. However, the Shulammite refuses to play the role of the victim. Every trace of self-pity, self-justification and anger have been purged from her. She does not blame others for the injustices, the misunderstandings, the lost opportunities nor the betrayals, for she realizes, like Joseph who suffered at the hands of his brothers, that what others may have intended for evil, God was able to use for good.[1]

The Shulammite has learned to be thankful for the fiery furnace of bitter life circumstances through which God refined her like gold. Far from holding her beloved responsible for the pain necessitated by her own stubbornness and pride, she realizes that through it all, he was with her, partaking of the pain, providing strength and ministering comfort.

| Beloved to Shulammite: | 8:13 | **O you who sit in the gardens, My companions are listening for your voice— Let me hear it!** |

Laboring in the vineyard of Baal-hamon, the Shulammite is portrayed as abiding[2] *in the gardens,* that is to say, she is continually ministering to the souls of men. She is well received by those hungry to know God; they long to hear the words of wisdom, comfort, encouragement, exhortation and revelation that flow from

---

[1] Genesis 50:20

[2] The Hebrew word translated *sit* is in the present participle verb form and can also be translated *sitting, abiding,* or *dwells.*

her lips. Even the faithful shepherds, *companions* of her beloved (1:7), eagerly anticipate hearing her *voice*.

Having matured significantly, the Shulammite is most precious to her beloved, and he is here taking great care that she does not labor in his vineyards at the expense of her own soul, as happened at the start of this song (1:6).

Praising the Shulammite for having acquired such a depth of wisdom and understanding so as to be a great blessing to the church, her beloved begs that he too might hear her voice. He wants to hear her songs of love, her intercessions and her praise.[1] Most of all, he longs to hear her pleadings for that which is his fundamental desire— ultimate union.

| Shulammite to Beloved: | 8:14 | **Hurry, my beloved,**
And be like a gazelle or a young stag
On the mountains of spices. |

Hesitating long enough for a wave of pent-up desire to surge naturally from within, the Shulammite implores her beloved to *hurry* to her. The word translated *hurry* is literally *flee*,[2] giving the following connotation to the Shulammite's plea: "Come as swiftly as a *gazelle or a young stag*, like a prisoner making his escape, as though held captive in heaven."

The ache of separation in the bride's heart will never subside until she is fully joined to her beloved, until she is where he is and beholds his glory unveiled.[3] Meanwhile, she longs to know him more fully,[4] to know the love of Christ which surpasses knowledge that she might be filled up to all the fullness of God.[5] This fullness is her divinely prescribed destiny, the unimaginable purpose for which she was created.

---

[1] This is not an invitation for her to preach the gospel as in 2:14.
[2] The Hebrew *barach* is also translated *pass through* and is used to describe the joining of boards to one another (Exodus 26:28; 36:33), an allusion to the bride's desire to be joined with her beloved.
[3] John 17:24
[4] Philippians 3:10
[5] Ephesians 3:19

So the song ends with the incessant cry of the end-time bride, the voice that her beloved longs to hear— the voice of desire. The Shulammite's supplication corresponds with the final prayer in Scripture in which the bride joins together with the Holy Spirit in crying, "Come, Lord Jesus."[1] This is the prayer that will release the Lord Jesus from his voluntary captivity where he dwells among *the mountains of spices* in heavenly places.

Here again, *spices* speak of the character of Christ (3:6; 4:14), and *mountains* speak of their abundant supply (4:6). This concluding phrase reveals the Shulammite's awareness of who her beloved is and what he values. He is the Christ, the Son of the living God, full of mercy and grace, abounding in lovingkindness and truth. As such, he is also able to perfect the fragrant aroma of his nature in her that, being conformed to his image, she might know him more fully.

The song is not intended to end, but to linger in the mind of the reader, who is left to wonder and to enter into the unfulfilled longing that resides in the bosom of the Shulammite.

---

[1] Revelation 22:17, 20

ABOUT THE AUTHOR

Michael Walsh was born in Los Angeles, California. In 1973, after serving in the Air Force and graduating from college, he and his wife, Denise, made a commitment of their lives to Christ. Six years later, Michael felt the Lord leading him to leave his CPA practice and move to Conroe, Texas in order to plant a church. Michael continues to serve as Senior Pastor in what is now called Mercy Christian Fellowship, a multi-congregational church. Denise travels extensively, preaching, teaching, and coordinating the foreign missions activities of the church. Together they share the joy of three children and five grandchildren, who also live in the Conroe area.

www.MercyChristianFellowship.com